D1446926

University of Cambridge Department of Applied Economics
OCCASIONAL PAPER 45

DEVELOPMENT, INCOME DISTRIBUTION AND SOCIAL CHANGE IN RURAL EGYPT (1952–1970)
A Study in the Political Economy of Agrarian Transition

Development,
Income Distribution and
Social Change in
Rural Egypt

1952 – 1970

A Study in the Political Economy of Agrarian Transition

MAHMOUD ABDEL-FADIL

Research Officer
Department of Applied Economics

CAMBRIDGE UNIVERSITY PRESS

CAMBRIDGE

LONDON : NEW YORK : MELBOURNE

Published by the Syndics of the Cambridge University Press
The Pitt Building, Trumpington Street, Cambridge CB2 1RP
Bentley House, 200 Euston Road, London NW1 2DB
32 East 57th Street, New York, NY 10022, USA
296 Beaconsfield Parade, Middle Park, Melbourne 3206, Australia

© Department of Applied Economics, University of Cambridge 1975

First published 1975

Typeset by EWC Wilkins Ltd., London and Northampton
Printed in Great Britain at the University Printing House Cambridge
(Euan Phillips University Printer)

Library of Congress Cataloguing in Publication Data
Abdel-Fadil, Mahmoud, 1941 –
    Development, income distribution, and social change in rural
Egypt (1952–1970)

    (University of Cambridge. Department of Applied Economics.
Occasional paper; 45)
    Includes bibliographical references.
    1. Agriculture – Economic aspects – Egypt. 2. Egypt – Rural
conditions. 3. Egypt – Economic conditions – 1952– I. Title.
II. Series: Cambridge. University. Dept of Applied Economics.
Occasional papers; 45.
HD2122.A54   338.1'0962   75–17114
ISBN 0 521 21000 3 hard covers
ISBN 0 521 29019 8 paper back

Contents

Tables and figures

APPENDIX TABLES

FIGURES

List of Currency, Weights and Measures used

Currency
1 Egyptian pound (£E)
  = 100 piastres (PT)
  = 1000 milliemes (m/m)
1 tallaris = 20 PT

Exchange Rates
Sept. 1949 – June 1962 £E1 = U.S. $2.872 (parity)
June 1962 – March 1972 £E1 = U.S. $2.286 (effective selling rate)

Weights and measures
1 feddan = 0.42 hectare = 1.04 acres
1 kantar (metric) = 50.0 kg.
1 kantar of unginned cotton = 157.5 kg.
1 kantar of ginned cotton = 44.9 kg.
1 ardeb = 198 litres of crops
1 ardeb of wheat = 150 kg.
1 ardeb of maize = 140 kg.
1 ardeb of beans = 155 kg.
1 ardeb of millet = 120 kg.
1 ardeb of peanuts = 75 kg.
1 ardeb of sesame = 120 kg.
1 dariba of rice (in husk) = 945 kg.
1 ardeb of rice (in husk) = 292.5 kg.
1 ardeb of rice (husked and bleached) = 200 kg.

Abbreviations used

ACO   Agricultural Credit Organisation (Cairo)
CAPMS Central Agency for Public Mobilization and Statistics (Cairo)
CBE   Central Bank of Egypt (Cairo)
ECC   Egyptian Cotton Commission
FAO   Food and Agriculture Organisation (Rome)
ILO   International Labour Office (Geneva)
IMF   International Monetary Fund (Washington)
INP   Institute of National Planning (Cairo)
NBE   National Bank of Egypt (Cairo)
UAR   United Arab Republic (Egypt)
UN   United Nations

Preface

This research work was first conceived during the academic year 1972/3, but the major part of it was completed during 1974 when I took it up as part of a larger study on "Development, Income Distribution and Social Change in Egypt, 1952–1970",[1] made possible by a research grant from the Social Science Research Council (SSRC).

It is impossible to acknowledge all those who gave me help and encouragement while I was working on this study. But I should like to express my particular thanks to Dr. Samir Radwan and Mr. Robert Mabro of the University of Oxford Institute of Economics and Statistics, Dr. Rodney Wilson of Durham University, Dr. Amr Mohieldine of Cairo University, and Dr. M. Sultan Abu-Ali of Ain-Shams University (Egypt). Without the welcome help of these colleagues the amassing of statistical material needed for this study would have been impossible.

I owe a great debt to Professor Krishna Bharadwaj of the Jawaharal Nehru University, New Delhi, Dr. Charles Feinstein and Mrs. Suzanne Paine of the Faculty of Economics, Cambridge, and Professor Ashok Rudra of the Indian Statistical Institute, who have read extensive parts of the original manuscript of this paper, and provided many helpful comments. The revised version owes a lot to their suggestions.

I have also benefited greatly from discussions with colleagues in Cambridge. I should like to thank in particular Angus Deaton, Michael Ellman and Myles Mackie who generously gave their time to discuss points with me and brought sources to my attention. I am much obliged to Marion Hughes for computational assistance, to Mrs. Lilian Silk and the typing staff of the Department of Applied Economics for typing out various versions of the manuscript, and to Jo Bradley who suggested many stylistic improvements.

Finally, I am grateful to the Department of Applied Economics and its Director, Wynne Godley, for having offered me the opportunity to work on this project; to the Provost and Fellows of King's College, Cambridge for financial support during the academic year 1972/3.

M A-F

Department of Applied Economics
Cambridge
June 1975

---

1 I hope to treat these subjects with reference to the 'urban sector' in a subsequent monograph.

Introduction

"If one is still obliged to make bricks without straw, mud
bricks are better than no bricks."
Charles Elliot (1970)

The main purpose of this study is to analyse and assess the various dimensions of
the process of agrarian transition in Egypt over the last two decades. The analysis
concentrates on the period 1952—70. The choice of 1952 as a starting point should
be obvious, for that year has the greatest political significance since it was then that
the *ancien régime* was overthrown and a new chapter of Egyptian history inaug-
urated. On the other hand, the choice of the terminal year is equally significant, for
Nasser, who led the 1952 revolution, died in 1970. This work could thus be regarded as an appraisal of the socio-economic transformations brought about in rural
Egypt under Nasser's regime.

Much has been written on the land reforms and agrarian policies in Nasser's
Egypt, but no overall assessment of the dynamics of the process of agrarian transition has yet been attempted. The present study arose out of my belief that such
an overall assessment is much needed.

In order to reach an analytically meaningful characterisation of the complex
production relations prevalent in rural Egypt, and to identify the respective
positions of and prospects for the different sections of the peasantry, we needed to
analyse, in concrete terms, the different policies and mechanisms underlying the
process of agrarian transition in Egypt during the period 1952—70, and to assess the
extent to which this process, with its inherent logic, has transformed the material
and social basis of production in the Egyptian agriculture.

In the course of this study, several conceptual and methodological problems
have been raised as a result of the general lack of relevant statistics. For neither
national nor international agencies have ever troubled to establish systematic statistical series on the main indicators of income distribution by the major social
classes as opposed to the national accounting aggregates. As Dudley Seers has
pointed out:

> "Lack of data on poverty, unemployment and inequality reflects the
> priorities of statistical offices rather than the difficulties of data collection.
> The conceptual problems of these measures do not seem to be more for-
> midable than those of the national income. We have just grown accus-
> tomed to ignoring them."[1]

This general bias in economic statistics may be attributed to the fact that many
economists believe that economics is concerned with *the allocation of resources
between products* rather than *the distribution of products between people.*

---

1 D. Seers, "The Meaning of Development", *International Development Review* Vol. 11
   (1969), pp. 2—6.

Nonetheless, in recent years there has been a growing recognition that not only the absolute level, but also the distribution between different socio-economic groups of a country's national income is crucial to a real understanding of the historical processes of growth and development. This late recognition has created a growing need for more information on the existing distribution patterns of national income, on the determinants of the distribution of income, and on the interrelation between distributional shifts in income and changes in the pattern of power and property in the developing countries.[2]

The present paper seeks to make a modest contribution to this area of research with special reference to the case of rural Egypt. It is hoped that more serious studies will be undertaken in the future as more disaggregated data and improved analytical techniques become available.

The study is arranged as follows. Chapter 1 sets the scene by surveying the basic changes in the agrarian structure which followed the implementation of the two major land reforms in 1952 and 1961. The themes discussed include changes in the matrix of landownership, changes in the size distribution of landholdings, and changes in tenurial conditions.

Chapter 2 provides a framework for understanding the dynamics of the process of agrarian transition. The relative positions and socio-economic characteristics of the various sections of the peasantry are described, and the key determining factors in the process of differentiation of the peasantry are identified.

Chapter 3 traces the income distributional shifts associated with the new agrarian structure. The relative 'losses' or 'gains' in income have been examined for the different groups of the peasantry during the period under review. It should be noted, however, that the state of available statistics is such that in many instances only fragmentary assessments of income distributional shifts are possible.

Chapter 4 attempts to evaluate the changes in consumption patterns and standards of living in rural Egypt that may be associated with the changed distribution of agricultural income under the new agrarian structure. It also sketches a profile of 'rural poverty'.

Chapter 5 discusses governmental policies relating to *co-operativisation,* pricing and procurement of farm produce. Two different questions will be distinguished in this chapter. On the one hand, the question of agricultural prices, as such, is discussed, largely in relation to the system of co-operative marketing. On the other hand, the question of the *relative* terms of trade between agriculture and other sectors (exporting and manufacturing sectors) and own-inputs is also examined in considerable detail.

The final chapter discusses rather briefly basic trends and the major determinants in the process of *rural out-migration* in Egypt.

The study comes up with a number of tentative results concerning the salient features of the process of agrarian transition in Egypt over the past two decades. Nevertheless, although the study is essentially concerned with the case of Egypt, the research results are of relevance to the understanding of different aspects of the political economy of agrarian transition in other parts of the Third World.

2 See, for instance: UN, *Economic Development and Income Distribution in Argentina* (New York, 1969); UN, *Income Distribution in Latin America* (New York, 1971); UN, *Economic Survey of Asia and the Far East 1971* (Bangkok, 1972), ch. 111.

1

Land Reforms and the Transformation of the Agrarian Structure

"Here man belongs to the land; it is not land that
belongs to him."
H.H. Ayrout
The Egyptian Peasant
(Boston, 1963), p. 53

1.1 Introductory survey: the pre-reform agrarian system

A land tenure system defines a set of complex social relationships which exist among people as to their rights to the occupancy and the use of land. More precisely, it involves the relationship between the 'owner' of the land – or the one who has *possessory* claim to the land – and the actual *land user* or *cultivator.*

There is a particularly long and involved history of land tenure in Egypt. While a complete discussion of this history of land tenure in Egypt lies beyond the scope of the present study,[1] it is important to sketch very briefly the most important features of Egypt's agrarian structure before the July 1952 revolution.

By far the most striking feature of the agrarian structure in Egypt before 1952 was the heavy concentration of landownership and the rapid increase in the number of small owners in relation to the area of land possessed by them. In 1952, the very big landowners (owning over 200 feddans), represented less than 0.1 per cent of the total number of landowners, and possessed about 20 per cent of the cultivated land; large and medium-sized landowners (over 5 feddans), together possessed about 65 per cent of the cultivated land. At the other end of the spectrum, only about 35% of the total cultivable land was owned by the great majority of landowners, (i.e. 94.4%).

Table 1.1 illustrates the persistence of this lopsided agrarian structure over the first half of the twentieth century. Remarkably, the average size of medium ownerships and their share in the total cultivated area remained fairly constant over the period 1900–52. The number of small owners more than tripled in fifty years, and although their share of the total cultivated area increased from some 22 per cent to 35 per cent, the average size of their ownership fell by 45 per cent.[2] The share of large owners in the cultivated area fell from 44 per cent at the turn of the century

---

1 There are a number of excellent studies of the agrarian question and land-tenure system in Egypt; see in particular: Yacub Artin, *La Propriété Foncière en Egypte* (Cairo, 1883); Mohammed Kamel Mursy, *L'Evolution Historique du Droit de Propriété Foncière en Egypte* (Cairo, 1935); Gabriel Baer, *A History of Landownership in Modern Egypt, 1800–1950* (London, 1962); Ibrahim Amer, *Al-ard wa'l-fellah: Al-mas'ala al-zira'iyya fi Misr* (The Land and the Peasant: The Agrarian Question in Egypt), in Arabic (Cairo, 1958); A.R. Abdel-Meguid, "The Agrarian Structure in Egypt", *L'Egypte Contemporaine,* Vol. LI, No. 300, (April 1960); Anouar Abdel-Malek, *Egypt Military Society,* translated by Ch. Lam Markmann (New York: Random House, 1968), pp. 52 and ff.
2 R. Mabro, *The Egyptian Economy 1952–72.* (Oxford: Clarendon Press, 1974), p. 60.

Table 1.1 Changes in distribution of landownership, 1900–1952

Year	Small Ownerships (Less than 5 feddans)				Medium Ownerships (5 and less than 50 feddans)					Large Ownerships (50 feddans and over)					All Ownerships	
	Owners (000's)	% of total land-owners	Area (000 feddans)	Average size of owner-ship (feddans)	Owners (000's)	% of total land-owners	Area (000 feddans)	%	Average size of owner-ship (feddans)	Owners (000's)	% of total land-owners	Area (000 feddans)	%	Average size of owner-ship (feddans)	Owners (000's)	Area (000 feddans)
1900	761	84	1,113	1.46	141	15	1,757	34	12.5	12	1	2,244	44	187	914	5,114
1906	1,084	88	1,293	1.19	134	11	1,662	30	12.4	13	1	2,476	46	190	1,231	5,431
1916	1,480	91	1,450	0.98	133	8	1,645	30	12.4	12	1	2,356	43	196	1,625	5,451
1936	2,242	93	1,837	0.82	146	6	1,747	30	12.0	12	1	2,254	39	188	2,400	5,838
1943	2,376	93.5	1,944	0.82	147	6	1,774	30	12.1	12	0.5	2,142	37	179	2,535	5,860
1952*	2,642	94.3	2,122	0.80	148	5.3	1,817	30	12.3	12	0.4	2,042	35	170	2,802	5,981

* Before the promulgation of the Land Reform Law.
Source: Eprime Eshag and M.A. Kamal, 'Agrarian Reform in the United Arab Republic (Egypt)'. Bulletin of the Oxford University Institute of Economics and Statistics, XXX, May 1968, p. 76.

4

to 35 per cent in 1952. Despite this change the distribution of landownership became even more unequal.[3]

There are, unfortunately, no such complete and precise set of figures for the number of *landless families* in rural Egypt. It is possible, however, to make some rough estimates for the number of such families (defined as neither owning nor renting land) by combining all the data available from the three agricultural censuses preceding the 1952 Revolution, namely 1929, 1939 and 1950. As a result of our calculations, we get the following tentative picture of the development of landless families in rural Egypt.

Table 1.2 *Number of landless families in rural Egypt before the Revolution*

(000's)

Agricultural census year	Rural population	Number of rural families	Number of landholding families	Number of landless families	Landless families as a percentage of total rural families
	(1)	(2)	(3)	(4)	(5)
					%
1929	10,579	2,116	1,207	508	24
1939	11,664	2,333	993	887	38
1950	13,700	2,740	997	1,217	44

Notes and sources:

Col. (1) Rural population figures were obtained by interpolating between Population census years.

Col. (2) Figures obtained by applying a uniform average size of a rural family of 5 persons. See, UN, *Demographic Yearbook* (1962), Table 12. The process of 'rural out-migration' may have contributed to a stabilisation of the average family size in rural areas during the period under investigation.

Col. (3) Figures for the total number of landholders as given in the three agricultural censuses after the exclusion of landholdings of 100 feddans and over all of which are assumed to belong to *absentee* landholders.

Col. (4) Figures for the landless families (after allowance is made for those who are engaged in non-agricultural activities) are obtained as *residual* figures. In the light of the population decennial census data we considered that about 19% of the rural population are engaged in other non-agricultural activities, and thus excluded from the figure for landless families.

Needless to say the figures for 'landless' shown in Table 1.2 must be treated as representing only rough orders of magnitude rather than precise estimates. Nonetheless the implication of these calculations is quite obvious, for the increasing number of *landless families* as a proportion of the total rural population is the best indication of the dimension of the mounting agrarian crisis in rural Egypt before the Revolution.

Three main institutional factors contributed to aggravate the lopsidedness of the agrarian structure in Egypt. *First,* the monopoly power of big landlords over land and water resources resulted in payments of exorbitant rents by small peasants and insecurity of tenure. Rents between 1948 and 1952 varied between £E20 and £E60 per feddan according to region, and were so high as to absorb about 75 per cent of the net income per feddan, leaving hardly anything for the tenant or the

3 *Ibid.*

sharecropper.[4] It was thus more advantageous for the landlord to lease his lands out rather than to cultivate it themselves. *Second*, most of medium and short-term credit had been monopolised by the large landowners, while small peasants — who constitute the vast majority of the Egyptian peasantry — had virtually no access to the modern credit market.[5] Small landowners and tenants were therefore compelled to turn to village moneylenders, merchants and brokers who extorted interest rates often exceeding 100 per cent per annum.[6] These rates represented a heavy burden on the meagre income of these small farmers, and have resulted ultimately in their complete ruin. From time to time, peasants were compelled to sell their own land and to join the ranks of landless peasants.[7] *Third,* heavy speculation in the rural land market had resulted in a tremendous inflation of land prices without any actual increase in 'productive' investment in land. For, in general, land in Egypt was not valued for its income-generating capacity alone. Its possession stood as a symbol of social prestige and a form of political power.[8]

Such high prices for land made it even more difficult for small tenant-cultivators to purchase more lands, resulting therefore in a further aggravation of the lopsidedness of the agrarian structure.

Nevertheless, despite the prevalence of large ownership in land, small-scale farming dominated most of Egyptian agriculture. The fact that the rents charged were in many cases higher than the average net income obtained from the land meant that it was more advantageous for the landlord to lease out his lands than to farm them. Leasing of large estates to intermediaries who divided them up into smallholdings allocated to sharecroppers or to tenants, was a common practice, and one of the most important reasons for the steady growth of *absentee landownership* in Egypt.

Such a divorce between ownership and operation of land on large estates (see Table 1.3) allowed for scores of rent jobbers and middlemen to be very active in the lease market. They would lease large areas under the auction system (*Mazad*) and then sublease them in small units to local small farmers at rents 50—70 per cent higher than those they paid to the original landlords or their agents (Nazir).[9] Thus there arose a whole chain of intermediaries between the small cultivators at the bottom and the statutory owners at the top. In other words, there was a whole *hierarchy of tenures* on the same parcel of land.

4   Cf. G.S. Saab, *Egyptian Agrarian Reform, 1952–1962,* (London: Oxford University Press: 1967) pp. 11–12.
5   In fact commercial banks were mainly concerned with financing trade in the principal export crop — cotton — by advancing short-term loans to big landlords, merchants and exporters, and were unwilling to undertake small credit transactions with the mass of small farmers. The *Agricultural Credit Bank* established in 1931 for the provision of short-term credit to small and medium-sized cultivators was precluded by statute from dealing with tenants or sharecroppers without the written approval of their landlords or the provision of some other collateral. See Saab, *op. cit.*, p. 8.
6   Saab, *ibid.*
7   On this point see: Baer, *A History of Landownership in Modern Egypt,* Ch. 11, pp. 25–38; and Jean G. Economides, 'Le Problème de l'Endettement Rural en Egypte', *L'Egypte Contemporaine,* (1952), pp. 35–65.
8   Cf. J.S. Oweis, 'The Impact of Land Reform on Egyptian Agriculture: 1952–1965', *Intermountain Econ. Rev.,* 11, No. 1, (Spring 1971), p. 50.
9   M.R. El-Ghonemy, 'Economic and Institutional Organization of Egyptian Agriculture since 1952', in *Egypt since the Revolution,* P.J. Vatikiotis (ed.), (New York: Praeger, 1968), p. 69.

Table 1.3 *The proportion of rented area in some large estates in Egypt 1949–50*
(Area in feddans)

Estate	Total	Operated by owners or their agencies	Rented	
			Area	Per cent
1. Royal Estate of Kafr-El-Sheikh	16,035	6,863	9,172	57.2
2. Estate of Sheikh-Fadl Agricultural Company in Menia	6,600	600	6,000	90.9
3. Large Estate at Nag Hamadi, Qena	14,075	2,680	11,395	80.8
4. Government Department of Public Domains	150,832	12,000	138,832	92.0

Source: El-Ghonemy, 'Economic and Institutional Organisation . . .', *op. cit.,* p. 69.

The mounting agrarian crisis in Egypt reached a dramatic point at mid-century, as the living conditions of the mass of the landless and small peasantry has become unbearable, coupled with the dim prospects of getting employment in the industrial sector. In the years 1950–52 the so-called 'passivity' of the Egyptian peasantry was wearing thin and signs of unrest were spreading everywhere in the countryside.[10]

Against this background, the leaders of the coup of 23 July 1952 sensed, right from the very beginning, the urgent need to tackle the 'agrarian question'. They had immediately realised that, if their revolution were to persist, they had both to destroy the power of the entrenched class of big landlords and to win the support of smallholders and the poor rural masses. The land reform law of September 1952 represented a frontal assault on the chronic problems of rural Egypt, and was intended to bring about radical changes in the agrarian structure. It is the purpose of the following sections of this chapter to examine these changes in some detail.

1.2 The land redistribution programme

Land reform was the first act of radical social change placed on the political agenda of the new regime. It took it only a month and a half to prepare the first land reform law, which was enacted on 7 September 1952. The land reform programme. was designed with the clear intention of bringing about a major redistribution of wealth, income and social power in the Egyptian countryside.

The most immediate objective of the land reform law was to break the power of the old ruling oligarchy, with its roots in big estates. From a longer term viewpoint, the far-reaching objective was to break the institutional barriers to a broad restructuring of the social and economic relations in the rural areas.

However, we shall confine out analysis here to a broad assessment of the impact of the two major land reforms in Egypt on the agrarian structure.[11]

10 The years 1950 and 1951 witnessed violent peasants' uprisings on large estates, especially at *Bahut* and *Kufur Negm*. The peasants attacked the private guards and set fire to stores and offices.

11 It is not our intention here to describe fully the Egyptian land reforms, which has been dealt with in several publications and studies. See in particular, Riad El-Ghonemy, *Resource Use and Income in Egyptian Agriculture Before and After the Land Reform with Particular Reference to Economic Development*, unpublished Ph.D. thesis, (North Carolina State University, U.S.A.: 1954); Sayed Marei, *Egyptian Agrarian Reform* (Cairo, 1957); Doreen Warriner, *Land Reform and Development in the Middle East* (London, 1957); Saad Gadalla, *Land Reforms in Relation to Social Development in Egypt* (Univ. of Missouri, 1962); and Gabriel Saab, *The Egyptian Agrarian Reform* (London, 1967).

The first land reform law of September 1952 was the starting point in a long process of radical transformation of the Egyptian agrarian structure. It set the maximum limit of landownership at 200 feddans for a single person, with 100 feddans extra allowed for his dependant children, provided that the total did not exceed 300 feddans. Any land held in excess of this was to be requisitioned and redistributed by the state to small farmers, tenants and labourers. Big landowners were allowed, however, a short time in which to sell lands in excess of this maximum limit.[12]

Expropriated owners (except for members of the royal family) received compensation in the form of non-negotiable government bonds[13] bearing 3 per cent interest, and redeemable in thirty years. The compensation was calculated at seventy times the basic land tax as assessed in 1949 (which averaged about £E3 per feddan). This amounted to about half the 'market value' of land which was commonly valued in 1951 at an average of £E400 per feddan.

The expropriated land was to be distributed within a period of five years among small tenants and farmers owning less than five feddans of agricultural land (article 9 of the law). In practice, priority in distribution was first given to the person who actually farmed the land, whether tenant or owner; thereafter to the landless inhabitants of the village who had the largest families, then to the less wealthy inhabitants.[14]

The distribution was made in plots of two to five feddans depending upon the fertility of the soil and the size of the beneficiary's family. *The size of holdings allotted by the land reform authorities was calculated in such a way as to give each beneficiary and his family an annual income just sufficient to meet bare subsistence expenses.*[15]

The expropriated land was sold by the government to the new beneficiaries, who were to pay for it in equal instalments over 30 years. The selling price was supposed to be equal to the compensation paid to expropriated owners plus a 15 per cent overhead charge to cover the administrative costs of the new Agrarian Reform Department. *It was thus clearly intended that the land distribution programme should be self-financing.*

In 1958, the administrative overheads were reduced from 15 to 10 per cent of the purchase price, the annual interest rate was reduced to $1\frac{1}{2}$ per cent, and the redemption period was extended to 40 years.

12   In this way many landowners were able to escape expropriation through private sales and other transactions.

13   These bonds may be used in payment of certain government taxes such as succession duties and the supplementary land tax.

14   For a complete description of the main stages of the execution of the first land reform law see the important article on 'The agrarian reforms in Egypt' by Sayed Marei, who was then chairman of the Committee responsible for carrying out the reform, and published in the *International Labour Review*, Vol. LXIX, No. 2 (Feb. 1954).

15   According to Sayed Marei, a calculation of the cost of living of different families — with varying sizes — showed that the cost of living for a family of seven was about £E116 per annum. On the basis of these calculations, the individual's average share in land distribution worked out at 14 kirat (0.6 feddans).
    He further states: "since the income of 5 feddans under normal conditions is nearly £E120 a year and the cost of living of a family of eight invididuals is £E128 per annum, a family of eight should be the maximum limit for the distribution of 5 feddans. It can just live on the income of these 5 feddans, supplemented by some other help from outside." cf. Marei, *Int. Lab. Rev.*, *op. cit.*, pp. 145–6.

The expropriated land available for distribution totalled a little more than *half a million* feddans. Thus the redistribution of land enforced by the first land reform law law, seems to have been a fairly moderate measure, involving no more than 8.4% of Egypt's total cultivated land.

Nonetheless, by far the most significant impact of the land reform law was on *tenancy regulations* – including the reduction of rents and the legal protection of tenancy – which affected larger sections of the rural population (i.e. tenant-cultivators). As Doreen Warriner has rightly emphasized: "The improvement in *income* and *legal status* for a very large section of the farm population is by far the most valuable achievement of the reform, greatly exceeding in importance the benefits of distribution."[16]

With the new radicalization derive in July 1961, a second Land Reform Law was promulgated (Law No. 127 of 1961) lowering the limit for a single owner to 100 feddans.[17] Under the new law the redistributed lands were sold to new beneficiaries at a price equal to half the value of the lands as assessed for compensation. In 1964, a new law (Law No. 138) stipulated that the redistributed land was to be sold to new beneficiaries at a price equivalent to one fourth of the value as assessed for compensation to ex-proprietors. Interest charges and payments for government expenses were also abolished.[18] These new concessions were extended to all beneficiaries under the first land reform law of 1952 and all subsequent legislation.

Table 1.4 *Agrarian reform lands distributed among small farmers, 1953–70*

Year	Area (feddans)	Number of beneficiaries (families)	Average amount of distributed land per family (feddans)
1953	16,426	4,784	3.4
1954	65,285	24,295	2.7
1955	66,687	31,588	2.1
1956	35,558	15,678	2.3
1957	42,067	19,701	2.1
1958	42,920	17,045	2.5
1959	5,982	2,447	2.4
1960	23,426	10,345	2.3
1961	28,381	9,291	3.0
1962	106,150	31,605	3.6
1963	90,172 ⎫		
1964	121,645 ⎬	107,286	2.2
1965	26,013 ⎭		
1966	25,668	12,013	2.1
1967	58,107	31,298	1.9
1968	20,531	8,295	2.5
1969	22,743	9,056	2.5
1970*	19,777	7,255	2.7
Total	817,538	341,982	2.4

* Data up to 1/11/1970.

Sources: Statistical Handbook of ARE (1952–1970), Cairo, June 1971.
  Cultivated Areas in ARE in 1969, Reference No. 30/413, Nov. 1972, p. 88.
  Statistical Atlas (1962).

16 Warriner, *Land Reform and Development in the Middle East,* p. 39. This question will be explored in some detail in Chapter 3.
17 This law was amended further in 1969 to limit maximum ownership to 50 feddans (see Appendix A).
18 cf. Oweis, 'The Impact of Land Reform on Egyptian Agriculture: 1952–1965', p. 54.

Table 1.5 *Areas acquired and distributed by land reform laws, 1953–69*

Origin of acquired land	Area (feddans)	Number of beneficiaries (families)
1. Original Land Reform Law No. 178 of 1952	365,147	146,496
2. Law No. 152 of 1957 and Law No. 44 of 1962 for transfer to land reform of *wakf* lands.	189,049	78,797
3. Second land reform, Law No. 127 of 1961	100,745	45,823
4. Purchase of lands sequestrated in 1956 including those of companies and other institutions.	112,641	49,390
5. Law No. 15 of 1963 excluding foreigners from land ownership.	30,081	14,172
6. Other confiscated land.	98	49
Total	797,761	334,727

Source: CAPMS, *Cultivated Areas in ARE in 1969*, Reference No. 30/413 (Cairo, Nov. 1972), p. 91.

As a result of various land reform laws enacted between 1952 and 1970, 817,538 feddans (about 12.5 per cent of the cultivated land) have been distributed among 341,982 families comprising about 1.7 million persons, or about 9 per cent of the rural pupulation in 1970. (See Table 1.4)

1.3 The impact of land reforms on the matrix of land ownership

1.3.1 Changes in the pattern of landownership by size class

The change in the matrix of landownership in Egypt in the last two decades can be regarded as a direct result of the implementation of the two land reforms in 1952 and 1961. It is possible to trace the changes that have taken place in the pattern of landownership during the period 1952–65, as official statistics on the distribution of landownership are available on a comparable basis.[19]

Table 1.6 gives the basic data concerning the evolution of the distribution of landownership over this period. A cursory glance at the data in this table indicates that the most notable change that followed the implementation of the agrarian reform law of 1952 is that, while the relative number of small ownerships remained nearly unchanged (94.4%), their share of land increased substantially from 35.4% to 46.4% (an increase of 11.2% in acreage). It is also worth noting that the number of *medium-sized ownerships*, namely *ownerships* of 20 to 50 feddans, increased in *absolute* terms from 22,000 to 30,000 after the enactment of the first agrarian reform law, with an area rising from 650,000 to 800,000 feddans (an increase of 23% in acreage.[20]

As little of the newly distributed land sold by the state went to the medium-scale owners, the growth in the absolute numbers and acreage of these ownerships largely reflects acquisitions of new land through 'distress' or 'crash' sales by the big landowners. This explanation is supported by the fact that the medium ownerships of smaller size (i.e. 5 to under 10 feddans and 10 to under 20 feddans) remained

19 1965 is the latest year for which data are available on a *comparable* basis.
20 Cf. "Changes in the Pattern of Landownership in U.A.R. (1952–1965)". *CBE Economic Review*, **VIII**, No. 384 (1968), pp. 147–8.

Table 1.6 *Developments in landownership in Egypt, 1952–65*

(000's)

Size class (feddans)	Distribution before: 1952 law				Distribution after: 1952 law				Situation in 1961*				Situation in 1965†			
	Land-ownership		Total area		Land-ownership		Total area		Land-ownership		Total area		Land-ownership		Total area	
	Number	%	Feddans	%	Number	%	Feddans	%	Number	%	Feddans	%	Number	%	Feddans	%
Small ownerships																
< 5	2,642	94.3	2,122	35.4	2,841	94.4	2,781	46.6	2,919	94.1	3,172	52.1	3,033	94.5	3,693	57.1
Medium size ownerships																
5– < 10	79	2.8	526	8.8	79	2.6	526	8.8	80	2.6	526	8.6	78	2.4	614	9.5
10– < 20	47	1.7	638	10.7	47	1.6	638	10.7	65	2.1	638	10.7	61‡	1.9	527	8.2
20– < 50	22	0.8	654	10.9	30	1.0	818	13.6	26	0.8	818	13.4	29	0.9	815	12.6
Large ownerships																
50– < 100	6	0.2	430	7.2	6	0.2	430	7.2	6	0.2	430	7.0	6	0.2	392	6.1
100– < 200	3	0.1	437	7.3	3	0.1	437	7.2	5	0.5	500	8.2	4	0.1	421	6.5
≥ 200	2	0.1	1,177	19.7	2	0.1	354	5.9	–	–	–	–	–	–	–	–
Total	2,801	100.0	5,984	100.0	3,008	100.0	5,984	100.0	3,101	100.0	6,084	100.0	3,211	100.0	6,462	100.0

Source: CAPMS, *Statistical Annual Book* (June 1968).
Notes: * After the promulgation of Law No. 127/1961.
† Excluding government properties.
‡ There is some doubt as to the accuracy of this figure since the average size of ownership in this bracket works out at 8.6 which is clearly inconsistent with size class of 10 to less than 20.feddans. The same applies to the situation in 1961.
§ The increase in the area of cultivated land between 1961 and 1965 is mainly due to large-scale land reclamation schemes.

almost unchanged both in number and acreage, in *absolute* as well as in *relative* terms, after the land reform.

With regard to the big landowners (owning more than 100 feddans), their number remained unchanged (5,000 owners) while their share of land declined to 13%, as against 27% before the application of the law.

Further changes in the pattern of landownership took place after the promulgation of Law No. 127 of 1961 and other contractual transactions. By 1965 the total acreage of small ownerships (less than 5 feddans) reached 57% of the total cultivated area. At the other end of the spectrum, large ownerships (50 feddans and over) retained 12.6% of the total cultivated land.

It is a notable feature of the Egyptian agrarian reforms that changes in the pattern of landownership were mainly confined to small and large ownerships (the tails of the distribution) rather than medium-sized ones. More significant still is the fact that, after two major attempts at redistributing the land, the *scale of relativities* remains remarkably constant. In fact, despite two major land reforms, the size distribution of landownerships remained *invariant* over time except for a 'shift' parameter, leaving the relative numbers of big landowners, medium-scale and small landowners almost unaltered.

1.3.2 Shifts in the degree of concentration in landownership

One familiar way of detecting the redistributive effects of land reforms is to construct *Lorenz curves* relating to the distribution of landownership at different points of time.[21] Fig. 1.1 shows that the *Lorenz curve* has uniformly moved outwards to a considerable degree, thus indicating a great reduction in the degree of concentration of landownership in Egypt over the period 1952–65.[22]

The Gini coefficient,[23] reflecting the degree of concentration in landownership, shifted from 0.611 before the promulgation of the 1952 law to 0.492 afterwards. After the enactment of the second land reform law of 1961, the Gini coefficient reached 0.432 and declined further to 0.383 in 1965, indicating a moderate decline of concentration of landownership during the first half of the 1960s.[24]

Nonetheless one should indicate the main limitations of the source-data used in our analysis in this section. A major deficiency of the official data on the distribution of landownership in Egypt lies in the fact that they tend to understate the degree of concentration of landownership (in particular for medium and large landowners). In fact, landownership statistics relate mainly to the number of *landed properties* (ownerships) in each village and not of *proprietors*, and thus disregard the existence of multiple ownership.[25] In other words, a landowner possessing

21 A *Lorenz curve* is a graphical representation of the relationship between the cumulative percentages of the number of owners and the corresponding cumulative percentages of owned land.

22 It should be emphasised however that although these changes in the distribution of landownership mainly reflect the impact of the two agrarian reforms, they may also include other dealings, such as legacies and donations.

23 *The Gini coefficient*, attributed to the Italian economist Gini (1912), has been widely used as a familiar measure of the *degree of inequality* in wealth and income as calculated from Lorenz curves. The Gini coefficient can be roughly defined as *a measure of dispersion:* the mean difference divided by twice the mean.

24 Cf. CBE, *Economic Review*, **VIII**, No. 3/4 (1968), p. 151.

25 See: Baer, *A History of Landownership in Modern Egypt*, p. 77.

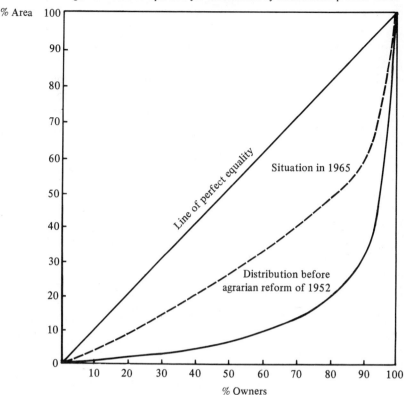

Fig. 1.1 *Lorenz comparison for distribution of landownership 1952–1965*

% Area

Line of perfect equality

Situation in 1965

Distribution before agrarian reform of 1952

% Owners

a piece of land in each of several villages is counted not as one owner, but as several. This certainly distorts the true picture of the distribution of landownership, and thus leads to an understatement of the degree of concentration of landownership in the medium and large brackets.[26]

Moreover, it is worth noting that many big landowners avoided having their land expropriated by registering land in the names of different members of their families, while still themselves retaining effective control and the ultimate possessory claims to land.

However, these data limitations and distortions are not serious enough to affect the validity and real significance of the foregoing analysis of the distribution pattern of landownership in Egypt during the period under review.[27]

1.4 Changes in the distribution of land by size of holdings

A more reliable guide to an analysis of changes in the agrarian structure is to look at the distribution pattern of *landholdings* rather than *ownerships*. A *holding* or a *farm*

---

26 Cf. A. Mohieldine, *Agricultural Investment and Employment in Egypt since 1935*, unpublished Ph.D. thesis, (London: 1966), pp. 50–51.
27 It might be argued that the same degree of *statistical bias* was common to all analysed data on the distribution of landownership.

Table 1.7 *Distribution of land-holdings by size, 1950 and 1961*

Size of holdings (feddans)	1950				1961			
	Number of holdings (000's)	%	Area (000 feddans)	%	Number of holdings (000's)	%	Area (000 feddans)	%
< 1	214.3	21.4	111.8	1.8	434.2	26.4	211.2	3.4
1 – < 2	248.3	24.8	335.7	5.5	385.9	23.5	505.3	8.1
2 – < 3	161.7	16.1	373.9	6.1	286.8	17.5	647.9	10.4
3 – < 4	99.1	9.9	328.7	5.4	174.6	10.6	566.4	9.1
4 – < 5	63.3	6.3	272.7	4.4	99.7	6.1	423.6	6.8
5 – < 10	122.4	12.2	818.4	13.3	170.0	10.4	1100.7	17.7
10 – < 20	52.5	5.2	705.3	11.5	56.7	3.4	742.6	12.0
20 – < 50	26.5	2.6	792.1	12.9	23.8	1.5	689.3	11.0
50 – < 100	8.4	0.8	579.1	9.4	6.4	0.4	429.9	7.0
⩾ 100	6.5	0.7	1826.3	29.7	4.0	0.24	905.9	14.5
Total	1003.0	100	6144.0	100	1642.1	100	6222.8	100

Sources: 1950: Department of Statistics and Census, Ministry of Agriculture, *Agricultural Census 1950*, Vol. 1, (Government Press: Cairo 1958), Table 3, pp. 34–5; 1961: *Fourth Agricultural Census 1961* (Cairo, 1967), Part I, section 1.

can be defined as an operational unit of cultivation, regardless of whether the land — operated as a single unit — is owned or leased. Thus the basic characteristic of a holding is 'operation' not 'ownership': *operational holding* = owned land + (leased-in land — leased-out land).

The third and fourth agricultural censuses, conducted in 1950 and 1961 respectively, provide valuable statistical material on the size distribution of farm-holdings in Egypt.[28] Table 1.7 gives the basic data about the number and area of farm-holdings classified by size.

An examination of the data in this table reveals the highly skewed nature of the distribution of farm-holdings in Egypt, which is even more skewed than the size distribution of landownership.

It is easy to see that the land tenure system in Egypt is largely dominated by small-holdings: small farm-holdings represented 78.5% of the total number of holdings in 1950 and 84% in 1961, while the farm area they covered amounted in 1950 to 23.2% and in 1961 to 38% of total cultivated land.

The group of medium-sized holdings (from 5 to less than 50 feddans) represented 20% of total holdings in 1950 and 15.3% in 1961, while their cultivated area rose from 37.7% in 1950 to 40.7% in 1961. The third group of large farm-holdings (50 feddans and over) shows a perceptible decrease in farm area, from 39% to 21.5% of the total cultivated land, as a result of land reform measures.

A simple comparison of the size-distribution of *landholdings* with the distribution pattern of *landownerships* (see Table 1.8) brings out quite clearly that one of the basic features of the land tenure system in Egypt is *the tendency to concentrate the land into larger holdings than the freeholds.*[29] In this respect, the economic function

28 According to the agricultural census of 1950, a holding is defined as one of more pieces of land devoted to agricultural activity operated by one holder or farmer, whether he is an owner or tenant or both together, cf. *Agricultural Census of 1950*, p. 1.
29 Cf. Hansen and Marzouk, *Development and Economic Policy in the UAR (Egypt)*, (Amsterdam: North-Holland Publishing Company, 1965), p. 87;

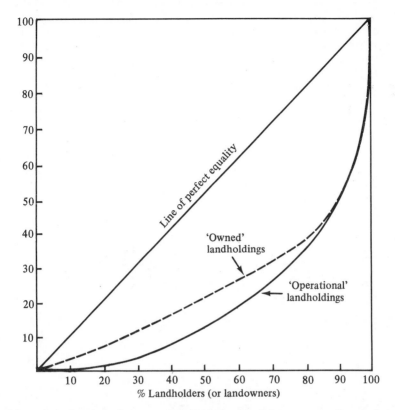

Fig. 1.2 *Lorenz comparison for distribution of 'owned' and 'operational' holdings, 1961*

% Farm Area

Line of perfect equality

'Owned' landholdings

'Operational' landholdings

% Landholders (or landowners)

of tenancy is to break up large ownerships and consolidate very small parcels into holdings of operational size.[30] This fact is further illustrated by a Lorenz comparison of the size distribution of operational landholdings and the size distribution of landownerships in 1961, as displayed in Fig. 1.2.

As can be seen from Table 1.8, recourse to tenancy was widespread among both large landlords and the small absentee owners — who could not draw a living from their minute plots. The large discrepancy between figures for *landownerships* and those for *holdings* in the size-class of 'less than five feddans', illustrates the fact that these small landowners tend to be the net *out-leasers* in the system. This is mainly attributable to the fact that there is more absentee ownership among the very small proprietors (in particular owners of less than one feddan) than among the medium and large-scale proprietors.[31]

On the other hand, medium-scale owners (owning between 5 and 10 feddans), as

30 Mabro, *The Egyptian Economy. . , op. cit.,* p. 62.
31 In fact, only about *one-fourth* of the owners of 'less than one feddan' can be classified as geniune owner-cultivators. This is hardly surprising, since plots of less than one feddan are too small to provide even a bare subsistence existence for a peasant, and their proprietors tend to rent their plots to other small proprietors — mainly those who own 5–10 feddans.
   Moreover, ownership of land represented for decades the chief form of economic security and prestige; the small employee who inherited a small piece of land clung to its ownership even when he could not operate it.

Table 1.8 *Comparison of 'ownerships' and 'landholdings' distribution patterns in Egypt, 1961*

Size-class (feddans)	No. of ownerships (000's)	No. of holdings (000's)	No. of holdings as a percentage of number of ownerships %	Total area of ownerships (000 feddans)	Total area of holdings (000 feddans)	% Area of holdings / Area of ownerships
< 5	2,919	1,381	47.3	3,172	2,354	74
5 – < 10	80	170	212	526	1,101	209
10 – < 20	65	57	88	638	743	117
20 – < 50	26	24	92	818	689	84
50 – < 100	6	6	100	430	430	100
⩾ 100	5	4	80	500	906	181
Total	3,101	1,642	53	6,084	6,223*	100

* The total area of holdings exceeds the total area of ownerships by 2%. A possible source of the discrepancy between the two figures – apart from any statistical and definitional differences – may be that the figure for the total area of ownerships is exclusive of *government properties.*

Sources: Tables (1.3) & (1.6)

well as the very large landowners (owners of 100 feddans and over) tend to be the most intensive net *in-leasers*. More generally, it is fair to say those who are usually able to lease-in more land are those who are initially better endowed in terms of land and other assets.

At any rate, this distribution pattern of farm-holdings has important negative implications for resource allocation in Egyptian agriculture. To alleviate the negative effects of small-scale farming, the government has been led to pursue a vigorous policy of 'land consolidation', aiming at the restructuring of land holdings into efficient large units through *co-operative organisation*.[32]

1.5   Distribution of holdings according to type of tenure

Land tenure systems embrace a complex set of relationships which involves many forms and bundles of *land-use rights*. In particular, we shall focus here on the relationship between the 'owner' of the land, the one who has a *possessory* claim to the land, and the land user or immediate cultivator.

1.5.1   Distribution of landholdings by types of tenure

Fortunately the agricultural census data for Egypt incorporate some useful material on the distribution of landholdings by types of tenure. The total area under tenancy constituted about 40% of the total cultivated land according to the 1961 census data. Table 1.9 gives the overall picture of the distribution of farm-holdings and cultivated land according to type of tenure in 1950 and 1961.

Table 1.9 *Distribution of holdings according to type of tenure, 1950 and 1961*

Types of tenure	1950				1961			
	Area		Holders		Area		Holders	
	000 feddans	%	000 feddans	%	000 feddans	%	000 feddans	%
1. Pure Ownership	3,720	61	657	66	2,665	43	623	38
2. Pure Tenancy	1,223	20	207	20	1,214	19.5	524	32
3. *Mixed:*								
Ownership	494	8	139	24	1,088	17.5	495	30
Tenancy	706	11			1,255	20		

Source: Third & Fourth Agricultural Censuses.

It is important to note at the outset that no general conclusion can be reached, on the basis of these data, about the actual changes in areas under tenancy. For it is difficult, in the Egyptian situation, to draw any sharp distinction between *owned* and *leased* land, as many owner-cultivators, who generally reserve the cash crops for themselves, often lease-out large areas, divided into small plots, to tenants or agricultural labourers on a *seasonal basis*.

As a matter of fact, seasonal tenancy arrangements are not usually taken into account in agricultural censuses. This is particularly true of 1950 agricultural census data, for all the available evidence points to a serious understatement of the area

---

32   See Chapter 5

under tenancy.[33] According to Sayed Marei, tenancy regulations enacted by the agrarian reforms, affected an area of about 3.1 million feddans,[34] which amounted to more than 50% of the cultivated land in 1952. This estimate seems to be more accurate than the census figure and comes closer to other information provided by the Egyptian Ministry of Agriculture, putting the area under tenancy at about 59% of the cultivated land in 1950.[35]

At any rate, the unreliability of the data and their defective coverage are such that tenure statistics can only be illustrative of the fact that about half of the cultivated land in Egypt is usually leased or share-cropped. Moreover, as about 50 per cent of landholdings are of less than two feddan — considered by the ILO report to be the minimum size to support a small rural family — many of these smallholders find themselves compelled to lease-in more land from larger proprietors as well as from small owners who do not cultivate their land.[36]

1.5.2   Distribution of farm area by type of tenure and size of holding

The analysis has been conducted so far in aggregate terms without any regard to the size of holdings. In fact, an analysis of different types of tenure, which relates to different size-classes of landholdings, is likely to be more revealing than a highly aggregative analysis. Tables 1.10 and 1.11 show the distribution of holdings and farm area by size of holdings for the three basic types of tenure.

The various types of farm holdings, enumerated in the 1961 census, are run on three tenure systems: owner's self-operation, cash tenancy, and share-cropping. In the light of the data given in Tables 1.10 and 1.11, it appears that 39% of the total number of holdings of under one feddan are 'purely leased holdings', the highest proportion among all size-classes. This result is hardly surprising, for most of the nominal small landowners (of less than one feddan) are *absentee landowners* as we stated earlier.

Holdings in the size-class 1—3 feddans are distributed rather more evenly between the three tenure categories. A large proportion of holdings in the range 3—10 feddans tends to be concentrated in the 'mixed' category, where *owned* and *leased* land are combined together in one operating unit. For holdings of larger size (over 10 feddans), the proportion of 'purely leased' holdings and farm area tends to decline very sharply with the increase in the size of holding, leaving 'owner-occupied' and 'mixed' farms as the two most dominant forms of land tenure. The fact that emerges here is that the relative share of 'purely leased holdings', as a distinct tenure category, tends to decline with increasing holding size. In fact this category of tenure becomes almost negligible for the largest holdings (over 50 feddans).

These findings highlight some basic facts characterising the Egyptian agrarian structure: *first*, families with holdings of less than one feddan are not always able to lease-in more pieces of land, since they are among the least credit-worthy

---

33 It seems also that in the case of many sharecropping arrangements, holdings were frequently classed as owner-operated. Cf. Saab, *op. cit.*, p. 14.
34 S. Marei, 'U.A.R.: Overturning the Pyramid', *CERES — FAO Review*, vol. 2, No. 6 (Nov.—Dec. 1969), p. 50.
35 See: *Bulletin of Agricultural Economics*, published by the Egyptian Ministry of Agriculture (issues of 1950/51).
36 Cf. ILO, *Rural Employment Problems in the U.A.R.*, p. 36.

Table 1.10 *Distribution of holdings of different sizes by type of tenure, 1961*

Size of holding (feddans)	Total Number of holdings	%	Number of 'purely owned' holdings	%	Number of 'purely leased' holdings	%	Number of 'mixed' holdings	%
< 1	434,219	100	204,942	47	168,791	39	60,486	14
1 — < 2	385,901	100	124,479	32	138,635	36	122,787	32
2 — < 3	286,804	100	106,017	37	86,894	30	93,893	33
3 — < 4	174,595	100	58,827	34	51,109	29	64,659	37
4 — < 5	99,722	100	32,271	32	27,154	27	40,297	41
5 — < 10	170,019	100	56,193	33	40,292	24	73,534	43
10 — < 20	56,705	100	23,329	41	8,254	15	25,122	44
20 — < 50	23,811	100	11,295	48	1,991	8	10,525	44
50 — < 100	6,424	100	3,479	54	440	7	2,505	39
⩾ 100	3,960	100	2,338	59	266	7	1,356	34
Total	1,642,160	100	623,170	38	523,826	32	495,164	30

Source: 1961 Agricultural Census: Part I, Section A, Table III.

members of the rural community. *Second*, there is an upper limit to the size of farm area to be operated by a tenant-farmer as a 'purely leased holding' (almost ten feddans). *Third*, those who are able to lease-in more land, to be operated within the framework of 'mixed holdings', are those who are initially better endowed (i.e. owners of more than 10 feddans).

1.5.3   Changes in tenancy arrangements

It is well known that land may be leased under two main institutional arrangements: share-cropping or cash tenancy. The choice of a specific type of tenancy arrangement in a country like Egypt tends to depend on institutional factors as well as pure economic considerations involving risk and uncertainty.[37]

The agricultural censuses provide some data on the division of holdings and rented land by type of rent. Table 1.12 shows the aggregate distribution of holdings and farm area by types of tenancy arrangement in 1950 and 1961.

Under a standard sharecropping arrangement, the landlord supplies the land and buildings and half of the expenditure on seeds, chemical fertilisers, irrigation, pest control and harvesting, in addition to paying the land tax. The tenant provides his labour, manure, canal and drain maintenance in addition to the other half of the production expenses as mentioned for the landlord. At harvest time, the owner receives half of the crop and the tenant the other half. These terms for sharecropping are laid down by the agrarian reform laws.[38]

We now turn to consider the relationship between the size of farm-holdings and the choice of a specific type of tenancy arrangement. Table 1.13 shows the distribution of leased holdings and farm area allocated to the two major types of rent by holding sizes.

37 The usual explanations for the existence of *share-rent* contracts (as opposed to *fixed rent* contracts) is that they provide a method of sharing risk. In the case of Egypt, *sharecroppers* are usually related to their landlords by various bonds (i.e. relatives, debts, etc . . .), and the *share-rent* does not represent the only form of renumeration for the land-use. Thus the choice of a specific type of tenancy arrangement is part of the complex social structure of the Egyptian village.
38 The land reform law required all rental arrangements to be in writing and the minimum compulsory period of tenancy to be 3 years.

Table 1.11 *Distribution of farm area by types of tenure and size of holding, 1961*

Size of holding (feddans)	Total area (feddans)	%	'Purely owned' holdings (feddans)	%	'Purely leased' holdings (feddans)	%	'Mixed' holdings (feddans)	%	Ratio of rented to owned land in 'mixed' holdings
< 1	211,155	100	92,044	44	79,658	38	39,453	18	1.2
1 – < 2	505,325	100	160,898	32	173,707	34	170,720	34	1.3
2 – < 3	647,912	100	236,665	36	192,006	30	219,241	34	1.3
3 – < 4	566,407	100	190,513	34	162,737	29	213,157	47	1.2
4 – < 5	423,622	100	137,176	32	113,471	27	172,972	41	1.2
5 – < 10	1,100,669	100	363,125	33	253,500	23	484,044	44	1.2
10 – < 20	742,619	100	307,802	41	103,498	14	331,319	45	1.2
20 – < 50	689,267	100	328,373	48	56,193	8	304,701	44	1.1
50 – < 100	429,952	100	232,611	54	29,193	7	167,925	39	1.0
≥ 100	905,911	100	615,342	68	49,740	5	240,829	27	0.9
Total	6,222,839	100	2,664,549	43	1,213,926	19.5	2,344,364	37.5	1.55

Source: Agricultural Census 1961: Part I, Section A, Table III.

Table 1.12 *Distribution of holdings and far area by type of rent, 1950 and 1961*

Type of rent	1950				1961			
	No. of holdings (000)	%	Area (000 feddans)	%	No. of holdings (000)	%	Area (000 feddans)	%
1. Cash rent	305	87	1,626	84	938	92	2,179	88
2. Share-Cropping & other types of leases	46	13	303	16	81	8	292	12
Total	351	100	1,929	100	1,019	100	2,471	100

Source: (1950): D. Mead, *Growth and Structural Change in the Egyptian Economy* (Illinois: 1967) *statistical appendix*, Table III–C–5 (1961): *Fourth Agricultural Census*, Section A, Table VI.

Table 1.13 *Distribution of holdings and leased land by types of rent, 1961*

Size of holding (feddans)	Total leased		Cash rent				Share cropping and others			
	No. of holdings (000)	Area (000 feddans)	No. of holdings (000)	%	Area (000 feddans)	%	No. of holdings (000)	%	Area (000 feddans)	%
< 1	229.3	101.2	222.7	97	98.0	97	7.0	3	3.3	3
1 – < 2	261.4	269.4	247.4	95	253.3	94	15.3	5	16.0	6
2 – < 3	180.8	314.3	165.1	91	283.0	90	17.4	9	31.3	10
3 – < 4	115.8	280.7	101.9	88	240.0	85	15.7	12	40.5	15
4 – < 5	67.4	207.5	58.2	86	127.4	83	10.4	14	35.1	17
5 – < 10	113.8	517.5	97.0	85	426.3	82	19.1	15	91.2	18
10 – < 20	33.4	285.5	29.7	89	247.0	86	3.6	11	38.5	14
20 – < 50	12.7	216.5	11.7	92	200.2	92	1.0	8	16.3	8
50 – < 100	2.9	114.3	2.7	93	106.6	93	0.2	7	7.7	7
≥ 100	1.6	163.5	1.5	94	151.8	93	00.1	6	11.7	7
Total	1,019	2,470	938		2,178.8		90.6		291.8	

Source: Fourth Agricultural Census (1961), Section 'A', Table V.

These data clearly reveal a certain pattern in the distribution of holdings of different sizes between the two major types of tenancy arrangements. The area under share-cropping tends to be negligible for small-holdings of less than 3 feddans. By contrast, the area held under share-cropping tends to be significant (14% to 18% of total leased land) for small farms of 3–5 feddans as well as for medium-size holdings (5 to 20 feddans). The proportion of share-cropping as a form of tenancy averages only 7% of the total leased land for larger farm-holdings, comprising over 20 feddans.

It is difficult, however, without access to more empirical evidence, to offer any precise explanation for the significance of share-cropping in the tenancy arrangements of medium-sized holdings (5 to 20 feddans). Nonetheless it might be argued that, for larger holdings of more than 20 feddans, crop-sharing may cease to be a beneficial arrangement as modern profitable inputs assume some significance. The incentives for increased investment as well as for capturing the returns on such investment may explain the preference for fixed contractual payments.

Undoubtedly, any explanation one might offer for the behaviour patterns of the tenant-farmers of any size of holding is bound to indicate only one of the numerous ways in which these tenancy arrangements have come about in reality.

1.5.4 The impact of agrarian reforms on the area under tenancy

Keeping in mind the above-mentioned shortcomings of tenancy statistics, we propose here to examine the extent to which the tenancy regulations enacted by the agrarian reforms have contributed to an *increase* or *contraction* of the area under tenancy (see Table 1.14).

Table 1.14 *The impact of the agrarian reforms on the area under tenancy*

Year	Area of land owner operated (feddans)	%	Area of land leased (feddans)	%
1950	2,481,933	41	3,492,640	59
1951	2,423,000	40	3,601,878	60
1952	2,388,479	39.5	3,668,978	60
1953	2,672,181	44	3,337,027	56
1954	2,623,833	44	3,560,497	56
1958	2,615,683	46	3,081,728	54
1959	2,929,106	49	3,028,780	51
1960	2,960,257	49	3,020,790	51
1961	2,833,680	47	3,142,819	53
1962	2,938,636	49	3,064,767	51

Source: Ezz-el Din Hammam, *The Real Impact of the Agrarian Reform on the Distribution of Income between Landowners and Tenants in U.A.R.*, INP Memo. 492, (Cairo, Sept. 1964), Table 1, p. 6.

The data in Table 1.14[39] suggest that there was a moderate drop in the total area of rented land from 59% in the agricultural year 1950/51 to 51% in 1960/61, *as the 'rental terms' for land in the lease market became less beneficial to the landowners as a result of the tenancy regulations enacted by the agrarian reforms.*

Perhaps one could conjecture that land reforms may have led to a resumption of cultivation of some tracts of land by owners, partly because they wanted to cultivate the extra land and largely owing to the new desire of many owners to safeguard themselves against rent avoidance and future encroachments by tenants.

1.6 Summing up

Few would deny that the suppression of the political power exercised by big landlords and the social liberation of large sections of the peasantry have been the most impressive achievement of the Egyptian agrarian reforms. For reasons stated earlier the land reform was a political necessity in Egypt at the time it occurred and hence became an integral part of the new power structure, laying the base for new social, political and economic institutions in rural Egypt.

Land reform measures were welcomed by the 'enlightened' business circles in Egypt as timely measures, long overdue, to redirect investment into industry and to avert the risk of a more radical solution to the agrarian question, which was looming large on the horizon. The National Bank of Egypt greeted the reforms in the following striking terms:

"Egypt may consider herself happy that after so many disappointing promises and empty talk, the matter has not slipped out of the hands of an orderly

---

39 These data are exclusive of 'seasonal leases' per crop.

government dealing with it within the framework of Law, and has not fallen into the sphere of "mass initiative", violence and disorder.

Looked at from this angle, almost any reform, no matter how radical, is preferable to the anarchy of a mass movement. Critics, and especially foreign critics, of the reform should keep this in mind".[40]

The principal aim of the Egyptian land reforms was to abolish the large estates and to create a vast class of small-holders.[41] Thus, the reform was, in principle and practice, more akin to the *liberal* ideal of 'a regime of small peasant properties' rather than to any *collectivist* or *socialistic* ideals.[42]

Table 1.15 gives a summary view of the changes in the structure of landownership in Egypt and traces the sources of change in the total area owned in each size-class over the period 1952–65. A comparison of the structure of ownership in 1952 with that in 1965 reveals that by 1965 about 671,000 feddans had been distributed in full ownership to small landowners as a result of the 1952 and 1961 land reform measures. However, the area finally transferred from big landowners to small land-owners as a result of the agrarian reform measures was much greater. According to our estimates the area sold by big landowners to small farmers, according to provisions of Article 4 of the 1952 agrarian reform law (enabling landlords to sell land in excess of the ceiling to their tenants in small plots not exceeding 5 feddans), amounts to 107,000 feddans. Moreover, about 453,000 feddans had been sold to small farmers by land reclamation organizations and companies (including Nile Deposit lands and the land distributed by the Egyptian Organization for Desert Development).

The increase in the area owned by medium-sized landowners in the size-class 20–50 feddans is totally accounted for by the crash sales and other private deals in the land market which occurred immediately after the implementation of the 1952 agrarian reform. The explanation of this is that many big landowners sold estates they were legally entitled to keep, fearing a subsequent reduction of the limit on residual holdings, or more drastic tenancy regulations. These estates were generally purchased in lots of 20–100 feddans by farmers who either kept them or broke them up further and sold them to medium or smaller farmers.[43] Some 249,000 feddans changed hands in this way.

Nevertheless, in spite of two major land reforms, the distribution of landownership remains highly skewed. Nonetheless, the most notable trend over the period 1952–65, has been the steady improvement in the relative position (increase in *numbers* and *acreage*) of the medium-sized properties, and in particular owners of 20 to 50 feddans. As a matter of fact these medium landowners owned almost *one-third* of Egypt's cultivated land in 1965, while they made up only 5.2% of the total number of landowners.

Under the conditions prevailing today, this stratum of rich peasants (medium-sized proprietors of 20 to 50 feddans) carries a decisive political weight in the Egyptian countryside, as they have been elevated in the social hierarchy by gaining

40   'Agrarian Reform in Egypt', *NBE Economic Bulletin*, V, No. 3 (1952), p. 167.
41   cf. Marei, 'The Agrarian Reform in Egypt', p. 148.
42   cf. Doreen Warriner, *Land Reform in Principle and Practice* (London, Oxford Univ. Press: 1969), p. 32.
43   See: Saab, *The Egyptian Agrarian Reform*, pp. 28–9.

Table 1.15 Summary of changes in the structure of landownership, 1952–65

Ownership classes by size (feddans)	Number of landowners			Total area owned			Sources of changes in total area owned	
	1952[1] (000's)	1965 (000's)	Change Δ (000's)	1952[1] (000 feddans)	1965 (000 feddans)	Change Δ (000 feddans)	(a) Transfers of land as a result of land reform programme (000 feddans)	(b) Private sales & other transactions (000 feddans)
1. *Small ownerships*								
< 5	2,642	3,033	+391	2,122	3,693 (3,353)	+1,571 (+1,231)	+671[4]	+218[5]
2. *Medium-sized ownerships*								
5 – < 10	79	78	−1	526	614	+88	—	+88
10 – < 20	47	41[2]	−6	638	527[3]	−111	—	−111
20 – < 50	22	29	+7	654	815	+161	—	+161
3. *Large ownerships*								
50 – < 100	6	6	—	430	392	−38	—	−38
100 – < 200	3	4	+1	437	421	−16	—	−16
≥ 200	2	—	−2	1,177	—	−1,177	−875[6]	−302
Total	2,801	3,191	+390	5,984	6,462 (6,326)	+478 (+342)	−204[7]	—

Notes: 1 Situation before the implementation of the agrarian reform law No. 178/1952.

2 Adjusted figure (see notes to Table 1.6).

3 These are doubtful figures. In the absence of firm evidence, we assume that the decrease in the area in this size class (111,000 feddans) has its counterpart in the 111,000 feddans sold by public organizations to small farmers (see footnote 5).

4 The figure represents the cumulative distributions of land reform lands up to 1965.

5 Including 111,000 feddans sold by other public organizations to small landholders (see: UAR *Statistical Handbook*, June 1970, p. 53).

6 The figure represents the total area requisitioned from 1952 to the end of year 1966 (see Mabro, *The Egyptian Economy 1952–1972*, Table 4.2, p. 68).

7 Figure represents the surplus of the *requisitioned* area over *the actually distributed* land.

8 The numbers in parentheses under the official figure in the size-class of less than 5 feddans represent our own estimates of the *effective* increase in the total areas of small ownerships derived by referring to figures of the annual agricultural survey published by the Ministry of Agriculture for the years 1961–64 and other sources. In fact, official figures for this class reflect *scheduled* rather than *effective* transfers of full rights of ownership in land. The increase in the total area owned by small landowners between 1952 and 1965 as reported in official statistics amounts to 1,571,000 feddans, a figure which is inconsistent with the maximum possible acquisitions of new land through land redistribution programmes, private sales and land reclamation taken together. We finally note that we assume here that all new additions to the cultivated area through land reclamation schemes accrue automatically to the small landowners.

possession of more land to till or control. In fact, all significant agrarian policy measures — whether technological or institutional — have tended to shift the centre of politico-economic gravity away from the old landed aristocracy and in favour of this new privileged stratum of rich peasants, as we shall see in the next chapter.

On the other hand, the agrarian reforms have had considerable favourable effects on agricultural production, insofar as a large class of tenant-farmers found themselves in a much better position to make output-raising improvements. With regard to small tenants, acquiring land in their own name and cultivating it themselves, that land reforms in Egypt has had its greatest success.

On the whole, one could argue that the tenurial land reforms in Egypt were mainly designed as *transitional means* towards a new progressive, and more dynamic, agrarian structure conducive to more growth and development.

2
Agrarian Classes and the Differentiation of the Peasantry

"To analyze a nut is to crack it"
Hegel, *Science of Logic*

In order to focus our attention on the restructuring of relationships among the different groups of the peasantry in the post-agrarian reform period an attempt is made in this chapter to study in some detail the *class composition* of the farm population in Egypt. The respective positions occupied by different sections of the peasantry in the complex socio-economic structure of the farm sector are identified with reference to their relations vis-à-vis the means of production. No implications about income distribution are considered here; the changes in income distribution that may be associated with the new agrarian structure are discussed in detail in the next chapter.

2.1   The process of differentiation amongst the peasantry

We propose to conduct our analysis of the process of differentiation in terms of:
(i) the magnitude of *wage employment*; (ii) the degree of *farm mechanization;* and (iii) differences in *crop-mixes*. The justifications for our choice of such criteria can be summarised as follows.

(a)   The magnitude of wage employment on 'medium' and 'large' farms may be regarded as the most important manifestation of the degree of differentiation amongst the peasantry. For an increasing degree of differentiation amongst the peasantry (which is usually associated with less equitable distribution of land between different groups of the peasantry) has its counterpart in the growth of the pool of landless peasants seeking wage employment.

(b)   The intensity of use of improved farm equipment represents a good index of the degree of differentiation amongst the peasantry. For it is almost impossible for 'small' and 'poor' peasants to use improved farm equipment, such as *tractors* and *irrigation motor pumps* because of the small area involved. In addition, farm mechanisation gives rise to economies of scale and thus lead to a notable increase in labour productivity, and in the incomes of mechanised farms. The process of farm mechanisation tends therefore to be a self-perpetuating one, as an increasingly larger fraction of income is ploughed back in the farms and is reflected in the permanent switch to the highly productive agro-technology.

(c)   Differences in crop-mixes tend to reflect, in the main, different degrees of transition to 'capitalistic agriculture'. The presence of economies of scale in fruit cultivation and other higher-valued crops has led an increasing number of *rich* farmers to specialise in their cultivation.

Table 2.1 *Distribution of labour force by size of farm, 1961*

Size of farm (feddans)	(1) Number of holders working on their own farms		(2) Unpaid family-labour		Hired wage-labour			
					(3) No. of Permanent wage-labourers (000's)	%	(4) No. of casual farm labourers (000's)	%
	numbers (000's)	%	numbers (000's)	%				
< 2	810	50	844	33	52	8	231	12
2 – < 5	547	34	1,050	42	127	21	602	33
5 – < 20	222	14	564	22	217	36	549	30
≥ 20	33	2	89	3	212	35	468	25
Total	1,612	100	2,547	100	608	100	1,850	100

Source: Fourth Agricultural Census (1961), Vol. I, Part IV, Table 58, pp. 207–8.

Table 2.2 *Extent of wage employment by size group, 1961*

Size group (feddans)	Total permanent labour force (000's)	%	Percentage distribution of different categories of permanent labour force		
			Landholders	Unpaid family labour	Permanent wage-labour
< 2 (poor peasantry)	1,706	100	47	50	3
2 – < 5 (small peasantry)	1,724	100	32	61	7
5 – < 20 (middle peasantry)	1,003	100	22	56	22
≥ 20	334	100	10	27	63
Total	4,767	100	34	53	13

Source: Fourth Agricultural Census (1961), Vol. I, Part IV, Table 58, pp. 207–208.

Having outlined our main line of argument, we shall now substantiate our conjectures by drawing on a wide variety of source material in order to illustrate the extent and the degree of differentiation amongst the peasantry in Egypt.

2.1.1 The differentiation of the peasantry according to the magnitude of wage-employment

The extent of the employment of wage labour is generally considered to be the principal manifestation and the simplest measure of the degree of differentiation amongst the peasantry everywhere. In this connection it is interesting to analyse the extent to which different groups of the peasantry hire wage labour for their farms.

The data provided by the fourth agricultural census of 1961 shed some light on the *extent* and *pattern* of wage employment by size of farm. Tables 2.1 and 2.2 give a summary of the statistical indicators related to the magnitude and distribution pattern of wage employment by size of farm.

As expected, it can be seen from these tables there is a marked process of differentiation amongst the peasantry according to the magnitude of wage-employment. In assessing these figures, three broad structural facts emerge.

First, substantial wage employment (permanent wage labour) is to be found only on the holdings of 'middle' and 'rich' peasants (in the category above 5 feddans). In fact, the 'middle' and 'rich' peasants employed about 71 per cent of the total permanent wage labour force in 1961.

The recent empirical evidence from the ILO-INP sample survey of rural employment problems, conducted in 1964—5 confirms this trend of an increasing scale of hire of wage labour on 'medium' and 'large' farms in rural Egypt. The sample survey produced the information summarized in Table 2.3.

Table 2.3 *Percentage of holdings employing outside wage labour, 1964/65*

Size of farm (feddans)	Percent of holdings employing outside wage labour
0.5 – < 2	24*
2 – < 5	36
5 – < 10	53
≥ 10	85

* Mainly temporary labourers.
Source: R. Mabro, 'Employment and Wages in Dual Agriculture'.,
Oxford Economic Papers (Nov. 1971), Table II.

Second, it is evident from Table 2.2 that wage labour becomes the dominant form of labour in the case of holdings above 20 feddans (and belonging to the 'rich peasantry' and 'big landlords'), since it accounts for about *two-thirds* of the total permanent labour force in these holdings. It goes without saying that this mode of operation is one of the very characteristics of developed capitalist agriculture.

Third, employment of permanent wage labour on small farms (below 5 feddans) is rather limited, for these rely almost exclusively on unpaid 'family labour'. In particular, the farms in the size group between 2 and 5 feddans constitute family-operated farms *par excellence*.

2.1.2 Distribution of ownership of farm animals amongst different groups of the peasantry

Ownership of farm animals constitute a great asset to cultivators. Water buffaloes and cows are widely owned by almost all groups of the peasantry in the Egyptian countryside. According to the 1950 and 1961 agricultural censuses, with the notable exception of the 'poor peasantry', about 90 per cent of all groups of the peasantry owned one or more head of cattle (see Table 2.4).

These animals are in great demand primarily for their *ploughing services* as well as for their *milk* and *dairy products*.[1] A small peasant usually needs at least a pair of draft animals to tackle the basic farm work of tillage and turning the water wheel. In addition, animal urine and dung provide valuable *manure* for his crops and the nutrients needed for the development of soil organisms.

Moreover, the dairy products obtained from these animals occupy a rather important place in the diet of the *fellah*. It has been said with some justification in this connection that farm animals serve as 'shock absorbers', consuming surplus grass and grain in periods of abundance and providing food for peasants in lean years.[2]

Initial cost is always a great obstacle to greater animal ownership among the 'poor' and 'small' peasantry, as compared with the number of head of cattle owned by the 'middle' and 'rich' peasants (see Table 2.4). As a result of these financial difficulties, joint ownership of cattle is quite common amongst the 'poor peasantry' in rural Egypt, and this adds a new dimension to the process of differentiation amongst the peasantry.

However, quite apart from the initial cost involved in obtaining a head of cattle, the economics of the maintenance of a cow or a buffalo are also of great importance for the 'poor' and 'small' peasant. The expense depends largely on how much of their food requirements can be met from low opportunity cost sources, such as the farmer's clover field,[3] as well as on the supply of family labour available to graze these animals (the guarding task usually falls to either the very old or the very young).

Finally, it should be noted that one further and important reason why buffaloes and cows are so widely owned or shared by small and poor peasants in Egypt lies in the fact that these animals, apart from land itself, are the major items of rural wealth and stores of value. This is particularly true for the 'small' and 'middle' peasantry. Whenever these farmers are faced with a major financial crisis, animals are sold in order to meet their obligations.

1 Both cows and water buffaloes are used as *draft* and *dairy* animals in Egyptian agriculture. While both cows and buffaloes can tackle the basic farm work, the Egyptian buffalo (gamusa) is a milk-giving animal of great importance to the fellah. A buffalo can give around 3,000 pounds of milk per year on average. This milk is usually richer than cow's milk, containing around 10 per cent fat as against 3.5 per cent fat in cow's milk. Cf: H.H. Ayrout, *The Egyptian Peasant*, (Boston: Beacon Press, 1963), p. 30.

2 cf. P. Sanghvi, *Surplus Manpower in Agriculture and Economic Development*, (London: Asia Publishing House, 1969), pp. 15–16.

3 In the winter and spring an Egyptian buffalo should graze on a meadow of about half a feddan of Egyptian clover. In summer it requires about 25 pounds of fodder daily, consisting of crop residue such as straw, cottonseed cake and bean stalks. cf. Ayrout, *The Egyptian Peasant*, p. 38.

Table 2.4 *Distribution of draft & dairy animals by size of holding, 1950 and 1961*

Strata of the peasantry by size of holding (feddans)	1950					1961				
	No. of holdings possessing one or more head of cattle	As a percentage of the total number of holdings in the size group	No. of head of cattle (cows & water buffaloes)	%	No. of head of cattle per holding	No. of holdings possessing one or more head of cattle	As a percentage of the total number of holdings in the size group	No. of head of cattle (cows & water buffaloes)	%	No. of head of cattle per holding
< 2	316,344	68	438,496*	24	1.4	567,904	69	958,468*	30	1.7
2 – < 5	285,748	88	530,432	28	1.9	485,644	87	1,162,119	36	2.4
5 – < 20	167,246	95	488,245	26	2.9	206,042	91	759,367	24	3.7
20 – < 50	25,115	95	145,120	8	5.8	19,745	83	147,196	5	7.5
50 – < 100	7,815	93	80,937	4	10.4	4,894	76	72,395	2	15.0
> 100	6,017	92	181,529	10	30.0	2,910	73	100,150	3	34.0
Total	808,285	81	1,864,759	100		1,278,139	78	3,199,695	100	

* The dairy cows and water buffaloes in this size-class are usually shared among a number of landholders.

Source: Figures computed from *The Third Agricultural Census* 1950, Part I, Table (32), p. 358; and *The Fourth Agricultural Census* 1961, Part I, Sec. IV, Table (41), p. 259.

2.1.3   Differentiation of the peasantry by degree of farm mechanisation

The overwhelming majority of Egyptian farmers use hand tools and draught animals in farming operations (i.e. ploughing, irrigation, etc.)[4] The use of improved farm equipment on a significant scale is mainly confined to the groups of 'rich peasantry' and 'big landlords'.

Data on the use of improved farm equipment for *traction* and *irrigation* by size of farm is summarised in Tables 2.5, 2.6, and 2.7 for the years 1950 and 1961. The 1950 Census figures refer to the period immediately preceding the 1952 land reform, and the figures for 1961 summarise the situation after almost 10 years of agrarian reforms.

It is evident from these tables that, in general, the use of improved farm equipment is positively correlated with increasing holding size. The use of tractors assumes some measure of importance only in holdings in the category above 20 feddans — owned by the 'rich peasantry' and 'big landlords' — which may be fairly regarded as 'tractorised' in the Egyptian context. The data also show how vigorous is the use of tractors on large farms, as more powerful tractors (i.e. more than 25 or 35 h.p.) are used, because of the indivisibilities involved.

A similar trend is observable in connection with the use of improved methods of irrigation, as the use of mechanised irrigation techniques (i.e. motor pumps) tends to intensify with increasing holding size. In 1950, as in 1961, motor pumps could be found on medium farms and large estates and only very rarely on small holdings.[5]

Nonetheless, by far the most notable trend in the use of tractors and improved irrigation methods in rural Egypt is that the stratum of 'rich peasantry' — cultivating from 20 to 50 feddans — succeeded in consolidating its economic power and gained new strength in the post-reform agrarian structure. This is strikingly illustrated by the fact that in 1961 the 'rich peasants' were already in possession of the largest number of tractors (29% of all tractors against only 13% in 1950). Moreover, the percentage of 'tractorised farms' in this stratum, which was no more than 5% in 1950, reached 15% in 1961. A similar trend is revealed in connection with the use of irrigation machined: the percentage of rich peasants' holdings using irrigation machines increased more than twofold between 1950 and 1961 (from 11 to 27 per cent).

The 'middle peasantry' also made some progress in the use of improved farm equipment for traction and irrigation. In fact, the 'middle peasantry' increased its share in the total number of tractors from 5% in 1950 to 19% in 1961, and its share in the total number of irrigation machines from 28% in 1960 to 36% in 1961. Moreover, mechanical variations of the water wheel, such as the *tabut* and *tambusha* are

4   The mass of 'poor' and 'small' peasantry employ the Egyptian wooden plough (*al-mihrath*) which can plough up to half a feddan a day. This plough consists of a wooden frame with a flat ogival plowshare about ten inches long and a shaft about eleven feet long, to which the draft animals are attached by a straight yoke. The animals may be two buffaloes, cows, a buffalo and a donkey, or any two animals hired for the occasion (see Ayrout, *ibid.*, p. 36). On the other hand, much of water-pumping is done through simple devices such as the water screw (shadouf) and the Archimedean screw (tambur), powered in most cases by human muscle.
5   It should be emphasised that water-pumping assumes particular significance in the Egyptian situation. Rich peasants who can afford to buy mechanically-powered water pumps find themselves in a much more powerful position to compete for irrigation water in *low-water periods*.

Table 2.5 Degree of use of tractors by size of holding, 1950

Size class (feddans)	Total holdings		No. of tractorised farms	% (3/1)	No. of tractors of less than 35 hp	No. of tractors of more than 35 hp	Total No. of tractors (5 + 6)	% of all tractors	Tractor/land ratio (No. of tractors per 000 feddans) (7)/(2)	% (6)/(7)	Percentage share of total number of tractors / % share of total area
	No.	Area (feddans)									
	(1)	(2)	(3)	(4)	(5)	(6)	(7)	(8)	(9)	(10)	(11)
< 5	786,780	1,422,817	175	0.0	165	77	242	2.4	0.17	32	0.10
5 − < 10	122,365	818,382	166	0.1	96	74	170	1.7	0.21	43	0.13
10 − < 20	52,517	705,331	330	0.6	235	122	357	3.6	0.5	34	0.31
20 − < 50	26,488	792,082	1,284	5.0	952	385	1,337	13.3	1.7	29	1.02
50 − < 100	8,372	579,053	2,333	30.0	1,771	632	2,403	24	4.2	26	2.53
≥ 100	6,520	1,826,259	4,329	66.0	2,709	2,754	5,463	55	3.0	50	1.83
Total	1,003,023	6,143,924	8,617	0.9	5,928	4,044	9,972	100	1.6	41	1.00

Source: Third Agricultural Census (1950), Part I, Table (43), p. 477.

Table 2.6 Degree of use of tractors by size of holding, 1961

Size class (feddans)	Total Holdings		No. of tractorised farms	% (3/1)	No. of tractors of less than 25 hp	No. of tractors of more than 25 hp	Total no. of tractors (5 + 6)	% of all tractors	Tractor/land ratio (No. of tractors per 000 feddans) (7/2)	% (6)/(7)	Percentage share of total number of tractors / % share of total area
	No.	Area (feddans)									
	(1)	(2)	(3)	(4)	(5)	(6)	(7)	(8)	(9)	(10)	(11)
< 5	1,381,241	2,354,421	736	0.05	432	416	848	7	0.36	49	0.18
5 − < 10	170,019	1,100,669	793	0.5	350	453	803	6	0.7	56	0.33
10 − < 20	56,705	742,619	1,638	2.9	714	993	1,707	13	2.3	58	1.08
20 − < 50	23,811	689,267	3,550	15.0	1,437	2,234	3,671	29	5.3	61	2.64
50 − < 100	6,424	429,952	2,384	37.0	791	1,774	2,565	20	6.0	69	2.86
≥ 100	3,960	905,911	2,277	57.5	937	2,306	3,243	25	3.6	71	1.79
Total	1,642,160	6,222,839	11,378	0.7	4,661	8,176	12,837	100	2.0	64	1.00

Source: Figures calculated from the Fourth Agricultural Census (1961), Part I, Sec IV, Table (54), p. 76.

Table 2.7 *Use of irrigation machines by size of holding, 1950 and 1961*

Size of holding (feddans)	Number of farms using irrigation machines (1)		As a percentage of total number of holdings in the size-class (2)		Total number of irrigation machines (3)		As a percentage of total number of irrigation machines (4)	
	1950	1961	1950	1961	1950	1961	1950 %	1961 %
< 5	957	4,795	0.1	0.3	1,097*	5,039*	7*	17*
5 – < 20	4,116	10,306	2.3	4.5	4,213	10,530	28	36
20 – < 50	2,973	6,364	11.0	27.0	3,125	6,632	21	22
50 – < 100	2,019	3,059	24.0	48.0	2,284	3,443	15	12
⩾ 100	3,334	2,633	51.0	66.5	4,451	3,742	29	13
Total	13,399	27,157	1.3	1.6	15,170	29,386	100	100

* Irrigation machines in this size-class are usually shared by a number of landholders.

Source: Figures computed from *The Third Agricultural Census* (1950), Part I – Table (43), p. 474, and *The Fourth Agricultural Census* (1961), Part I, Sec. IV, Table (54), p. 76.

to be found on a significant scale in the holdings of the 'middle peasantry'.

Lastly, it should be stressed that availability of finance appears to be a major factor responsible for pushing ahead this particular aspect of the process of differentiation amongst the peasantry, since the capacity to invest in improved farm machinery is only conceivable for rich or capitalist farmers who enjoy investible surpluses.

2.1.4   Differentiation of the peasantry in terms of differences in 'crop-mixes'

Field crops dominate the agriculture of Egypt. In 1952 they occupied 98 per cent of the cropped area, with only 1 per cent each in vegetables and fruit. During the 1960s the relative share of fruit doubled, but this still left 98 per cent in field crops and vegetables (see Table 2.8).

Table 2.8 *Crop areas in Egypt, average 1960–4*

Crop	Acreage (000 feddans)	% of total cropped area
Wheat	1,443	13.5
Maize	1,795	17.0
Millet	488	5.0
Rice	830	8.0
Cotton	1,816	17.0
Sugarcane	125	1.2
Vegetables	566	5.3
Fruits	195	1.8
Berseem clover	2,532	24.0
Other crop	879	7.2
Total cropped area	10,669	100.0

Source: M. Clawson, H. Landsberg and L.T. Alexander (eds.), *The Agricultural Potential of the Middle East*, (New York: American Elsevier Publishing Company, Inc., 1971), Table 8-1, p. 66.

Cotton continues to be the leading cash crop of the country. However throughout the 1960's other cash crops such as rice and sugar-cane assumed an increasing share of the cropped area at the expense of cotton cultivation. Wheat, maize and millet are the main subsistence crops, providing the peasant with his daily bread.

2.1.4.1   Differentiation in terms of cash vs. subsistence crops

The allocation of cropped land in most of the 'poor' and 'small' peasants' crop rotation systems is mainly governed by a simple trade-off between *subsistence requirements* (in terms of cereals)[6] and *cash requirements* in terms of one cash crop (mostly cotton). To switch from a *subsistence* to a *cash* crop, the 'poor' and 'small' peasant is faced with a serious dilemma. If he grows a subsistence crop, and is successful, his family's subsistence needs will be met regardless of the crop's market price. However, if he chooses to grow more cotton, for example, he may fail to provide adequate food for his family (assuming a successful crop), either because

---

6 Cereals in general provide the basis of the average diet of lower income people. The non-food uses of cereals are also important: some is used for seeds and some to feed dairy cows and chickens.

cotton prices decline or because maize or wheat prices rise unexpectedly.[7]

On the other hand, the transition to higher-valued crops (i.e. fruit, flowers and vegetables) can be undertaken on a significant scale only by prosperous 'medium' and 'rich' peasants.

This can be easily evidenced in the case of Egypt by comparing changes in relative shares of fruit acreage with other cash and subsistence crops for different groups of the peasantry over the period 1950–61 (see Tables 2.9 and 2.10). By far the most significant trend which emerges from these data is that the 'small' and 'middle' peasantry were expanding their relative acreage of cash crops at the expense of the old 'big landlordship'. On the other hand, the 'poor' and 'small' peasants were resolving their dilemma by relying a bit more on 'subsistence crops'. This situation is neatly illustrated in Figs. 3.1 and 3.2.

Undoubtedly these differences in crop-mixes and rotations add a new and significant dimension to the process of differentiation amongst the peasantry in Egypt.

2.4.1.2   The growth of commercial fruit cultivation

Fruit cultivation represents another aspect of the process of differentiation amongst the peasantry, since one of the main vehicles of income growth in 'capitalistic agriculture' is the transition to higher-valued crops.[8] Such a transition can be undertaken only by prosperous 'rich farmers' and 'big landlords', for a variety of reasons.

First, fruit cultivation is land-intensive and its technical characteristics make it a feasible commercial venture only for the big landowner. *Second*, the prospective fruit cultivator should be financially able to generate a surplus for a number of years ahead not only to support his family but also to make the necessary investment to

7   See on this point: Walter P. Falcon, 'Farmer Response to Price in a Subsistence Economy: The Case of West Pakistan', *American Economic Review,* vol. LV–no. 3, (May 1964), pp. 582–3. Falcon's analysis is illuminating in many respects, since he found that the supply response to sugarcane price-increases was dampened because, to grow sugarcane, farmers had to forgo growing wheat the main subsistence crop. More significant still is that the supply-price response coefficients between *cash crops* were found to be larger than those between *subsistence* and *cash crops.*

8   In the 1960s it was estimated that income from orchards provided an average rate of return on invested capital amounting to 9 per cent per annum, compared with no more than 5 per cent in the case of traditional field crops. (cf. Saab, *Egyptian Agrarian Reforms,* p. 129). This can be further illustrated by considering the following comparative figures for the annual gross income per feddan for different crops in the 1960s.

Crop	Gross income per annum per feddan (£E)	Index of yield differentials (Cereals = 100)
Cereals	40	100
Cotton	80	200
Rice	80	200
Sugarcane	100	250
Fruit	150	375
Flowers	1000	2500

Source: M. Hassanein Heikal, "Le problème agraire: horizons nouveaux", in *la Voie Egyptienne Vers Le Socialisme,* (Cairo: Dar al-Maaref), pp. 192–3.

Table 2.9 Allocation of the cropped area of leading cash crops by size of holding, 1950 and 1961

Size of holding (feddans)	(1) Allocation of cotton area		(2) Allocation of rice area		(3) Allocation of sugar-cane area		(4) Allocation of fruit area	
	1950	1961	1950	1961	1950	1961	1950	1961
	%	%	%	%	%	%	%	%
< 2	7	10.5	3	3	2	9	5	7
2 – < 5	17	27.5	11	23	15	24	10	10
5 – < 20	26	31.0	26	37	25	31	20	17
20 – < 50	14	12.0	13	13	13	14	14	15
⩾ 50	36	19.0	47	24	45	22	51	51
Total	100	100	100	100	100	100	100	100
Total cultivated area per crop ('000 feddans)	1,964	1,960	685	519	83	156	107	144

Source: Third Agricultural Census (1950), Vol. 1, Table (14), pp. 150–155.
Fourth Agricultural Census (1961), Vol. 1, Sec. 2, Table (27), pp. 275–327.

36

Table 2.10 *Allocation of the cropped area of the main subsistence crops by size of holding, 1950 and 1961*

Size of holding (feddans)	(1) Allocation of wheat area		(2) Allocation of Nili* maize area		(3) Allocation of Seifi (summer) maize area		(4) Allocation of Nili* millet area		(5) Allocation of Seifi (summer) millet area		(6) Allocation of broad beans area	
	1950	1961	1950	1961	1950	1961	1950	1961	1950	1961	1950	1961
	%	%	%	%	%	%	%	%	%	%	%	%
< 2	10	15	12	16	8	12	8	12	10	23	4	6
2 – < 5	20	31	21	33	16	27	19	27	23	28	15	23
5 – < 20	27	30	25	28	23	32	30	30	40	28	31	36
20 – < 50	12	9	12	9	13	11	15	12	8	10	16	14
> 50	31	15	30	14	40	18	28	19	19	11	34	21
Total	100	100	100	100	100	100	100	100	100	100	100	100
Total cropped area per crop (000 feddans)	1,385	1,717	1,439	1,539	46	442	55	69	343	460	365	368

* A *Nili* crop is a fall crop cultivated at the time of high Nile, from August to October. With the completion of the High dam the original reason for the *Nili* round crops – i.e., the additional water from Nile river floods – largely ceased to exist.
Source: *Third Agricultural Census* (1950), Vol. 1, Table (14) pp. 150–155.
Fourth Agricultural Census (1961), Vol. 1, Sec. 2, Table (27), pp. 275–327.

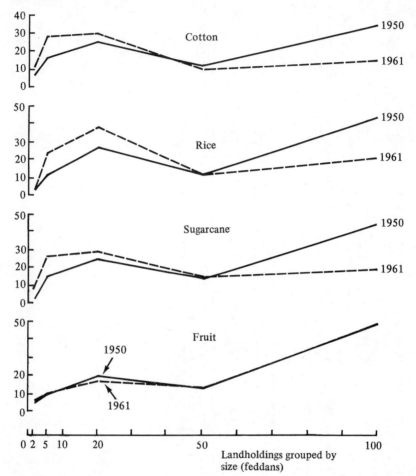

Fig. 2.1 *Allocation of cropped area of the leading cash crops by size of holding, 1950 and 1961*

Share of different groups of
holdings as a percentage of
the cropped area

begin fruit cultivation.[9] *Third*, the production of fruit is normally associated with long gestation periods between initial investment and the beginning of cash flow from the investment (for example, some fruit trees require from five to seven years before there is any measurable return from orchard plantations).

The extension of fruit cultivation among different groups of the peasantry may be indirectly inferred from Table 2.11, giving comparative figures for the relative acreage of the basic fruit varieties (citrus fruit, grapes, bananas and mangoes) for the years 1950 and 1961. An overall and consistent picture emerges very clearly from this table, that no less than 60 per cent of the grape, banana and mango agreage, and about 50 per cent of the citrus fruit acreage, is concentrated in farms

9 The planting of *orchards* in the sixties required an amount of initial investment ranging from £E50 to £E450 per feddan according to the variety of fruit planted. Cf. Saab, *op. cit.*, p. 129.

Fig. 2.2 *Allocation of cropped area of the main subsistence crops by size of holding, 1950 and 1961*

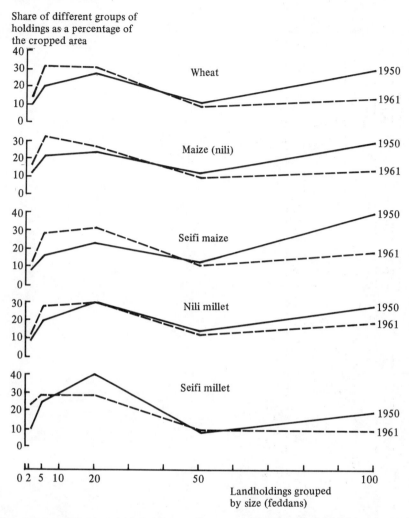

Share of different groups of
holdings as a percentage of
the cropped area

Landholdings grouped
by size (feddans)

falling in the size class of 20 feddans and over — belonging to the 'rich peasantry' and 'big landlords'.

As for the stratum of the 'middle peasantry', the relative fruit acreage of this group recorded a slight decline during the period under review. By contrast, the persistence of a relatively high percentage of fruit acreage in the size group of 'less than 5 feddans' may be partly explained in terms of a long process of increasing fragmentation of orchard holdings due to orchard land being passed on to successive generations of cultivators through inheritance. As for the increase in the *absolute* fruit acreage in small holdings of less than 5 feddans between 1950–1961, there can hardly be any economic justification for this increase, but only a political explanation. Many small landowners, who wanted to safeguard their small plots — in the post-land reform era — against any future encroachments by their tenants, began to plant orchards, since orchard land was exempted from the tenancy regulations enacted by the first land reform law.

Table 2.11 Cultivated areas under the main fruit crop by size of holding, 1950 and 1961

Size of holding (feddans)	Citrus fruit				Grapes				Bananas				Mangoes			
	1950		1961		1950		1961		1950		1961		1950		1961	
	Area (feddans)	%	Area (feddans)	%	Area (feddans)	%	Area (feddans)	%	Area (feddans)	%	Area (feddans)	%	Area (feddans)	%	Area (feddans)	%
< 5	10,883	29	18,488	25	3,874	20	3,869	22	931	14	9,803	21	1,619	22	2,601	22
5 – < 20	9,095	24	16,158	22	2,716	16	2,131	12	1,842	26	1,618	19	1,530	21	2,173	18
≥ 20	17,918	47	39,118	52	11,378	64	11,740	66	4,123	60	5,047	60	4,220	57	7,130	60
Total	37,896	100	73,764	100	17,968	100	17,740	100	6,896	100	8,468	100	7,369	100	11,904	100

Source: Third Agricultural Census (1950), Vol. I, Table (22), p. 252.
Fourth Agricultural Census (1961), Vol. I, Table (32), p. 109.

In sum, the expansion of fruit acreage continued with some vigour throughout the 1960s, and the total area under commercial fruit cultivation almost doubled (increasing from 131,000 feddans in 1960 to 244,000 in 1970).[10]

2.2 A broad stratification of agrarian classes

Having examined the extent (or the degree) of the process of differentiation amongst different groups of the peasantry over the period 1950–61, we propose here to sketch, in the light of the statistical evidence analysed in the previous section, a highly simplified stratification of the main agrarian classes in the Egyptian country-side; namely: (1) 'landless peasants'; (2) 'poor peasantry'; (3) 'small peasantry'; (4) 'middle peasantry'; (5) 'rich peasantry' or 'capitalist farmers'. This broad categorisation is based on three basic indicators related to the application of capital and the extent of wage employment, as well as differences in crop mixes, while retaining *the size of holding* as the main *stratification variable*.

Our analysis in this section is confined to the different strata of the 'landed peasantry'; later in this chapter we shall attempt to identify the main groups of 'landless peasants'. (See Sec. 2.3).

The poor peasantry[11] (below 2 feddans)

There is little doubt that the overwhelming majority of the 'landed peasantry' in Egypt falls into this category of 'poor' or 'ruined' peasantry, which embraces about 50 per cent of all landed families. The 'landless' who lease-in a tiny piece of land in search of some secure income also fall into this category of 'poor peasants'.

These 'poor peasants' are in fact not far removed from the ranks of 'landless peasantry', as they cannot raise sufficient produce for the maintenance of their own families, and have to supplement their income by hiring-out labour. As the gross output of the previous harvest may fall short of the family subsistence requirements, these poor peasants find themselves compelled to draw permanently upon 'consumption loans' on onerous payment terms. Such consumption-loans are in fact the main cause of the perpetual indebtedness of these poor peasants.[12] In other words, for these peasants crop success means freedom from starvation and a temporary escape from indebtedness until the next planting season.

The small peasants (2–5 feddans)

This group of the peasantry, with somewhat larger holdings constitute about 25 per cent of total number of landed families. They usually operate on a family basis, and

---

10 cf. *ARE Statistical Handbook,* (Cairo, June 1971).
11 An alternative stratification of agrarian classes in Rural Egypt has been suggested by Samir Amin in *L'Egypte Nasserienne* (Paris, 1964), pp. 10–11; as follows:
(a) landless peasants;
(b) poor peasants (below 1 feddan)
(c) middle peasantry (1–5 feddans)
(d) rich farmers (5–20 feddans)
(e) rural capitalists (above 20 feddans)
We think, however, that our stratification approaches much closer to the realities of rural Egypt.
12 The same analysis applies to the 'very small farmers' in India. See Krishna Bhardawaj, *Production Conditions in Indian Agriculture*, (University of Cambridge Dept. of Applied Economics: Occasional Paper No. 33), Cambridge University Press, 1974, p. 62.

in most cases manage to raise most of their own subsistence food requirements. In other words, they are under somewhat less pressure to resort to 'consumption loans', and hence are less indebted to money-lenders.

In a typical small farmer's family, the wife, the children, the buffalo and the donkey are the cultivator's most valuable assets. The head of the family works full-time on the land. His wife lends a hand at seed time and harvest, rears poultry at home, and makes butter and cheese for sale. The children look after the animals and work for wages five or six weeks a year at cotton picking or fighting the cotton worm. The buffalo draws the plough, turns the water-wheel, and produces milk cheese and butter. The donkey transports manure, crops and the peasant himself.[13]

The middle peasantry (5–20 feddans)

Having somewhat larger holdings than that of the 'small peasantry', this group is usually more prosperous and employs permanent wage labourers to some extent. These peasants produce mainly for the market and their crop-mixes normally cover a wider and more profitable variety of crops (i.e. cash crops and vegetables). In general, their holdings are 'technically' more efficient in terms of the use of better irrigation facilities, improved seeds and more intensive use of bullock labour and farm equipment.

They generally enjoy a surplus over and above their consumption requirements after meeting other fixed money obligations. Often these 'middle peasants' are also engaged in other gainful activities such as retail trade and money-lending. In other words, these farmers have a fallback source of income in case of low yields.

The rich peasantry (over 20 feddans)

The 'rich peasants' rely mainly on hiring wage-labour to cultivate their land and use capitalistic farming methods on a significant scale. The presence of economies of scale in some high-valued crops (i.e. fruit, flowers and vegetables) has led a good many of them to specialise in their cultivation.

In general, the *propensity to invest* among this group of the peasantry is quite high, and most of them are virtually engaged in entrepreneurial activities involving the improvement of agricultural techniques. In the Egyptian context, this class of 'rich peasants' is becoming increasingly identified with the formation of a class of 'capitalist farmers' or 'rural bourgeoisie.'

It must be admitted that the above stratification remains very crude and schematic, and that our broad 'agrarian classes' are perhaps too much identified in purely economic terms without allowing for regional variations. Nonetheless, on the whole, our broad categorisation corresponds to a real process of socio-political differentiation between, on the one hand, the stratum of 'middle peasantry' (owing or cultivating up to 20 feddans) which tends to be more traditionalist in its outlook and stand on public affairs and, on the other hand, the stratum of 'rich peasants' or 'capitalist farmers' (cultivating over 20 feddans), who are less traditional in their outlook and more capitalist-minded.[14]

13 Cf. Ayrout, *The Egyptian Peasant, op. cit.*, pp. 58–9.
14 Cf. Mahmoud Hussein, *Class Conflict in Egypt: 1945–1971*, (New York: Monthly Review Press, 1973), pp. 26–7.

The 'middle peasants' are numerically superior; and judged in the light of historical evidence they usually have a vested interest in maintaining semi-feudal ideological and socio-political superstructures in the Egyptian countryside. The *omdas* (village heads) and *a'yans* (village notables) were largely drawn from the ranks of this middle peasantry.[15]

2.3   The landless peasants

The existence of a sizeable pool of landless peasants is a notable feature of the Egyptian agrarian scene. These landless peasants, being the least credit-worthy members of the rural community, find themselves unable to rent land and can only sell their labour power for subsistence. They are thus compelled to take casual day-to-day employment or to enter longer-term commitments as permanent labourers.[16]

2.3.1   The size of the pool of landless peasants

Landless peasants constitute a sizeable proportion of the rural population in Egypt, and the high rate of population growth in rural areas adds year after year to their numbers.

Although hard data on landless peasants are virtually non-existent, it is possible to make some tentative estimates of the number of landless families (defined as neither owning nor renting land) on the basis of crude assumptions about the age and occupational structure of the rural population, the average composition of the rural family and the increase in the number of landed families. The results of our calculations are given in Table 2.12.

It should be stressed however that, in the absence of firm data, our figures for the landless can only be taken as a rough order of magnitude. There are, however, many indicators, which corroborate the general trends among the landless expressed by the percentages given in Table 2.12, even if the exact numbers may have been somewhat different.

The major fact which emerges from these calculations is that there has been a steady fall in the *absolute* number of landless families in rural Egypt since 1952 and up to the mid-1960s. *The sub-period 1965–70 witnessed a new increase in the absolute number of landless families.* This reversal of the trend in the late sixties may be attributed to the growing population pressure on land, as well as to the freeze of agrarian reforms.[17]

2.3.2   Cateogries of landless peasants

In order to appreciate the overall employment and income distribution situation in rural Egypt, it is necessary to know a little more about the different categories of landless peasants.

---

15   In fact, a man aspiring to the position of village head (omda) is not eligible for the post unless he owns at least ten feddans. Cf. Ayrout, *The Egyptian Peasant*, p. 31.

16   See Ayrout, *op. cit.*, p. 55.

17   The situation could undoubtedly have improved had the 1969 Land Reform proposals, for lowering the ceiling on individual landownership to 50 feddans, been implemented (see Appendix A). In fact, the reform proposals were not put into practice until 1970.

Table 2.12 *The number of landless families in rural Egypt, 1950–70*

	1950	1961	1965	1970
(1) *Rural population* (000's)	13,700	16,120	17,000*	19,331
(2) *Number of rural families* (000's)	2,740	3,224	3,345†	3,866
(3) *Number of families engaged in non-agricultural activities* (000's)	520	613	635	734
(4) *Number of landed families* (i.e. landholders) (000's)	1,003	1,641	1,785‡	1,853 §
(5) *Number of landless families* (000's)	1,217	970	925	1,279
(6) *Landless families as a percentage of total number of rural families*	44%	30%	28%	33%

Notes and sources:
* Direct figure based on the *FAO's Indicative World Plan for the Near East* (Rome, 1966).
† Direct figure derived from *the 1966 Population Census* Vol. II. Ref. 711/01, July 1967, Table 4.
‡ This figure is obtained by adding to the number of landed families in 1961 the 143,300 families receiving new land distributed by the Agrarian Reform Authority between 1962 and 1965.
§ The number of landed families in 1965 increased by 68,000 families which benefited from the distribution of agrarian reform land during the period 1966–70.
The figures in row 2 are obtained by applying the standard size of *five persons* per family. See U.N., *Demographic Yearbook* (1962), Table 12.
The figures in row 3 are obtained according to the ratio given in *the 1960 Population Census,* which works out at 19% of the rural population. We admit that this ratio may have an *upward bias*, thus leading to an understatement of the number of the really landless families.

Landless peasants are broadly divided into *permanent* and *casual* labours. Among the former are included permanent agricultural labourers hired on an annual or longer basis. As to the *casual* labourers we must distinguish between two categories of casual labourers: 'farm' casual labourers engaged in casual (or temporary) employment in the farm sector; and casual migratory or 'tarahil' labourers who are usually recruited for the maintenance of canals and other rural public works on a temporary or seasonal basis.

Permanent agricultural wage-labourers

The bulk of permanent wage labourers are employed on medium and large farms. Employment of permanent wage labour on small farms (below 5 feddans) is rather limited, for these farms rely almost exclusively on 'family labour'. Nonetheless some permanent farm labourers are usually attached to small farms by kinship or traditional ties (they are usually among the farmer's relatives).[18]

The category 'permanent agricultural labourers' mainly include those who perform the manual operations on the fields and who used to be known as 'tamilia'. However, on large farms, the category 'permanent wage labourers' should be broadly defined so as to include all groups of specialised agricultural labourers, such as the 'kallaf' who looks after the livestock, the tractor driver and other farm machine operators.

18 The usual practice in this case is to assign the permanent agricultural labourer a small piece of land of about 16 kirats (2/3 feddan) to cultivate on his own, in exchange for his labour services.

Permanent labourers — unlike casual labourers — are more or less fully employed throughout the year and hence enjoy steady incomes all the year round. Nonetheless, the nature of their remunerations tend to vary a good deal from region to region, and in many cases they are paid partly in kind and partly in cash according to the prevailing custom and tradition.[19]

Casual farm labourers

Casual farm labourers are those landless peasants who enter into the labour force in the farm sector for short periods in response to additional demand for labour in the peak seasons, like sowing or harvesting, and thus supplement the permanent regular labour force in the farm sector.[20] These labourers are not tied to any particular farm and the major part of their income is derived from 'casual' employment opportunities offered to them on a temporary basis.

The 1961 agricultural census for the first time provides information about temporary (or casual) farm labour by different sex and age groups. According to the census figures, the number of 'temporary' farm labourers (of both sexes and over the age of 11) had reached 1.2 million in 1961, of whom about one quarter were females and one half in the age group between 12 and 18 (See Table 2.13).

Table 2.13 *Casual 'temporary' labour in the farm sector, 1961*

Age group	Sex group		Both sexes	Percentage of total casual farm labour force
	Male	Female		
12 – < 18 years	406,111	215,374	621,485	50.5%
⩾ 18 years	506,208	103,936	610,144	49.5%
Total	912,319	319,310	1,231,629	100

Source: 1961 Agricultural Census, Vol. I, Part IV, Table 58, p. 208

It can be seen from the table that female participation rates are quite high for both age groups: 35% of the age group 12 to 18 years and 17% in the age group 18 years and over. We may further observe that since there is no alternative source of income for landless families, young boys and girls in the age group 12 to 18 years form about 51% of the total casual labour force in Egyptian agriculture.

19 In Mounifia region, for instance, the permanent wage labourer receives his wages according to the following formula: in the first six months he receives 3 ardebs (420 kgs) of maize and one ardeb (150 kgs) of wheat and thereafter 150 P.T. monthly in cash. Cf. Mohiedin, *Thesis* . . ., p. 71.
20 In the past, when there was less differentiation amongst the peasantry, *the system of mutual exchange of labour* played an important role in meeting labour requirements during the harvesting period. The difference in times of sowing and in crop-patterns of the individual cultivators enabled them to help each other during the harvesting period.
    A fairly equitable distribution of land amongst the peasantry constituted an essential precondition for the proper functioning of this system in the past. With the increasing degree of differentiation amongst the peasantry this precondition tended to break down, because of the growth in the numbers of landless peasants, although its survivals are to be found in some Egyptian villages to this day.

According to Mohie-eldine,[21] the casual labour force is concentrated in certain provinces where the majority of farms are large (38% of the casual labour force in Lower Egypt is concentrated in Beheira and Kafr-el-Sheikh provinces). The reverse is true for Mounifia and Qalubia provinces, where the majority of the farms are small family farms, and the problem of landlessness is less acute. In other words, *there is a positive association between the degree of concentration of landholdings and the size of the casual labour force.* The higher the degree of landholding concentration, the larger the casual labour tends to be.

Casual farm labour is hired-in by farms of all sizes as shown in Table 2.14. However, 'medium' and 'large' farms together provide employment opportunities for some *one million* casual agricultural labourers.

The tarahil casual labourers: the poorest of the rural poor

A substantial proportion of landless peasants (mostly adult males) work as casual labourers within a system known as *tarhila* by which labour is recruited for 4 to 8 weeks for the maintenance of canals and other rural public works. This group of rural labourers — recruited mainly from the highly-populated provinces of Upper Egypt and the Delta — is freely mobile, willing to enter casual employment not only in the vicinity of their villages but sometimes in distant localities.[22]

The employers of these casual labourers usually have recourse to special labour contractors (*mokawil anfarr*) who guarantee a regular supply of casual labour for a commission. The *tarahil* labourers suffer from the combination of two modes of exploitation, namely usury and employers' exploitation, for the usual practice is that the contractor deducts a number of commissions which could add up to about 12 per cent of the wages paid to *tarahil* labourers. Moreover, most of the *tarahil* labourers are under strong pressure from their contractors to work extra unpaid days at the end of *tarhila* for the contractor's own account.

It was not until 1960, eight years after the Revolution, that the appalling conditions of *tarahil* labourers began to attract the attention of the government. In the 1960's many attempts were made to set up *governmental agencies* designed to compete with (or to subsisute for) the labour contractors in recruiting casual labourers for rural public works. These attempts all failed to undermine the strong position of the labour contractors in the rural labour market.[23]

The failure of these official initiatives revealed the extent to which the power of labour contractors arises from their position in the nexus of the agrarian economic power structure; for most of the *tarahil* labourers are not free agents. They are normally attached to their contractors by various bonds (kinship, debts, money advances during the slack season and various other social relationships). In practice, no state-financed agency was empowered to lend money to *tarahil* labourers, as the contractors normally do, for such occasions as births, deaths, sickness and marriage — which are the regularly recurring occasions for expenditure which the desparate *tarahil* labourer can neither avoid nor afford to meet out of his meagre resources. Ignoring this, the government schemes were never effective in breaking the power of the contractors.

21 Mohie-eldine, *Thesis*, p. 73.
22 cf. Ayrout, *The Egyptian Peasant, op. cit.*
23 For a critical appraisal of these experimental government-financed agencies see Hosni Hussein, "Tarahil Labourers" (In Arabic), Al-Ta'lia, vol. 7 No. 1, (Jan. 1971).

Table 2.14 *Distribution of casual farm labour force in Egypt by size of holding, sex-age groups, 1961*

Size of farm (feddans)	Casual temporary labourers (by age group)						All age groups			% of Total
	6 – <12 yrs		12 – <18 yrs		≥ 18 years					
	Male	Female	Male	Female	Male	Female	Male	Female	Total	
< 2	51,933	30,705	50,957	20,828	68,737	7,919	171,627	59,452	231,079	12.5
2 – < 5	121,430	85,930	130,000	68,383	166,295	30,400	417,718	184,713	602,431	32.5
5 – < 20	110,704	76,186	119,560	67,291	141,060	34,418	371,322	177,895	549,219	30.0
≥ 20	84,813	57,184	105,601	58,872	130,116	31,199	320,530	147,255	467,785	25.0
Total	368,880	250,000	406,118	215,374	506,208	103,936	1,281,197	569,315	1,850,514	100

Source: Figures computed from *1961 Agricultural Census*, Vol. I, Part IV, Table 58, p. 208.

More important still is the crucial problem of survival for each labourer, from *tarhila* to *tarhila*, which can be overcome only by borrowing money from his contractor to meet his regular consumption requirements. These *consumption-loans* are in fact the main cause of the perpetual indebtedness of the *tarahil* labourer, and hence of his inability to break free from the *tarhila* system dominated by the contractors. Thus the *tarahil* labourer finds himself caught in a system of perpetual bondage as he is always compelled to supply his labour services to the same man, to whom he is perpetually indebted.[24]

More generally it is important to emphasise that the *tarhila* system of labour-hire retains certain features peculiar to the feudal labour-service system, namely the bondage and the usurious character of the mode of labour-hire.

On the other hand, the existence of such a *reserve army of tarahil labourers* illustrates the acuteness of the crisis of transition from feudalism to capitalism in modern Egypt, for this growing mass of labourers, while separated from their principal means of production, the land, are unable as yet to find regular wage employment in the developing capitalist sector of the economy. In other words, these 'free' landless peasants are prevented from becoming a *proletariat* in the modern sense, and are thus compelled to fall back upon semi-feudal modes of exploitation based on a bonded labour-hire system.

It should be emphasised however that the power of labour-contractors does not derive solely from their activities as intermediaries in the rural labour market, but is buttressed by their ancillary roles in the Egyptian rural community as merchants or landlords. For the contractor is either himself the local shopkeeper, produce merchant, landowner, and/or moneylender; or is closely allied with this group of village functionaries. Hence a labour-contractor acting as a moneylender-cum-merchant may extract a very high rate of interest by giving 'consumption loans' in kind to his labourers and stipulating in return more exploitative conditions of work in the forthcoming *tarhila*. Such interlocking of markets increases the exploitive power of the labour contractors over the landless rural labourers, and it would thus be misleading to ignore the pervasive nature of this exploitation, which is inherent in the 'relations of production' in the Egyptian countryside.

Finally it should be noted that it is almost certainly a mistake to conceive of 'farm' and tarahil' labourers in terms of mutually exclusive categories. In fact, it is quite common to be a casual 'farm' labourer and a casual 'tarahil' labourer at the same time; as the seasonal pattern of agricultural activities in Egypt allows the same labourer to be recruited as a 'tarahil labourer' in the *slack season*, and to become a temporary 'farm labourer' later during the peak season.[25]

24 For a similar perpetual indebtedness mechanism among the small tenants in the Indian villages of West Bengal, see A. Bhaduri, "Agricultural Backwardness under Semi-Feudalism", *Economic Journal* (March 1973).

25 A typical casual labourer in rural Egypt would go on four 'tarhilas' per year, each lasting for an average of one month. The same labourer hires-out his labour services during the peak season in the farm sector for a period not exceeding 3 months. Thus all in all he finds work for a period extending to 7 months a year (210 days). For the rest of the year (5 months), he stays almost unemployed or just recovering from the physical exhaustion of the hard tarhila work. At times he may be lucky enough to get some casual work in the farm sector for an extra month or so.

2.4   Summary and conclusions

The foregoing analysis enables us to establish conclusively that there is a marked degree of differentiation amongst the peasantry in Egypt.

It can hardly be a coincidence that the evidence presented in this chapter on the differentiation of the peasantry – gathered from diverse sources and analysed by multiple indicators – has given compatible results. Table (2.15) gives a summary view of the process of differentiation based on selected statistical indicators computed from the 1961 agricultural census data. It can be readily seen that in every respect, and on all counts, measures of the degree of differentiation amongst the peasantry are remarkably consistent with each other.

This is not surprising, since the different aspects of the process of differentiation are closely related. For instance, the use of agricultural machinery on a significant scale presupposes the existence of a sizeable pool of landless wage labourers. Moreover, the introduction of agricultural machinery gives rise to a certain hierarchy amongst wage labourers themselves (i.e. tractor drivers, farm machine operators etc.,), thus strengthening the capitalistic features of the process of cultivation.

It is unfortunate that *the fifth agricultural census*, originally scheduled for 1971, was not carried out. Had this census been conducted, the process of the differentiation of the peasantry in the Egyptian countryside would have come out even in more pronounced terms than it did in 1961. There are strong indications however that under the agrarian system of today, the stratum of rich peasants (holders of 20 to 50 feddans) carry a decisive weight in the nexus of the new agrarian power structure. Over the longer term, a successful innovative push by capitalist farmers and rich peasants in the field of new crop varieties will almost certainly lead them to ask for more means of mechanizing on an extensive scale. This will greatly accelerate the process of differentiation among the peasantry. There is also clear evidence that this new privileged stratum of rich peasants (i.e. the kulak class) has gained great bargaining power in recent years.[26]

On the other hand, the new agrarian policies have had some favourable and positive effects on the 'middle peasantry' as well as on the large class of 'small peasants' insofar as they have found themselves in a much better position to make output-raising improvements.

Nonetheless, in *structural* terms, the basic dualism in the agrarian system remains inviolate, and the new agrarian changes did not help much to solve the *structural* problems of the 'landless' and 'poor peasants' – sustaining themselves on minute plots of land. For the great majority of rural casual labourers were no better off in 1970 than they had been when they rejoiced at the overthrow of the old regime in 1952.

---

26 In 1972 the government presented to the people's assembly a bill imposing a tax on
    fruit orchards of £E20 per feddan, but this was rejected by the assembly under
    pressure from the pro-rich peasants' lobby.

Table 2.15 *Summary indicators of the degree of differentiation of the Egyptian peasantry, 1960–61*

Size of holding (feddans)	Percentage distribution of total number of holdings		Percentage shares of total farm area (owned or leased-in)		Percentage shares of total agricultural labour force		Percentage of hired wage-labour to total permanent labour force		Percentage shares of tractors in use		Percentage shares of fixed tools of irrigation		Percentage shares of total fruit area	
	1950	1961	1950	1961	1950	1961	1950	1961	1950	1961	1950	1961	1950	1961
	%	%	%	%	%	%	%	%	%	%	%	%	%	%
1. < 5 (poor and small peasantry)	78	84	23	38	n.a.	73	n.a.	10	2.4	7	7	17	15	17
2. 5 – < 20 (middle peasantry)	18	14	25	30	n.a.	20	n.a.	22	5.3	19	28	36	20	17
3. > 20 (rich peasantry and big landlordship)	4	2	52	32	n.a.	7	n.a.	63	92.3	74	65	47	65	66
Total	100	100	100	100	–	100	–	13.0	100	100	100	100	100	100

Source: Detailed tables in the text.

3

Changes in the Distribution
of Agricultural Income

In the preceding two chapters we have tried to examine the major socio-economic changes which have taken place in Egypt's agrarian structure since 1952, and to identify the major groups among the peasantry. The central concern of this chapter is with the impact of these changes in the agrarian system on *structural shifts* in the distribution of agricultural income between various groups of the peasantry.

Neo-classical economists prefer to study the distribution of income earned in agriculture by *factor shares*. In such an analytical framework the distributive shares are related to (or determined by) the marginal products of factors engaged in agriculture. The acceptance of such a marginal productivity approach to income distribution is usually supplanted by the use of production functions. The Cobb-Douglas production function is the one generally used in this type of analysis.[1]

In the present author's view — quite apart from the particular analytical and empirical difficulties associated with the construction of an 'aggregate production function' for agriculture — such an approach appears to be an excessive abstraction from reality, and for a number of reasons is of limited use for the analysis of the interdependence between distribution of income, social change and economic growth. In the first place, it has proved impossible in practice to isolate 'factor incomes' except by making heroic simplifying assumptions, since it is almost impossible to isolate factor shares for the large section of the peasantry who cultivate their own land — where all factor incomes actually merge.[2] Secondly, even if the different types of income could be isolated, they no longer (if they ever did) correspond to distinct socio-economic groups.

---

1 This function may be simply written in terms of land and labour: $P = f(L, A)$, where P is the 'factor income' of agriculture, L the input of labour, and A area of land cultivated. The specific functional form of Cobb-Douglas may be written as follows

$$P = L^{\alpha} A^{\beta} \qquad \text{(where } \alpha + \beta = 1)$$

This functional form has the important property that the *marginal* product of any of the two factors is a given fraction of the *average* product of the factor:

$$f_L' = \alpha \left(\frac{f}{L} \right); \quad \text{and} \quad f_A' = \beta \left(\frac{f}{A} \right).$$

See C. Clark and M. Haswell, *The Economics of Subsistence Agriculture*, 4th ed. (London: Macmillan, 1970), ch. X; and B. Hansen, "Marginal Productivity Wage Theory and Subsistence Wage Theory in Egyptian Agriculture", *Journal of Development Studies*, II (July, 1966), pp. 367–407.

2 Professor Bent Hansen has attempted to estimate distributive shares in Egyptian agriculture within a neo-classical analytical framework ['Distributive Shares in

Hence the need to define homogeneous socio-economic groups with broadly similar types of incomes and broadly similar consumption and savings behaviour is not a matter of pure academic interest, but is central to the analysis of the relation between distribution and the socio-economic changes in the economy.[3] For the purpose of our analysis, it is important to be able to identify in the rural population such distinct socio-economic groups as rural labourers and tenant-farmers, and proprietors by size of holding. In doing so, we share the classical economists' main concern to focus on the process of distribution of income between broad social classes, in order to be able to explain the dynamic behaviour of the economy and society at large.[4]

In order to get a balanced view of the distributional shifts which have occurred within the agricultural sector since 1952, we shall first consider the impact of the agrarian reforms on the distribution of agricultural income. This will be followed by a more general analysis of the changes in the distribution of agricultural income by major socio-economic groups. Finally, we shall examine the trend in the development of real wages since 1952 for agricultural labourers, in order to gain some insight into the question of the direction and extent of changes in the standards of living of these labourers.

3.1   Income distribution effects of agrarian reforms

Although the distribution of wealth in the form of land was the most publicised aspect of the land reforms in Egypt, it represented in fact a less significant change than the notable 'income effect' arising from the rent ceiling.[5]

Egyptian Agriculture, 1897–1961', *The International Economic Review*, Vol. 9, No. 2 (June 1968)]. His analysis raises some awkward problems of a definitional and statistical nature: the absolute size of the *wages' share* in agricultural income was obtained by imputing average daily wages for labourers and by assuming that each person is working full time, an arbitrary assumption which introduces a systematic element of overestimation in the share of wages. Similarly, the *share of rents* was obtained as the ratio between the rental value of all cultivated land, whether actually rented or not, and total agricultural income. A *residual share* (amounting to about 13% of the agricultural income in 1951) emerges, which can be attributed − according to Professor Hansen − to the presence of some *overlapping* between rental values and wages on the one hand, and between rental values and usury interests on the other.

3 It is interesting to note that the recent trend in the literature on income distribution is towards a classification which will combine information on the source of income with a classification by socio-economic groups which share common patterns of behaviour. Of particular interest in this connection are the following works: Proceedings of the Conference of the International Economic Association J. Marchal and B. Ducros (eds.) *The Distribution of National Income*, (London: 1968); U.N. Research Institute for Social Development, *Distribution of Income and Economic Growth (Concepts and Issues)*, Report by Nancy Baster, (Geneva: 1970); Charles Elliott, 'Income Distribution and Social Stratification: Some Notes on Theory and Practice', *Journal of Development Studies*, Vol. 8, No. 3, (April 1972), pp. 37−56.

4 Such an approach to income distribution occupied a central place in the works of Quesnay, Ricardo and Marx. In a letter to McCulloch in 1820 Ricardo writes: "After all, the great questions of Rent, Wages, and Profits must be explained by the proportions in which the whole produce is divided between landlords, capitalists, and labourers." cf. Piero Sraffa's introduction to the *Works and Correspondence of David Ricardo*, Vol. I (Cambridge Univ. Press, 1951), p. xxxiii.

5 See Warriner, *Land Reform and Development in the Middle East*, p. 33.

3.1.1   The impact of agrarian reforms on the incomes of tenant-cultivators

It has been claimed that up to 1960 about 1,100,000 tenant-cultivators benefited from the first land reform law,[6] which would mean that the livelihood of about 5 million people in rural Egypt was affected.

If we assume that the average gross farm income per feddan remained much the same as in the pre-reform period, the increase in tenants' income due to the enactment of tenancy regulations would amount to the difference between the pre-reform rent level and the new 'statutory rent'. As the 1952 land reform law fixed the annual rent per feddan of tenants subject to cash rents at seven times the basic land tax (averaging about £E3 per feddan) the annual statutory rent was therefore fixed at about £E21 per feddan. This figure is at least some £E10 less than the average level of cash rent prevailing during the two years immediately preceding the enactment of 1952 agrarian reform.[7]

According to the most conservative estimates, the gain in income conferred on tenant-farmers by *the rent ceiling* should have mounted to about £E20 million annually (taking the area affected by tenancy regulations to be only 2 million feddans). On the other hand, according to the estimates of the Egyptian Ministry of Agriculture, the reduction of rents added as much as £E40 million annually to the income of tenant-farmers.[8] This great discrepancy between the two estimates may be attributed to differences in average rent per feddan between Lower and Upper Egypt in the pre-reform period, as well as to the non-inclusion of gains accruing to share-croppers in the first estimate.

Although the system of share-cropping before the 1952 reform varied widely from region to region and from one crop to another, a common practice for cotton cultivation was for the landlord to take all but a small fraction of the cotton crop and half or more of the wheat crop, leaving the maize and barseem (Egyptian clover) for the cultivator and his buffalo.[9] In other words, under such a feudal share-cropping arrangement, the landlord provided seed and fertiliser for the cotton crop and got the labour free.

The reform of 1952 stipulated that landlords and tenants should share equally in the cost of cultivation and in the produce of the land. The total area affected by these new regulations for share-tenancy amounted — according to the estimates of Sayed Marei — to about ¾ million feddans of agricultural land.[10]

As a result of these 'tenancy regulations' the main impact of the land reform was the alteration of relative shares in agricultural income in favour of the

6   Cf. Ezz-el-Din Hammam, 'The Real Impact . . . . .', p. 7.
7   Cf. Hansen & Marzouk, *op. cit.*, Table 4.5, p. 90.
8   See: UN Department of Economic and Social Affairs, *Progress in Land Reform*, (New York: 1956), p. 136.
9   Cf. Warriner, *Land Reform and Development in the Middle East, op. cit.*
10   Cf. *CERES, loc. cit.*, p. 50. Our figure here is based on Marei's estimate that the percentage of leased land against *payment in kind* amounted to 24% of a total leased area of 3.1 million feddans.

tenant-cultivators at the expense of big absentee landlords. Hansen and Marzouk have estimated that the drop in the absentee owners' share in agricultural value added amounted to almost half of its previous level before the land reform, thus allowing for a rise by about one-third in the share going to tenants.[11]

But it would be misleading to see this shift as a *permanent* structural change in the distribution of agricultural income, as recent investigations have shown that the margin between the 'statutory' and 'market' rates of rent tended to widen again on account of a rise in the latter.[12] A common practice to evade rent ceiling, as noted by Saab,[13] is to sign a lease calling for the legal statutory rent, but at the same time to compel the tenant to sign separate bills of exchange for the extra amount.

Thus, to an unknown extent, much of the initial income gain to the tenants (in the early years of land reform), which accrued in the form of reduced rents, had gradually been lost back to the landowners through "black market" rents and through various forms of evasion e.g. through shifting the burden of land tax and certain costs on to the tenant.[14]

3.1.2 The impact of agrarian reforms on the incomes of the beneficiaries of land distribution

Those who have avoided this "clawback" are those who have become full owners of redistributed land. By making use of the available official data on average gross income, average cost of cultivation per feddan and other overhead outlays — land taxes and contributions towards co-operative expenses — it is possible to estimate changes in the average net income of those new beneficiaries of land distribution, who cultivate their land with the aid of family rather than hired labour, and represent about one-fifth of the total number of landholders. Eprime Eshag and M.A. Kamal[15] have attempted such an estimate, and the broad figures obtained for changes in net income per feddan of the beneficiaries of land distribution for the crop years 1952/3 to 1964/5 are shown in Table 3.1. It can be readily seen that the trend of growing *money* incomes was uninterrupted throughout the period under review. Of the increase of about 50 per cent in *gross* money receipts per feddan between 1952/3 and 1964/5, about 30 per cent was accounted for by gains in land productivity (i.e. increase in crop yields) and about 20 per cent by the recovery in the prices of agricultural crops, in particular of cotton, from their post-Korean War low of 1952/3.[16] Nonetheless, if due allowance is made for inflationary pressures during this period, the *real* increase in average gross receipts per feddan would only amount to 36 per cent, which is still a substantial increase.

---

11 See Hansen and Marzouk, *op. cit.*, p. 94.
12 See Hansen and Marzouk, *op. cit.*, p. 85; and G. Saab, *op. cit.*, p. 145.
13 Saab, *op. cit.*
14 Hansen, 'Distributive Shares . . .' *op. cit.*, p. 191.
15 Cf. Eprime Eshag and M.A. Kamal, "Agrarian Reform in the United Arab Republic (Egypt)", *Bulletin of the Oxford Institute of Economics and Statistics*, XXX, (May 1968), pp. 96–8.
16 *Ibid.*

Table 3.1 *Income per feddan of the beneficiaries of land distribution during crop years 1952/3 to 1964/5 (£E.)*

	1952/3	1954/5	1956/7	1958/9	1960/1	1962/3	1964/5
Gross receipts	55	58	66	66	75	76	84
Less cost of cultivation	−10	− 7	− 9	−10	−10	−11	−13
Operating profit	45	51	58	57	64	65	71
Index (a)	100	113	129	127	142	144	158
Less: *Overheads* Taxes and cooperative expenses (b)	− 6	− 6	− 6	− 6	− 6	− 6	− 6
Purchase price of land	−12	−12	−12	−12	− 8	− 4	− 1
Net income per feddan	27	33	39	39	50	55	64
Index (a)	100	122	144	144	185	204	237

(a) Calculated by the author.
(b) Land tax is estimated at £E3, supplementary tax at £E0.3 and contribution towards cooperative expenses at £E3 per feddan; total is rounded to £E6 per feddan.
Source: Eshag and Kamal, p. 97.

On the other hand, overhead outlays were declining over time because of the down-scaling of the annual instalments paid for the purchase of land following a series of successive governmental decrees reducing the sale price of land to the beneficiaries, extending the indemnity period and lowering interest charges.[17]

Needless to say, these calculations are very crude and the margin of error is quite large. But the figures do give some reasonable idea of the order of magnitude of the changes in net income per feddan for the beneficiaries of land distribution. Yet it is noteworthy that the net disposable money income per feddan for the beneficiaries of land distribution is considerably lower than the estimated figures given in Table 3.1.[18] We may also remark that the assumption made about the fixity of the contributions to cooperative expenses throughout the period 1952/3–1964/5 is highly unrealistic, since contributions to cooperative expenses rose considerably during the sixties.

Now, if we assume that the level of average operating profit per feddan was the same in 1951/2 as in 1952/3, we can ascertain with a reasonable degree of certainty that there has been a straight financial gain to the class of new landowners (beneficiaries of land distribution), which could have amounted to about £E12 per feddan (i.e. the difference between the former rent paid by the farmer and the new payment instalments, taking to be £E18 per feddan). In order to get a clearer picture of the income distributional effects of the agrarian reforms, our findings may be summarized as in Table 3.2

17 In 1961 half of the instalment payments were written off.
18 An investigating team from the evening newspaper *Al-Missa*, led by Ali el-Shalakani, was able to ascertain, after a long series of field investigations carried out in 1958, that the peasant was obliged to pay something like £E40 per year for each feddan received from the state after deducting the cost of cultivation including £E14.45 for the annual instalment in respect of the purchase of land, £E12.06 to pay for irrigation facilities and other overheads, and £E10 to pay off earlier loans. *Al-Missa*, August 8 and Sept. 25, 1958, as quoted in Abdel-Malek, *Egypt: Military Society*, p. 73.

Table 3.2 *Income distributional effects of agrarian reforms*

	Increase in net annual income *per feddan* (£E)	Increase in annual income *per family* (£E)	No. of beneficiaries in 1961/2 (families) 000's	Beneficiaries as a percentage of total landless %
Changes in the income of the new beneficiaries of the land distribution[1]	+ 36	+ 93.6[2]	167[3]	10
Changes in the income of the tenant-cultivators	+ 10	+ 28.0[4]	1,114[5]	68
Total			1,281	78

Source: See text

Notes

(1)   All the beneficiaries of the land distribution are assumed to have been tenant-cultivators before the agrarian reforms.
(2)   Based on an average piece of 2.6 feddans per family, since most owners were sold very small plots (nearer the minimum of two feddans than the maximum of five).
(3)   Families benefiting from the distribution of land up to 1961/2 (See Table 1.4)
(4)   Assuming an average of 2.8 feddans of rented land per family, obtained by dividing the total area under tenancy (3.1 million feddans) by the number of families benefiting from the new tenancy regulations (1,114,129 families according to Hammam's estimate)
(5)   Hammam's estimate.

3.2   Distribution of agricultural income by socio-economic groups

To obtain any reliable set of figures on the distribution of agricultrual income by socio-economic groups is not any easy task. Not only are statistics in this respect scanty,[19] but the concepts and classifications used in official statistics are also highly ambiguous for the purpose of our analysis.[20] We propose however to offer in the following pages a tentative analysis of the socio-economic structure of income distribution in rural Egypt.

By drawing on a wide variety of source material, we have attempted to piece together various pieces of empirical evidence and statistics in order to draw up a *matrix of income distribution,* with relevant classes (or socio-economic groups) in the rows as shown in Table 3.3.

19   An interesting study was however undertaken by Samir Amin in *L'Egypte Nassérienne* (Paris: 1964, ch. 1), where he produced a set of figures on social stratification and the pattern of income distribution in rural Egypt for 1958. This study suffers from the following weaknesses concerning the data base:
      (a) Rural population was estimated at 19 million in 1959, whereas in fact it was about 16 million as late as 1960. This would certainly affect the number of 'landless' peasants, whose number should be brought down by at least two millions.
      (b) The figures quoted for the distribution of landholdings are for 1950, while reference is made to them as if they were for 1957.
      (c) The figures for agricultural income relate to 1958/9.
      See also: Saab, *The Egyptian Agrarian Reform, 1952–1962, op. cit.,* p. 13.
20   The published estimates of the income generated in the agricultural sector covering the period 1952–69 are based on *the value added method,* and thus are of little help to our enquiry. cf: CAPMS, *National Income Estimates for the Agricultural Sector,* Ref. 04/412 (Cairo: December 1971).

The broad socio-economic groups, retained in this matrix, are defined both in relation to the *earning process* and in relation to their *spending* and *saving* behaviour. The changing relative distributive shares of these socio-economic groups provide the link between the dynamics of social change, economic growth and the distribution of income.

The years 1950 and 1961 were selected as two bench-mark dates in order to assess the redistributional impact of the new social and development policies pursued in rural Egypt after the 1952 revolution. The choice of these two points of time was dictated by the fact that they correspond to agricultural census years, where reliable and firm data on landholdings are available.

On the other hand, it is unfortunate that the fifth agricultural census, scheduled for 1971, has not been carried out, hence no comparable set of figures is available after 1961; the most that we can hope to do is to make the best possible estimates of the developments which have taken place in the distribution of agricultural income since then, by making use of all available fragmentary evidence in this respect.

Using the figures on landholdings in the 1950 agricultural census, estimates of national income from agriculture for the years 1945—7 and a rough estimate of the average money rent per feddan before 1952, we are able to obtain a breakdown of agricultural income by the major socio-economic groups for 1950 as shown in Table 3.3.[21] For 1961, we use the census figures on landholdings, area under tenancy and the age-sex composition of rural labourers in that year in order to obtain a breakdown of agricultural income by the same socio-economic groups.

Needless to say, these calculations make no pretentions to accuracy, as the margin of error is large. But we do think however, given the available data, that they shed some new light on the distributional shifts in agricultural income by the major socio-economic groups in rural Egypt. A few remarks concerning the data base are, however, in order.

First, the year 1950 was the year of Korean war boom with a strong upward bias in the non-wage income share of agricultural income.[22] This gives some downward bias to the share of agricultural income going to wage labourers.

Secondly, the 'less than 5 feddans' holding bracket in 1961 included land reform beneficiaries. The interest payments to the government and the amortisations associated with the newly distributed land are left out of the picture, since they are a kind of compulsory savings.[23]

Thirdly, it should be stressed that the use of a uniform average income per feddan, regardless of the farm size, leads to some upward bias in the incomes of small owners and tenents. Observations made in most countries generally indicate that many small farmers are compelled to sell the whole of their crop immediately after the harvest, at a comparatively unfavourable price, even if they have to buy some back at a substantially higher price later.[24] These losses in income are mainly due to the lack of adequate storage facilities, as well as the pressing need for cash.

21 Compare our results with Mead's estimates, pp. 76—79.
22 cf. Mabro, *The Egyptian Economy 1952—1972*, p. 220.
23 cf. Hansen & Marzouk, *op. cit.*, p. 94.
24 See C. Clark & M. Haswell, *The Economics of Subsistence Agriculture*, p. 63.

Table 3.3 Distribution of agricultural income by socio-economic groups, 1950 and 1961

Major socio-economic recipient groups	1950						1961						
	£E million	Share in total income	No families (000's)	% of total farm population	Average income per head of family (£E)	(2)/(4)	£E million	Share in total income	No families (000's)	% of total farm population	Average income per head of family (£E) money / real		(2)/(4)
	(1)	(2)	(3)	(4)	(5)	(6)	(1)	(2)	(3)	(4)	(5)		(6)
1. Wages paid to agricultural labourers (income of landless peasants)	20	5.3	1,217	55	16.4	0.09	39	9.7	970	37	40	30	0.26
2. Income of landholders, by size of holdings													
< 5 feddans (poor & small peasantry)	55	15.0	787	35	70	0.43	113	28.0	1,381	53	82	81	0.53
5 – < 50 feddans (Middle & rich peasantry)	92	25.0	201	9	458	2.77	130	32.3	251	9	518	513	3.55
≥ 50 (big landowners)	144	39.0	15	1	9600	39.00	69	17.0	10	1	6900	6832	17.00
3. Rental payments for absentee landownership	58	15.7					52	13.0					
Net value added in agriculture (at current prices)	369	100.0	2,220	100	166	1.00	403	100.0	2,612	100	154	152	1.0

Notes and sources: 1950

1. All labourers are assumed to work 150 days per year (see Mead, *op. cit.*, p. 78).
2. Figures for the incomes of different groups of landholders are based on estimates of average gross value added per feddan for different size farms (see Mead, p. 67), multiplied by the acreage in each size-class as reported in the 1950 agricultural census.
3. Average rental is estimated at £E30 per feddan (see Hansen & Marzouk, *op. cit.*, p. 83). Rental payments refer to rent actually paid (in cash or kind), excluding imputed rent of owner-occupied land.
4. In col. 6 we have attempted a crude method of 'normalization' by computing
$$\frac{\text{The percentage share in income}}{\text{The percentage share in population}}\text{; for each income}$$
recipient group, in order to be able to draw more meaningful conclusions about changes in the distribution of agriculture income by socio-economic groups between 1950 and 1961.

Notes and sources: 1961

1. The wage share is derived from census data on the number and age-sex composition of paid labourers, combined with a rough estimate of the average number of days worked per year for each group, and a knowledge of wage differentials by sex and age (see appendix D).
2. Incomes of different groups of landholders were obtained by assuming the following uniform income levels: income of an *owned feddan*, net of land tax £E62; income of a *rented feddan*, net of land tax £E44. Wages paid to hired labour were netted out from the incomes of landholders, as the wage bill for both casual and permanent labourers were divided up between holdings of different sizes in proportion to their respective shares of both types of hired labour as recorded in the 1961 census. Appropriate deflators were then applied to figures on average money income by family.
3. Average rental is estimated at £E21 per feddan. The share of rent payments in total income in 1961 did not fall dramatically despite the enforcement of rent control. This was mainly because of the high degree of absentee land-ownership among the very small landowners.

With the above qualifications in mind, a number of important inferences on the distributional shifts within the agricultural sector over the decade of the 1950s can be drawn from the figures given in Table 3.3.

The introduction of 'rent control' after 1952 has had to a notable downward effect on average money rent per feddan, and in most cases average rents per feddan declined by some 25-30 per cent. This implied a fall in the income of absentee landlords, and an increase in the incomes of tenant-cultivators.

The biggest shift in the distribution of agricultural income was in favour of the 'middle and rich peasantry', whose share of total agricultural income rose from 25 per cent to over 32 per cent. This result is consistent with the general trends of differentiation of the peasantry discussed in Chapter 2.

There was also a substantial increase in the income received by the poorest groups of the rural population — wage labourers and those cultivating tiny pieces of land or small farms — with their share of total agricultural income rising from 20 per cent in 1950 to about 38 per cent in 1961. However, in order to be able to interpret this increase in the income received by the poorer strata from a welfare point of view, we should need to know something about the numbers of people with claims on the income in each of these categories.

For the group of "landless peasants" the increase in their share of agricultural income was accompanied by a substantial increase in money income per capita, on the count of the fall in the absolute numbers of landless families (as defined in Table 2.12) as well as the rise in the number of wage earners.

On the other hand, the increase in the income received by the "small" and "poor" peasantry was accompanied by a tremendous increase in the number of farmers falling into this category, as a result of the land redistribution programme. The transfer of landownership implied significant income increases for the beneficiaries falling in this size group. However, it is interesting to note that while their share of total agricultural income almost doubled over the decade, the increase in money income per capita has amounted to no more than 20 per cent.[25]

Let us finally note that an important feature of the redistributional shifts is that the absolute income received by the big landlords (over 50 feddans), as well as their relative share of total agricultural income, dropped markedly during the 1950s.

The main conclusion to be drawn from the preceding discussion is that, as a result of the significant redistribution of income within the agricultural sector over the decade of the 1950s, the 'middle' and 'rich' peasantry benefited most from the process. (i.e. had the biggest rise in per-capita income). It is also clear that the 'landless' and 'small' peasantry achieved significant gains in income, though to a lesser degree. For the remainder — the absentee landlords and the very big landlords — incomes declined very sharply, hitting a few of the first group (averages have little meaning here)[26] and hitting all of the second group quite hard.

Unfortunately, we are unable to obtain reliable comparable data on developments in the distribution of agricultural income after 1961. The principal difficulty

---

25 The increase in the income of the new owners (beneficiaries of land redistribution) is much more substantial than that of old owners in this group.

26 See Mead, *op. cit.*, p. 79.

Table 3.4 *Frequency distribution of rural households according to annual family income by economic type, (sample survey, 1964/65)*

Classification	Anuual income (£E)					
	< 50 %	50-99 %	100-149 %	150-199 %	⩾ 200 %	unknown %
Economic type of household:						
Farmers:						
< 2 feddans	32	38	20	4	3	3
2 − < 5 feddans	9	38	31	15	6	1
5 − < 10 feddans	3	9	31	23	32	2
⩾ 10 feddans	4	4	12	8	72	-
Farm labourers	54	27	12	4	1	2
Craftsmen	35	35	18	5	2	5
Salesmen	38	29	16	7	10	-
Service workers	27	40	28	3	1	1
Non-agricultural labourers	36	34	14	7	9	-
Other employees	17	7	33	17	23	3
Other households (i.e. widows, old people, etc.)	68	13	6	5	4	4

Source: ILO., *Rural Employment Problems in the U.A.R.*, p. 68.

encountered arises from the fact that there are no reliable figures on the distribution of landholdings and the age-sex composition of the agricultural wage labourers. The only piece of direct evidence which may be of some relevance to our inquiry is related to the pattern of income distribution in 1965, as revealed by a sample survey of rural households.

Table 3.4 presents data relating to the relative frequency distribution of rural households in the sample — classified into broad landholding and other occupational classes — by size class of annual incomes as recorded in 1965.[27]

Although the data are very incomplete, it is possible however to make some tentative comparisons of income disparities between different groups of the peasantry over the period 1950-65. A comparison of the average incomes (in money terms) accruing to various groups is summarised in Table 3.5.

Some broad tentative conclusions emerge from a simple inspection of the figures in the table:

(i) there is a definite, though mild, trend of improvement in the distribution of agricultural income, associated with the narrowing of the range of income differentials between different groups of the peasantry;

(ii) some large income disparities between landless labourers and the rich peasantry, as well as the remaining big landlords, persisted as late as 1965, after two major agrarian reforms.

(iii) the relativity scale of income differential between the three bottom groups of the peasantry (landless, poor and small) remained much the same after 1950.

27 From further breakdowns of the income survey conducted by ILO and INP, strong positive correlations between size of income and size of household and, in particular between size of income and number of labour units worked per household, can be obtained. Both correlations indicate that *per capita* income is much more evenly distributed than family income. See Report D: *Wages, Incomes and Consumption in Rural Areas,* (INP: Cairo), Table 2.2.

Table 3.5 *Income differentials in rural areas by socio-economic groups, 1950-65*

	1950 (£E)	income differential	1965 (£E)	income differential
Agricultural labourers (fully employed)	24	1	49	1
poor peasants (< 2 feddans)	34	1.4	68	1.4
small peasants (2 – < 5 feddans)	70	2.9	103	2.1
middle peasantry				
5 – < 10 feddans	260	10.8	350	7.1
10 – < 20 feddans	535	22.3	600	12.2
rich peasantry (20 – < 50 feddans)	1200	50	2100	43
big landlords (≥ 50 feddans)	over 2000	more than 83	over 3000	more than 61

Notes and sources:
1950: figures derived by combining estimates for gross value of output per feddan by size of farm (Mead, *op. cit.*, p. 67), and the data on average annual net income by size of holding given in El-Ghonemy, 'Economic and Institutional Organisation of Egyptian Agriculture since 1952', *op. cit.*, p. 74.
1965: figures based on estimates for net income per feddan for 1964/5 given in Table 3.1; adjusted in the light of the empirical evidence provided in Table 3.4, after averaging the annual income over frequency classes for each group of peasantry.

It should be remembered, however, that the data on income distribution presented in this section relate to *agricultural* population rather than to *rural* population, for rural areas contain a sizeable proportion of non-agricultural population (amounting to 19% of the total). We may further note that our estimates of the average annual incomes of the different groups of the peasantry do not account for the extra income which is derived by 'poor' and 'small' farmers from sources other than agricultural activities.[28]

On the other hand, information on the size of urban-rural income transfers is conspicuously absent in Egypt. There are, however, strong indications that some voluntary redistributional flows (in the form of cash remittances) are actually taking place through kinship bonds and operate in such a way as to ensure that the relatively wealthy urban income-receivers pass some of their earnings to poor relatives in the countryside.

3.3 Income distribution by factor shares in Egyptian agriculture

It may be of some interest to supplement our analysis of the distribution of agricultural income by socio-economic groups with some additional data on changes in the distribution of agricultural income by *factor shares* over the period 1951-70.

28 It is estimated that about 16 per cent of the total working time of the members of farm labourers' households were spent on non-agricultural work. cf. ILO *Report*, p. 39. Also, it should be noted that many small landholders derive some extra income from the sale of dairy products and poultry in the town market nearest to their rural residence. However, the extra income derived in this way is fairly small: a pilot survey, carried out in 1955, in three villages near Cairo showed that 18 per cent of the households did not own any poultry, and among the rest of the households the total value of the poultry owned did not exceed £E0.70 in 25 per cent; £E1.46 in 50 per cent of the cases. See: H.M. Hussein, 'Pilot Survey of Family Budgets in Egypt', *International Labour Review*, LXXVIII No. 3 (Sept. 1958) p. 286

Wages and property incomes (including rent payments) constitute the two major income sources of households, as they flow directly from the production process in agriculture. In Table 3.6 we have assembled all available data on the *functional* distribution of agricultural income by factor shares. Two broad trends in the development of distributive shares in Egyptian agriculture can be traced during the period under investigation.

First, the figures in Table 3.6 reveal a marked fall in the share of property returns from 1951/2 to 1969/71, the fall being of a magnitude of 15-16 percentage units. About half of this can be ascribed to the decline in the share of cash rents in total agricultural income as a result of rent controls. As we have already mentioned (section 3.1) money rent per feddan came under government control after 1952. This had a downward effect on rent per feddan, and in most cases the reduction was quite substantial, at least in the first years of the implementation of land reforms.

Second, the rise in the share of labour, the counterpart of the decline in the share of property income, is quite uncertain, since we have good reason to believe that the data on agricultural wages as reported in official statistics represent 'imputed' average annual wages for the whole labour force employed in agricultural (including unpaid family labour and landholders working on their own account), rather than wages paid (in cash or kind) to the *wage* labourers in agriculture. As we shall see in the next section, money-wage rates remained almost constant throughout the 1950s, and it is most unlikely that the increase in the absolute size of the share of wages between 1951/2 and 1960/1 reflects an increase in the employment opportunities for agricultural wage labourers. For, it is well known that, the land reforms, by splitting up big estates, for some time lowered the demand for hired labour in agriculture.[29]

At any rate, the figures presented in Table 3.6 give a fairly reasonable, though tentative, idea of the changes which occurred in the *functional* distribution of agricultural income by factor shares over the period 1952-70.

3.4 The movement of real wages for agricultural labourers

It seems unnecessary to stress the need for some knowledge of the trend in the development of real wages in rural Egypt during the period under investigation. Such knowledge would provide valuable insight into the question of the *direction* and *extent* of changes in the standards of living of agricultural labourers.

In this section we do not aim at a comprehensive analysis of the movement of real wages in rural areas. Our aim is the more modest one of obtaining some rough indicators of changes in the standards of living of agricultural labourers. This modest aim is partly explained by the inadequacy of available statistical material, and, more generally, by the conceptual and methodological difficulties associated with the very notion of a 'unique' measure (or index) of real wages.[30] We propose therefore

29 See: Appendix B on 'The impact of public developmental schemes on employment opportunities for casual agricultural labourers'.
30 In fact, all indices purporting to show a general movement in real wages are simply conventions and should always be treated as such. Only if we accept the convention that we shall call a number arrived at on the basis of the prices of articles, through weighting and averaging in certain way, a real wage index, can we manipulate it and draw conclusions which are true for such numbers.

Table 3.6 *Development of distributive shares in Egyptian agriculture, 1952-70*

(at current prices)

Financial years (ending 30 June)	Agri-cultural income[1] (£E million)	Wages (£E million)	Share in total income	Total property returns[3] (£E million)	Share in total income	Cash rents (£E million)	Share in total income
			%		%		%
1951/2	352	60	17	292	83	58	16
59/60	405	98	24	307	76	n.a.	-
60/1	403	99	25	304	75	47	12
61/2	373[2]	117	31	256	69	48	13
62/3	425	126	30	299	70	48	11
63/4	475	139	29	336	71	47	10
64/5	528	167	32	361	68	46	9
65/6	608	197	32	411	68	46	8
66/7	612	205	33	407	67	47	8
67/8	644	201	31	443	69	48	7.5
68/9	688	211	31	477	69	49	7
69/70	772	218	28	554	72	n.a.	-

[1] Net value added at current prices.
[2] The fall in agricultural income in this year was due to the failure of the cotton crop.
[3] Inclusive of rent payments.

Sources:
1951/52: Hassan Abdallah, *U.A.R. Agriculture* (Cairo, 1965), p. 92.
1959/60 – 1964/5: U.A.R. Ministry of Planning, *Follow-up and Evaluation Report on the First Five-Year Plan*, Part I, (Cairo, Feb. 1966), Tables 18 and 19.
1965/66 – 1969/70: Price Planning Agency, *Distribution of Personal Incomes*, Memo No. 18 (in Arabic), (Cairo: January 1973), Table 7, p. 14.
Rent payments: Ministry of Agriculture, *Agricultural Economics Bulletin*, various issues.

to derive more than one tentative index (or wage deflator), in order to be able to form some reasonably accurate idea as to the basic trends in the movement of rural wages in rural Egypt during the 1950s and 1960s.

Our first tentative measure is related to the idea that, in a surplus labour economy, the consumption needs of the agricultural labourer may be reducible to one basic subsistence good, which tends to dominate his diet over a relatively long period of time. Such a measure will be referred to in the text as the 'grain equivalent' measure of rural wages.

On the other hand, we shall consider two other indices which allow for a wider range of subsistence goods to be taken into consideration. These latter indices will be compared with that derived on the basis of the 'grain equivalent' method in order to find a reasonably unambiguous answer to our fundamental question: to what extent has the movement in money wages been associated with an increase (or a decrease) in real wages during the period under investigation?

3.4.1. The 'grain equivalent' method of deriving rural wages

The usual procedure in studies of 'rural poverty' is to derive estimates for a minimum level of living in rural areas on the basis of *nutritional calculations* (i.e. the calorific value for an adequate minimum diet).[31]

31 See, for instance, P.K. Bardhan, 'On the Minimum Level of Living and the Rural Poor', *Indian Economic Review* (April 1970), pp. 129–36.

Cereals (*maize* in particular) occupy a dominant place in the average diet of the rural poor in Egypt.[32] Maize is mainly consumed in Lower Egypt and millet in Upper Egypt; both are preferred to other foodstuffs by the poorer sections of the rural community, because they find them cheaper and more filling.[33] In fact, other food-stuffs – universally regarded as 'superior' cereals – are not offered to the rural poor on the same favourable price-calorie terms.

Because of the absolute dominance of maize – as the main staple crop – in the agricultural labourer's daily diet,[34] one feels justified in resorting to a familiar *Ricardian* procedure whereby one simple wage-good (i.e. corn) may be taken as representative of the subsistence requirements of a labourer. In the same current of ideas, Colin Clark and Margaret Haswell have suggested a new method for comparing the behaviour of real wages between countries, by concentrating on what they call the 'grain equivalent' of rural wages.[35]

The logic of this method is quite simple: the subsistence requirements of a labourer in terms of grain are to be used as a good 'proxy variable' for studying the behaviour of real rural wages, and hence circumventing the index number problem involved in considering the whole range of subsistence goods consumed by the labourer at a certain point of time. In this respect, Clark and Haswell assert that "a community living entirely on grain (with a few wild plants, or other source to supply vitamins and minerals) will require, at this rate, anything from 520 to 640 g./ person/day".[36] They further add that a person consuming grain at this rate would also obtain sufficient protective protein.

An estimate made by a committee of the FAO in 1957 indicated three levels of daily calorie requirements for a 'reference man' according to different degrees of activities as follows: sedentary work, 2,800; moderate work 3,200; heavy work, 4,400.[37] For the purpose of the present study, to be safe, we shall assume that the figure of 3,000 calories represents a good approximation of daily requirements of calories for a labourer in rural Egypt.

32   "Eighty per cent of the *fellah's* calories come from *maize bread*, of which he eats up to three pounds a day". cf. Peter Mansfield, *Nasser's Egypt*, 2nd ed., (London: 1969), pp. 202–3.
33   cf. G. Amin, *Food Supply and Economic Development with special reference to Egypt*, (London: Cass, 1966), p. 54.
34   Money wages in rural Egypt are so low that no significant surplus over food require-ments is produced for clothing, and other non-food items. According to the 1958/9 Household Budget Survey, textiles occupy no more than 3 per cent of the budget of the rural poor.
35   cf. Clark and Haswell, *The Economics of Subsistence Agriculture*, ch. IV.
36   *ibid.*, p. 58.
37   See: 'Calorie requirements, Report of the Second Committee on Calorie Requirements', *F.A.O. Nutritional Studies*, No. 15 (1957). A "reference man" is defined as a man of 25 years of age, healthy, weighing 65 kilograms, living in the temperate zone at a mean annual temperature of 10°C. The committee considered that the figures of 2,800 and 4,400 probably represent extreme limits.
       However, such estimates are now questioned. See the challenging paper by Leonard Joy, 'Food and Nutrition Planning', *Journal of Agricultural Economics*, XXIV, (January 1973).

Table 3.7 *The 'grain equivalent' of rural wages, 1950–71*

Year	Price of maize (piastres) Per Ardeb* (1)	Per Kg (2)	Money cost (piastres) of 3000 calories' worth of maize (3)	Index (4)	Daily money-wages (piastres) (5)	(5) ÷ (4) (6)
1951	245	1.75	1.45	100	11.0	11.0
1952	270	1.93	1.60	110	11.0	10.0
1953	270	1.93	1.60	110	11.0	10.0
1954	264	1.89	1.57	108	11.0	10.2
1955	378	2.70	2.24	154	11.0	7.1
1956	419	2.99	2.48	171	11.0	6.4
1957	350	2.50	2.07	143	11.0	7.7
1958	350	2.50	2.07	143	11.0	7.7
1959	350	2.50	2.07	143	12.0	8.4
1960	350	2.50	2.07	143	n.a.	-
1961	350	2.50	2.07	143	12.6	8.8
1962	360	2.57	2.14	148	n.a.	-
1964	490	3.50	2.90	200	18.0	9.0
1965	420	3.0	2.50	172	18.6	10.8
1971	360	4.0	3.32	229	25.0	10.9

Notes and sources:
* 1 ardeb of maize = 140 kgs.

Col. (1) and (2) prices for maize are in most cases wholesale prices, for years 1959–61 see NBE, *Econ. Bull.*, Xi/4, 1958; NBE., *Econ. Bull.*, XVi/1-2, 1963; years 1964–71: F. Shalaby and M.F. Moustafa, 'Nutritional Levels from viewpoint of prices', *Central Agency for Price Planning*, Memo. No. 12, (Cairo: June 1972), Table (7), p. 23.
Col. (3) obtained by multiplying figures in Col. (2) by the standard conversion factor 0.833.
Col. (5) for 1950s see Mead, p. 313, for the years 1960/61, 1964/5, 66/7 and 1969/70 data obtained from the Dept. of Agricultural Economics and Statistics, Ministry of Agriculture (Cairo), as cited in Raga Abdel-Rassoul, *Agricultural Price and Income Policies,* INP Memo 168 (Internal Series), (Cairo: June 1971), p. 25.

Accordingly, a labourer consuming *maize* at the rate of 304 kg per year would be obtaining some 3,000 calories/day, which may be regarded as providing a satisfactory subsistence minimum diet for a larger-bodied person working 8 hours a day on average.[38]

We have calculated the total money-cost of the normative subsistence requirements (in terms of the price of maize) over the period under investigation in order to compare it with the movement of daily money wages in rural Egypt. The results of these calculations are given in Table 3.7.

As to the movement of money wage rates for the agricultural labourers, it is now widely agreed that although a statutory minimum rural wage of 18 piastres has existed for men since 1952, the average level of daily money wages for men remained much the same throughout the 1950s (around 11 piastres).[39] As late as 1961 the average daily wage for men was reported to be still around 12 piastres.[40] Only in the mid-sixties did the average wage for men approach the level of the statutory

38 One kg of maize will provide about 3,600 calories. This means that a labourer needs to consume up to 833 g of maize per day in order to get 3,000 calories.
39 To evade the legal regulations for minimum wages for rural labourers, the proprietors, and even the state, used to fix unusually long half-days, thus paying half a day's wage rather than the full day's wage. Cf. Ayrout, *The Egyptian Peasant*, p. 27.
40 cf. *Rural Employment Survey*: Report D, *op. cit.*, p. 10.

minimum wages set in 1952. In fact, the increase in money wage rates for rural labourers was of the order of 40-50 per cent over the period 1960–65.[41] This big wage increase must be set against the background of the strong inflationary tendencies that developed in the Egyptian economy around the mid-1960s, as well as the 'tightness' of the labour market in rural areas as a result of the increased demand for wage-labour. The increased demand for labour was generated by the construction of the High Dam and the implementation of large-scale land reclamation schemes in the 1960s.[42]

It should be noted however that the years 1950–51 (the Korean boom) were already marked by a strong *upward* movement in the agricultural money wage rates. Hence, these years would seem inappropriate for intertemporal comparisons of the movement of money wages. However, if we remove this strong *upward* bias due to the Korean boom from our wage series, some investigators claim that money wage rates for rural labourers actually increased in the 1950s by about 25 per cent over the level which prevailed in the late 1940s.[43]

On the other hand, the main reason why the maize price remained fairly stable over the period 1957–61 is attributable to the fact that it was subject to price control by the government, which aimed at supplying maize to the rural population at stable (and often subsidised) prices.[44]

3.4.2. Movement in real rural wages: a summary view

The real wage rate is usually defined to be the rate of wages at some *constant purchasing power*. In other words, it is the money-wage rate deflated by some index of the cost-of-living for rural labourers.

A special cost-of-living index for rural labourers, based on a representative bundle of 10 commodities consumed by people in the lowest expenditure bracket (i.e. less than £E25 per annum), was computed at the Institute of National Planning in Cairo up to 1961. The weights used in constructing the index were derived from the 1958/9 family budget data, but on the whole the index remains heavily weighted in terms of food grains, as the weight of maize in this index amounts to 45 per cent.[45]

In order to get a clearer picture of the trend in the movement of real rural wages, we shall now try to utilise all the available indicators relevant to this point. In Table 3.8 we combine all three available indices: the 'grain equivalent' index, the official wholesale price index for cereals, and the INP special cost-of-living index for agricultural labourers.

41 ibid.
42 See Appendix B on 'The Impact of Public developmental schemes on employment opportunities for casual agricultural labourers'.
43 See Hansen, 'Marginal Productivity Wage Theory and Subsistence Wage Theory in Egyptian Agriculture', *op. cit.*; and ILO, *Rural Employment Problems, op. cit.*, p. 69.
44 cf. F. Zaghloul, *'A Cost-of-Living Index for Rural Labourers, 1913–1961'*, INP Memo. 557, (Cairo: April 1965), p. 7.
45 Family budget surveys are usually conducted by considering 'bundles' of goods or 'categories of expenditure' rather than individual commodities. But this does not help in constructing index numbers, since bundles are *composites*, i.e., mixtures of goods, and should thus be reducible to some simple commodity taken to be the most representative manifestation of each commodity group.

Table 3.8 *Movement in rural real wages, 1950–71*

Year	(1) Index of average daily money-wages for men (1950 = 100)	(2) Index of money cost of the 'grain equivalent' of rural wages in terms of maize (1950 = 100)	(3) Official wholesale price index for cereals (1950 = 100)	(4) Special cost-of-living index for agri-cultural labourers (1950 = 100)
1950	100	100	100	100.0
1951	100	100	106	100.0
1952	100	110	102	100.5
1953	100	110	112	101.7
1954	100	108	118	104.3
1955	100	154	125	112.0
1956	100	171	136	129.7
1957	100	143	134	128.6
1958	100	143	127	131.5
1959	109	143	128	126.0
1960	115	143	128	128.0
1961	115	143	134	136.0
1962	115	148	133	139.3
1963	164	148	131	144.0
1964	164	200	137	167.5
1965	169	172	149	198.1
1971	227	229	190	214.6

Notes and sources:
Col. (1) based on data on daily money-wage rate for agricultural labourers given in Mead, pp. 92 and 95, see also the *ILO Report on Rural Employment Problems,* p. 69, and other sources
Col. (2) data derived from Table 3.7.
Col. (3) See Mead, *Statistical Appendix,* Table V1-F-1 and other sources.
Col. (4) Zaghloul, Table 2, p. 5, after 1961 we used the official index number of retail prices for foodstuffs (including fuel and soap) as the closest substitute for the special cost-of-living index.

By all three measures, the table reveals a marked fall in rural real wages during the period 1952–62. It also becomes clear that food grain prices have risen much faster than the prices of other commodities over the period. In other words, the food grain price indices used as wage-deflators show a much greater fall in real wages during the period 1952–62.

45 Continued
Out of 20 commodity groups recorded in the 1958/9 budget survey in Egypt, *ten* 'representative' commodities were selected. These then commodities and their relative weights are as follows.

Commodity group	Expenditure percent of total	Representative commodity	Weights
Cereals	36.22	Maize	45.0
Pulses	3.01	Beans	3.7
Meat, fish and eggs	10.88	Beef	13.5
Oils and fats	2.31	Cotton seed oil	2.9
Dairy products	7.06	Butter (samna)	8.8
Vegetables	5.67	Onions	7.1
Fruits	1.27	Dates	1.6
Sugar and sugar products	4.75	Sugar	5.9
Beverages	3.74	Tea	4.3
Fuel and lighting	5.79	Kerosene	7.2

Source: F. Zaghloul 'A Cost-of-Living Index for Rural Labourers', p.3.

Unfortunately, no appropriate cost-of-living index for rural labourers exists for the period 1962–70. But judging on the basis of the large price rises since the mid-sixties, it may be safely assumed that the cost of living index for rural labourers rose by a further 40 or 50 per cent from 1961 to 1970.[46] The rise in prices of certain basic consumption commodities (i.e. maize, sugar, tea, tobacco, fuel) was felt most acutely by the landless peasants.

Fig. 3.1 *Movement of real rural wages, 1950–1971*

Key: 1. Index of average daily money wages for men
      2. Index of money cost of the 'grain equivalent' of rural wages in terms of maize
      3. Official wholesale price index for cereals
      4. Special cost-of-living for agricultural labourers

Indices of money-wages,
prices and cost-of-living

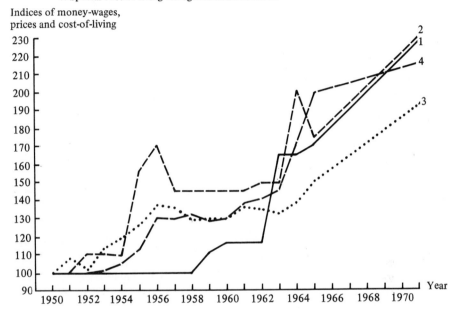

46 The development of the official index number of retail prices for foodstuffs (including fuel and soap) throughout the 1960s is reported as follows:

Year	Index (1959/60 = 100)
1961/2	101.5
1962/3	102.4
1963/4	105.9
1964/5	123.2
1965/6	145.7
1966/7	152.7
1967/8	147.7
1968/9	147.7
1969/70	157.8

Source: NBE, *Eco. Bull.*, XXV – No. 4 (1972), p. 280.

Finally, one should bear in mind that an important limitation of all three indices presented in Table 3.8 is that they were constructed with reference to official prices rather than actual (or black market) prices, and may thus give a somewhat misleading picture as to the relative stability of rural retail prices over the period under review.[47] We conclude, therefore, that all three indices tend to understate the rise in the cost of living for rural labourers (unless of course counterbalancing forces were operating).[48]

47 There is some fragmentary evidence in support of this contention, for the retail rural prices for maize as reported in *the household sample survey of 1958/59* (Table 5, p. 326) ranged from 2.74 piastres to 3.20 piastres per kg – according to *different* *fractile groups* – while the price recorded in official statistics amounted to 2.50 piastres.
48 In fact *the share of own produce* in total maize consumption for the lowest income group of the rural household is less than one per cent. cf. Central Statistical Committee, *Household Sample Budget Survey 1958–1959,* (Cairo: April 1961), Table 5, p. 326 (in Arabic).

4

Changes in Consumption Patterns in Rural Egypt

4.1   The general pattern of rural consumption

In the Egyptian national accounts private consumption appears only as a *residual* term, and no aggregate figures on rural consumption are available. The first full-scale sample survey of household consumption was carried out by the Central Statistical Committee (C.S.C.) during the period October 1958 to November 1959. The results of this survey were published in 1961.[1]

Table 4.1 shows the percentage distribution of expenditure by size of total annual expenditure groups in rural areas in 1958/9. This table reveals a very familiar pattern of expenditure distribution, with the percentage expenditure on food falling, and that on durable consumer goods services etc. rising substantially with increases in income.

The group of "stimulants", i.e. tobacco, coffee, tea, etc., shows a more complicated pattern. The percentage expenditure increases strongly with income, from below £E25 to £E75–100, indicating a very high expenditure elasticity, while for expenditure brackets higher than £E100 the percentage expenditure stays unchanged indicating unit elasticity.[2]

1   The data on consumption were collected over a period of 12 consecutive months (between 1.12.1958 and 30.11.1959) in order to eliminate seasonal variations in consumption patterns. A three-stage sampling system was adopted, the first stage being *the district* (Markaz), the second *the village* and the ultimate unit being the *the household.* Half the districts of each province were first selected at random. Then villages belonging to the selected districts were stratified according to the village size, and 1/40 of the villages were selected at random from each stratum. A proportion of households from each selected village were then systematically selected, bringing the ultimate sample in rural areas to a total of 3,037 rural families, comprising 16,468 persons. The sample thus includes *one in every thousand rural households.* For further details the reader is referred to the original publication (in Arabic), by the Central Statistical Committee, *Family Budget Sample Survey 1958–1959,* (Cairo, 1961), pp.13 et seq.
2   cf. Report D: *Wages, Incomes, and Consumption in Rural Areas,* p.45.

Table 4.1 *Consumption patterns for rural households: percentage distribution of expenditure for different income groups, 1958/9*

Annual expenditure brackets (£E)	Current consumption goods					Durable consumer goods	Services etc.	Other exp.	Total
	Food	Stimu-lants	Bever-ages	Others	Total				
< 25	73.5	1.4	3.5	7.9	86.3	3.2	2.5	8.0	100
25 — < 50	68.5	4.9	4.4	6.9	84.7	5.3	3.7	8.0	100
50 — < 75	67.7	6.4	3.9	6.2	84.2	6.3	4.6	4.9	100
75 — < 100	68.1	7.0	3.9	5.6	84.6	6.7	5.1	4.5	100
100 — < 150	65.7	7.0	3.7	5.5	81.9	7.7	5.9	4.5	100
150 — < 200	63.4	7.4	3.6	5.3	79.7	8.6	7.2	4.5	100
200 — < 250	63.2	6.8	3.2	4.9	78.1	8.9	8.4	4.6	100
250 — < 300	60.6	6.7	3.2	4.9	75.4	9.8	9.6	5.2	100
300 — < 400	60.6	6.5	3.3	4.7	75.1	10.2	9.6	5.1	100
400 — < 600	56.2	5.8	3.1	4.4	69.5	11.8	12.7	6.0	100
600 — < 800	54.1	6.3	2.9	4.5	67.8	11.7	13.6	6.9	100
800 — < 1000	53.1	6.4	3.0	3.6	66.1	10.8	19.0	4.1	100
≥ 1000	38.6	7.7	2.8	4.7	53.8	11.7	26.2	8.3	100
All households	63.0	6.7	3.5	5.2	78.4	8.6	8.2	4.9	100

Source: Report D on *Wages, Incomes, and Consumption in Rural Areas*, p.46

The second round of the National Sample Survey of Household Consumption was carried out in 1964/5.[3] As in the first round 'total expenditure' (rather than income brackets) was retained as the stratification variable.

The results of this more recent survey tended to confirm the picture of the pattern of rural consumption as derived from the first sample survey of 1958/9. The various 1964/5 survey results for rural areas are summarised in tables 4.2 and 4.3.

Table 4.2 *Percentages of average per capita expenditure on selected food items relative to per capita rural total expenditure, 1964/5*

Annual family income brackets (£E)	Total expenditure in rural areas (£E)	Percentage of expenditure on food and beverages %	Cereals and starches %	Meat, fish & eggs %	Milk & dairy products %	Fruit %
< 50	25.11	73.0	23.8	14.0	6.7	1.4
50 — < 100	26.60	70.3	24.5	14.4	6.6	1.7
100 — < 150	30.32	69.1	22.3	15.3	7.6	1.8
150 — < 200	33.75	67.3	21.7	15.1	7.6	1.8
200 — < 300	38.28	66.6	21.2	15.5	8.2	1.9
300 — < 400	41.85	62.4	19.8	14.5	7.4	2.1
400 — < 600	53.99	59.7	16.4	13.8	7.8	1.9
600 — < 1000	58.27	54.7	13.7	13.5	9.3	1.9
≥ 1000	103.32	57.0	10.6	17.7	8.7	2.6

Source: NBE, 'Food Consumption in the U.A.R,' *Eco. Bull.*, XXII — No. 4 (1969), Tables V & VI.

Table 4.2 gives the percentage distribution of expenditure for all rural households in the sample in 1964/5. The point to note here is the relatively high percentage of expenditure on cereals and starches in the consumption bundles of the rural poor (those with incomes of less than £E50 per annum). This may be attributed to the fact that the proportion of calorie intake from cereals and starchy foods is particularly high in relation to their prices.

3 The data for the study were collected over four rounds each starting on a different quarterly date in order to take account of seasonal changes in expenditure pattern. For the purpose of the study the country was divided into three major areas: (i) *Urban governorates,* consisting of the capitals of the the Egypt's 21 governorates; (ii) *District capitals* (Markaz), which numbered 98 towns representing the district capitals of the Governorates mentioned in (i) above; and (iii) *Rural areas,* comprising the 4000 existing villages; which were in turn stratified according to village size: "large villages" of 1000 or more households, and "small villages" with less than 1000 households. The total number of households comprising the sample amounted to 3,411 (in each round), distributed as follows: 1,654 from urban governorates, 649 from district capitals and 1,108 from rural areas. The *sample fraction* adopted for the rural areas worked out at 0.31 per thousand of the rural households. See: CAPMS, '*The 1964/65 Family Budget Survey,* Document No. 20/221, (Cairo, August 1969), pp.4—6.

Table 4.3 Income elasticities of demand for food and beverages in rural Egypt, 1964/5*

Annual income brackets (£E)	Cereals & starchy food	Dry beans	Meat, eggs & fish	Fats & oils	Milk & dairy products	Vegetables	Fruit	Sugar & products	Total food & beverages
< 200	0.673	1.123	1.147	0.647	1.415	0.474	1.436	0.979	0.747
200 — < 600	0.493	0.763	0.771	−0.123	0.846	0.385	1.486	0.474	0.638
≥ 600	−0.683	−0.733	0.972	−2.253	2.534	−0.443	1.144	0.727	0.554
Weighted Average	0.458	0.767	0.921	−0.03	1.186	0.348	1.462	0.674	0.670

* Raw figures obtained from Central Agency for Public Mobilization & Statistics "Family Budget Survey 1964/65" (Cairo), August, 1969
Source: NBE, "Food Consumption in the U.A.R.", Eco. Bull., XXII–4, (1969), Table VIII

From Table 4.3, it appears that the income elasticity of demand for food and beverages amounts to 0.75 for low-income groups, 0.64 for medium-income groups and 0.55 for high-income groups in rural areas. The higher income elasticity of demand for dry beans, cereals and starchy food for low-income groups demonstrates once again a striking difference from higher-income groups (£E600 & more), where income elasticities are *negative* for cereals, starchy foods and dry beans.

The average elasticity of demand for all income groups — based on the weighted average of the numbers of people in each income bracket — is particularly high for fruit (1.46), milk and dairy products (1.19), meat, fish and eggs (0.92), in contrast with the order of magnitude of these elasticities in developed countries.

Broadly speaking, historical evidence tells us that the tendency for the rural poor (as incomes grow) is to shift away from starchy roots or coarse grains and toward 'superior' foodstuffs (i.e. meat, dairy products and vegetables). In reality, meat, vegetables and other 'superior' foodstuffs are not offered to the rural poor on comparative price-calorie terms.

A 'normalised'calorie basis for comparison would demonstrate how limited is *the degree of substitution* between different goods in the consumption baskets of the rural poor, given the prevailing pattern of relative prices. This point is strikingly illustrated by the data in Table 4.4.

Table 4.4. *Comparative price – calorie terms for selected commodities*

Commodity	Money cost of 100 calorie worth of the commodity (in millièmes)*	
	1964	1971
Maize	1	1.1
Millet	1	1.1
Wheat flour	n.a	1.5
Beans	1.8	2.9
Onions	4.3	7.0
Dates	5.3	n.a
Grapes	9.3	n.a
Bananas	8.5	9.9
Buffalo meat	36.6	60.7
Mutton	15.4	22.8
Fresh fish	14.9	19.6
Eggs	–	24.7

* one piastre = 10 millièmes
Source: F. Shalaby and M.F. Moustafa 'Levels of Nutrition in Relation to Prices', *Central Agency for Price Planning,* Memo No.12, (Cairo, June 1972), Table (7), pp.23–4.

If one hundred calories' worth of maize (or millet) were to be taken as the *numéraire* in our system, it can readily be seen that the *physical[4] rates of substitution* in consumption are greatly constrained, and the choice open to the

---

4 In order to maintain the consuming unit at the same 'physiological' utility level in terms of calories.

rural poor is severely reduced. That is to say that, given the pattern of relative prices a poor rural family has to pay for foodstuffs, it becomes evident that there are a very limited (and rigid) number of combinations that will yield approximately the same calorific value, given the family's low income.

The consumption pattern of the rural poor is thus doomed to be marked by the endless monotony of a *cereal-based diet,* as there are few items that could add flavour to the diet which are not very expensive and beyond their reach. An increase in per capita real income may result in the consumption of more onions or some cheap fruit items (i.e. dates or melon), rather than a major shift from cereals to the consumption of some meat or fish or citrus fruit.

This also raises the more fundamental point that there is, in general, little room for 'substitutability' among different needs under the conditions on non-saturation of *prime needs* and necessities for low-income groups. In reality, there exists a very definite order of priority in consumers' needs, especially strong at low levels of income, where satisfaction of some prime need is a precondition for the appearance of all others.[5] The difficulties of *the marginal approach* become more apparent when applied to situations, which clearly are very prevalent, in which some available commodities are excluded entirely from the consumer's budget. Moreover, the concept of a marginal rate of substitution, the basic concept of the current theory of consumer's choice, cease to apply in such situations.[6]

4.2   Distribution of rural households according to annual consumption expenditure

In order to trace the changes in rural consumption over time it will be useful to examine the change in the frequency distribution of rural households according to annual consumption expenditure, Table 4.5 presents family budget data relating to the distribution of rural households according to frequency classes of annual consumption expenditure in 1958/9 and 1964/5, The data clearly indicate a notable change in the frequency distribution of rural households over the period under review.

This change can be evidenced from the fact that while the two sample distributions have the same *modal class* (see Chart 4.1), they differ from each other according to the degree to which the sample values of our variate cluster about their mean or spread from it. The data indicate that, between 1958 and 1965, the relative frequency of rural families falling in the expenditure class from £E150 to

5   The existance of a well ordered scale of priorities among wants, or what can be called *the hierachy principle*, is clearly explained by Professor Joan Robinson in the following way: "Generally speaking, wants stand in a hierachy (though with considerable overlap at each level) and an increment in a family's real income is not devoted to buying a little more of everything at the same level, but to stepping down the hierachy." See: *The Accumulation of Capital* (London: Macmillan, 1956), p.354.

6   See on this point R. Dorfman, P. Samuelson and R. Solow, *Linear Programming and Economic Analysis,* (New York: McGraw-Hill, Inc., 1958), pp.25 and 28;
L.L. Pasinetti, *A New Theoretical Approach to the Problem of Economic Growth,* Pontificiae Academiae, Scientirarum Scirpta Varia, (Rome, 1965), p.63;
and D.M. Nuti, 'Social Choice and the Polish Consumer', *Cambridge Review,* (May 1971), p.220.

Table 4.5 *Distribution of households in rural areas according to annual consumption expenditure, 1958/9 and 1964/5*

Annual expenditure brackets (£E)	Sample survey 1958/9			Sample survey 1964/5 (four rounds)		
	Average total expenditure (£E per household)	No. of households	%	Average total expenditure (£E per household)	No. of households	%
< 25	20.57	42	1.4	19.42	12	0.27
25 − < 50	39.41	279	9.2	38.57	125	2.79
50 − < 75	63.14	460	15.1	64.22	218	4.87
75 − < 100	88.30	442	14.6	88.41	344	7.68
100 − < 150	123.00	748	24.5	125.60	1007	22.48
150 − < 200	172.66	443	14.6	175.12	850	18.97
200 − < 250	221.98	246	8.1	223.75	613	13.68
250 − < 300	271.83	134	4.4	272.80	410	9.15
300 − < 400	338.69	127	4.2	342.32	466	10.40
400 − < 600	475.87	89	3.0	481.85	293	6.54
600 − < 800	707.61	18	0.6	678.65	84	1.88
800 − < 1000	866.50	4	0.13	889.50	24	0.54
≥ 1,000	1508.20	5	0.16	1512.44	34	0.75
Total	147.70	3,037	100.00	224.17	4,480	100.00

Source: Computed from the family budget surveys for rural households of 1958/9 and 1964/5. See: Osman A. El-Kholie, 'Disparaties of Egyptian Personal Income Distribution as reflected by Family Budget Data', *L'Egypte Contemporaine*, LXIV–No. 354 (October 1973), Tables (2) and (4); and CAPMS, *Bulletin of Public Mobilisation and Statistics*, Vol. 9, No. 81 (Nov. 1971) Table (3).

£E300 increased from 27% to about 42%. It is not justified however to compare the percentages of households in each expenditure class. To do this one needs to know the *interfractile price differences* between 1958/59 and 1964/65 in rural areas.

But in order to test whether this shift is associated with a fall (or increase) in the overall degree of inequality of the distribution of total consumption expenditure among the rural people, we need to compute some conventional summary measures of inequality. But different summary measures of inequality are usually concerned with measuring different aspects of variability in income (or consumption expenditure),[7] we have computed different summary measures of inequality in order to quantify the difference in overall inequality between the two sample distributions of consumption expenditure in rural Egypt.

The inequality measures most commonly used in empirical work include: *the coefficient of variation*, which attaches equal weight to transfers at different income levels; *the standard deviation of logarithms*, which attaches more weight to transfers at the lower end of the distribution; *the interquartile measures*, which

7   The important point to note here is that, in general, one will get a different notion of overall inequality if one compares two or more income distributions in terms of different summary measures of inequality. The relationship between cases where the conventional summary measures of inequality give conflicting rankings and the crossing of the Lorenz curves was suggested by K.R. Ranadive in "The equality of Incomes in India", *Bulletin of Oxford Institute of Economics and Statistics*, Vol. 27 (1965), pp.119–34. These ideas were further elaborated and generalized in A.B. Atkinson's paper "On the Measurement of Inequality", *Journal of Economic Theory*, Vol. 2 (1970), pp.244–63.

reflect the transfers affecting middle income classes (i.e. the middle fifty per cent of income recipients); finally, in the case of *Gini coefficient* more weight is attached to transfers in the centre of the distribution than at the tails.[8]

Table 4.6 summarises the main results of our computation of different summary measures of inequality for the two sample distributions of consumption expenditures.

In the light of these results, one could say that the shift in the frequency distribution of consumption expenditures in rural Egypt between 1958 and 1965 has been associated with a *slight* fall in the overall degree of inequality of the distribution of total consumption. Yet it should be noted that while the distribution shifted to the right, it remained highly peaked and positively skewed with a long tail to the right.

To illustrate more clearly the incidences of the process of redistribution of consumption in rural Egypt between 1958 and 1965, we have obtained a 'log-normalised' picture of the two consumption distributions as shown in Fig. 4.2. By looking at the graphical picture in both Figs. 4.1 and 4.2, it becomes clear that the equalising process has been mainly confined to the middle consumption classes (i.e. ranging between the 3rd and 7th deciles), rather than the lower or top ends of the distribution.

Table 4.6 *Summary measures of inequality of consumption expenditure distribution in rural Egypt*

Measures of relative dispersion	1958/9 sample distribution	1964/5 sample distribution	Change
Mean value (£E)	147.7	224.2	+76.5
		(203.8)	(+56.1)
Standard deviation	120.5	180.6	+60.1
		(164.2)	(+43.7)
Coefficient of variation[1]	0.816	0.806	−0.01
Standard deviation of logs[2]	0.670	0.639	−0.03
Interquartile ratio[3]	0.938	0.870	−0.07
Gini coefficient	0.373	0.354	−0.02

Notes:
(1) The coefficient of variation is the ratio of the standard deviation divided by the mean.
(2) In the case of highly skewed distributions – like our two sample distributions – it might be more appropriate to compute the standard deviation of the logarithms of the values of our variate (i.e. consumption expenditures).
(3) Defined as (first quartile – third quartile)/median.
(4) The figures in parentheses are deflated figures using the 1958 retail price index as a deflator.

4.3   Subsistence bundles for the rural poor

Because the notion of an average consumption level per capita in rural areas normally conceals tremendous inequalities, we think it is more appropriate to approach the question by focusing our analysis on the consumption baskets of the rural poor.

8 See: Atkinson; *Op. cit.*

Fig. 4.1. *Comparison of the percentage distribution of rural households by annual expenditure brackets – two sample surveys 1958/59 and 1964/65*

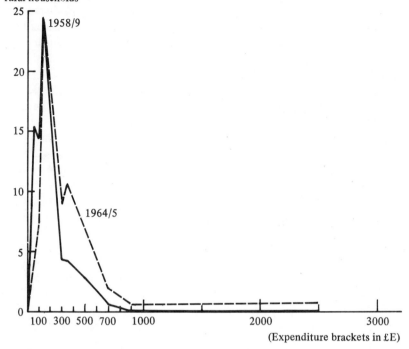

Fig. 4.2. *Comparison of the two sample-distributions after 'log-normalisation'*

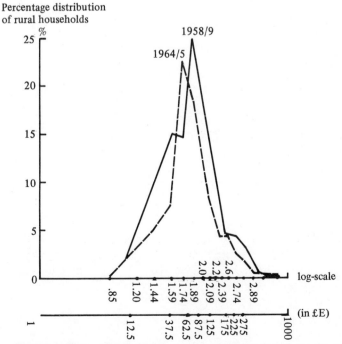

Data Source: CAPMS, Bulletin of Public Mobilisation and Statistics, Vol. 9, No. 81, (Nov. 1971
1971), Table (3), p. 846

From the first family budget survey carried out in 1958-9, it is possible to obtain direct information on the physical composition of consumption baskets for the rural poor in Egypt. The survey gives the quantity purchased of each good per head in each expenditure class. The two lowest expenditure brackets (less than £E25 and £E25 to less than £E50 per annum) are generally considered to comprise the bulk of Egypt's rural population, namely the 'landless peasants' and the 'poor peasantry'.

In Table 4.7, we have assembled the relevant figures relating to the physical composition of subsistence bundles for the rural poor (two lowest expenditure brackets) as revealed by the family budget data of 1958/9. Comparing these with the *normative* estimates suggested by the FAO Regional Office in Cairo regarding the composition of a minimum diet under Egyptian conditions as the basis of our comparisons, one can easily appreciate how wide is the gap which exists between the actual compositions of subsistence bundles for the rural poor and the normative subsistence diet as suggested by the FAO estimates.

On the other hand, we have calculated the calorie—protein contents of the subsistence bundles for the rural poor, falling in the lowest expenditure bracket of

Table 4.7 *Subsistence bundles for the rural poor (annual per capita figures)*

Commodities	Quantities consumed by people in the expenditure bracket of less than £E25 per annum, in 1958/9 (1)	Quantities consumed by people in the expenditure bracket of £E25 to less than £E50 in 1958/9 (2)	FAO estimates of per capita requirements of food stuffs, 1959 (3)
	(in kg. except eggs in number)	(in kg. except eggs in number)	(kg per year)
Wheat	32.3	39.7	60.5
Maize and millet	107.4	109.0	140.3
Flour	19.9	16.0	n.a.
Rice and potatoes	13.4	14.0	4.4
Beans and lentils	5.9	7.3	29.4
Meat, poultry & fish	6.7	7.6	4.8
Milk and cheese	8.9	10.8	18.1
Eggs	12	14	n.a.
Onions	10.7	9.5	15.5
Tomatoes (or other veg.)	10.5	9.7	14.9
Butter and animal fat	1.6	2.1	n.a.
Citrus fruit and dates	3.6	5.3	29.7
Sugar and molasses	9.2	10.8	11.5
Vegetable oils	2.5	2.3	4.4

Sources: Cols. (1) and (2): figures calculated from *The Family Budget Survey 1958/59* (Cairo, 1961), Table (2), pp.332—3.

Col. (3): estimates of the FAO Regional Office in Cairo, as cited in G. Amin, *Food Supply and Economic Development with Special Reference to Egypt.* (London: Cass, 1966), p.64.

Note: The excess of the·observed average annual intakes per head of meat, poultry and fish in the 1958/9 survey over the FAO estimate of the minimum per capita requirements of these food items is most surprising, since Egypt is generally reported to be one of the animal protein deficient countries. This may be due to an 'overstatement' of the consumption of meat, poultry and fish by the rural poor as recorded in the survey.

Table 4.8 *Calorie-protein contents of the subsistence bundles of the rural poor, 1964/5*

Commodity group	Daily calorie intake	%	Daily protein intake (in grammes)	%
Cereals and starch	1420	70.1	42.5	71.4
Pulses	158	7.8	10.8	18.2
Meat, fish and eggs	45	2.2	3.5	5.8
Fats and oils	143	7.1	0.1	0.2
Milk and dairy products	20	1.0	1.1	1.8
Vegetables	17	0.8	1.1	1.8
Fruits	26	1.3	0.4	0.8
Sugar and sugar products	197	9.7	–	–
Total	2026	100.0	59.5	100.0

Source: Computed from the *Family Budget Survey Data for 1964/5* – averages of the 'four rounds' of the survey.

less than £E25, in order to be able to compare it with the recommended minimum protein-calorie requirements. The results of our calculations are given in Table 4.8.

It can be seen from Table 4.8 that the subsistence consumption levels of the rural poor, falling in the expenditure class of 'less than £E25 per annum', are not sufficient to meet the generally 'recommended' protein-calorie minimum requirements for the working people:

	recommended levels	observed levels	level of deficiency
Calorie intake	3000	2026	−974
Protein (in grs.)	73	59.5	−13.5

Thus, despite the crudity of the empirical evidence, it would seem safe to contend that those sections of the rural population falling within the lowest expenditure bracket are living below the bare subsistence minimum. Moreover, this evidence of protein-calorie deficiencies should help to relate nutritional deficiency patterns to the socio-economic characteristics of the rural population.

5

The Movement in Agricultural Terms of Trade and the Disposal of Agricultural Surplus

"The single most important question in development policy in the poorer countries turns out to be the way in which the peasants are involved in the accumulation process. Peasants are strategically important not only because of their numbers, but also because they produce one of the most important material inputs associated with the process of capital accumulation, namely the *food* and *fibres* necessary to sustain any labour which is diverted to any other form of activity".

Wyn Owen (1966)

5.1 Economic development and problems of mobilisation of agricultural surplus

In the course of the development process a substantial proportion of the surplus available in the agricultural sector needs to be siphoned out as an *investment fund* to finance the development effort in the whole society. Hence, the fundamental developmental question becomes: what government policies must be devised and what institutional arrangement should be designed to effect the necessary extraction of the investible surplus from agriculture?

This long-standing problem in development literature is in fact twofold: there is the question of diverting the agricultural produce from the agricultural to the non-agricultural activities on the one hand, and that of enforcing the necessary savings among the farm population on the other[1]. Thus one could differentiate between what might be characterised, respectively, as, first, 'the production squeeze on agriculture', and, secondly, 'the expenditure squeeze on agriculture'. Under the first will be identified the "requisitioning" of parts of *farm production* through procurement policies and, under the second, the "taxation" of residual *farm income* via the manipulation of the intersectoral terms of trade. The general rule has been for the impact of this "double squeeze" on agriculture to be positive in both directions in most developing countries.[2]

In practice, the "double squeeze" on agriculture may take several forms. One classic instrument of policy is to devise a scheme to tax agricultural income directly. Yet, the effectiveness of direct taxation in the conditions of developing countries is becoming more questionable.[3] In fact, direct taxation has very definite limits: it

---

1 Dharm Narain, 'Ratio of interchange between agricultural and manufactured goods in relation to capital formation in underdeveloped economies', *Indian Economic Review,* Vol. III No. 4, (August 1957), p.47.

2 Cf. Wyn Owen, 'The double developmental squeeze on agriculture', *American Economic Review,* Vol. LVI, No. 1, (march 1966), p.44.

3 Cf. A. Eckstein, 'Land Reform and Economic Development', *World Politics,* Vol. 3 (1955), p.660

may be evaded; it is more easily felt by the cultivators and more likely to cause political complications.

There are several possibilities for taxing agriculture *indirectly*. First, the pricing policy of agricultural inputs (or the manipulation of terms of trade between agricultural outputs and inputs) can be used as an effective instrument for taxing agriculture.[4] A second well-known device is to tax farmers' consumption, by regulating the terms of trade between agricultural outputs and the consumer goods which farmers usually buy from the manufacturing sector (i.e. sugar, tobacco, clothes, tea, kerosene and other manufactured goods).

The significance of the first form of indirect taxation derives from the fact that a major proportion of agricultural produce has to be exchanged to meet fixed money obligations (i.e. the value of agricultural inputs bought on credit), and does not have its exchange counterpart in consumption goods. Thus it seems analytically useful to distinguish between that component of the marketed surplus with which the farmers buy the 'agricultural inputs' and that component which he exchanges for 'urban consumption goods'.

In sum, the most important issue involved here is what type of policy of the intersectoral terms of trade is to be associated with the intersectoral commodity flows. Within such a policy, manipulation of the domestic terms of trade make the transfers of the agricultural surplus, as a major source of accumulation and public finance, depend not only on the subjective preferences for saving or consuming of the independent cultivators or landlords, but more importantly, on the presence of appropriate institutional arrangements for intersectoral commodity flows.[5]

In the following sections, we shall discuss in some detail governmental efforts in Egypt during the 1960s to evolve a new accommodating institutional framework within which *pricing* and *procurement* policies for the main agricultural crops were devised in such a way as to give the state the greatest overall financial control over the surplus generated in agriculture.

5.2 Cooperative marketing and the disposal of farm products

5.2.1 *The setting-up of supervised farmers' cooperatives*

While at first *farmers' cooperatives* were promoted in the villages where land reform was a major factor.[6] Egyptian policy-makers shortly realised that a large scale mobilisation of agricultural surplus would be unsuccessful without a radical reorganization of the institutional environment in the agricultural sector, and that

---

4 On the importance of this instrument of policy see: Little—Scitovsky—Scott: *Industry and Trade in Some Developing Countries* (London: Oxford University Press, 1970), pp.347—8

5 See J. Fei and G. Ranis, *Development of the Labor Surplus Economy,* (Illinois: R. Irwin, Inc., 1964), pp.27—36.

6 According to Professor Bent Hansen the introduction of the cooperative system in Land Reform areas in Egypt was directly copied from the British Gezira Project in Sudan, and was adopted as a clever way of combining large-scale advantages in irrigation, crop rotation and marketing with small-scale production and private initiative. Cf. B. Hansen, 'Economic Development in Egypt, in C.A. Cooper and S.S. Alexander (eds.), *Economic Development and Population Growth in the Middle East* (Rand Corporation Study), (New York 1972).

pure *laissez-faire* policies could not accomplish this. The introduction of an intergrated system of agricultural cooperatives in all parts of the country appeared therefore as the only way of achieving an effective maximisation and mobilisation of agricultural surplus.

Persistent attempts were therefore made to introduce *voluntary* systems of cooperative farming outside the land reform areas from the late 1950s onwards. The motive behind the desire to setup agricultural cooperatives throughout the whole country was twofold.[7]

The *first* goal was to ensure a minimum level of efficiency in production by allowing the use of large-scale methods for small holdings. This was done by dividing the land in each village into three large blocks, each of 50 to 100 feddans, and introducing a single crop rotation. The beneficiaries of such a cooperative farming system were then allotted a holding in three pieces (i.e. one in each block), so that one would be under cotton, another under maize or rice, and the third under berseem (Egyptian clover).

Second, cooperatives had to become the primary channel through which the state sought to deal with farmers in matters related to the mobilisation and control of agricultural surplus. In reality, the new institutional framework was a clever device by means of which it became possible to transfer to the state the functions of the old landlord, as a money-lender and cotton marketeer. For the agricultural cooperatives have become over time the sole source of agricultural credit and farm inputs, as well as the only channel for marketing cotton.

At any rate, what really mattered for the Egyptian policy-makers was not so much the risk of squandering the agricultural surplus on consumption by small holders, but rather how to channel the surplus to the planned avenues of industrial expansion and other general social purposes. To that effect, they discovered that a more reliable way of mobilising the agricultural marketable surplus was to increase the peasnats' fixed money obligations and consequently their need for cash. In other words, the volume of marketed surplus would vary directly with the degree of peasants' indebtedness to the state, and more generally with the peasants' need for cash to meet their fixed money obligations.[8,9]

Table 5.1 shows the dramatic expansion of the membership of agricultural cooperatives during the period 1952-70. In fact, cooperatives sprang up all over the country so that today each village has, at least, one multi-purpose agricultural cooperative to serve its members' needs in production, marketing and other social services. Each of these cooperatives employs a trained agronomist to supervise

7   Cf. M. Abdel-Fadil, 'Les cooperatives agricoles en R.A.U.', *Options Méditerranéennes,* (Paris: April 1971), pp.43–4; Patrick O'Brien, *The Revolution in Egypt's Economic System from Private Enterprise to Socialism 1952–1965,* (London: Oxford University Press, 1966), pp.120–1 and 136–46.
8   G. Amin, *Food Supply and Economic Development . . . , op. cit.,* p.36
9   In this respect, one may call *obligatory* marketable surplus that part of the output which the cultivator is obliged to sell or give up to meet certain fixed money liabilities which he has incurred before the harvesting of the crops. The residual income, i.e., output *minus* obligatory surplus in money terms, is the net disposable income of the cultivator. See P. Sanghvi, *Surplus Manpower in Agriculture and Economic Development* (with special reference to India), (London: Asia Publishing House, 1969), p.139.

agricultural operations, a store-keeper and an accountant's clerk, as well as having a management board.[10]

Table 5.1. *Development of membership and the number of agricultural cooperatives, 1952-70*

Year*	No. of cooperatives	Members (million)
1952	1,727	0.5
1965	4,839	2.4
1966	4,879	2.5
1967	4,921	2.7
1968	4,955	3.0
1969	4,998	2.9
1970	5,013	3.1

*Agricultural years
Source: CAPMS, *Statistical Handbook,* (June 1971), p.51.

5.2.2   The disposal of farm products through cooperative channels

It is clear that the effectiveness of terms of trade as an instrument of policy, derives largely from the compulsion under which a farmer is to dispose of a fraction of his produce.[11] In other words, *the larger the fraction he sells cooperatively, the greater will be the effective range of policy.*

In order to ensure this, the government's policy consisted of two sets of measures: *first* the extension of the system of cooperative marketing to cover the most important crops, such as cotton, rice, onions, potatoes and groundnuts. This device was clearly intended to make sure that the supply of the main crops necessary for the *manufacturing* and *export* sectors would be secured.

Secondly, the delivery of some selected crops was punctually enforced through a system of 'compulsory deliveries'. These policy measures varied widely between different crops, and in this connection we propose to examine in this section the policy instruments used in the cotton trade and other crops as part of the policy package designed to tax away a substantial proportion of the surplus in Egyptian agriculture.

The disposal of the cotton crop through cooperative channels

The system of cooperative marketing of cotton was first introduced in 1953 in land reform areas.[12] In the year 1962 cooperative marketing of cotton was voluntarily

10 Under growing pressure from the rich peasants, the law of agricultural cooperatives, which stipulated that 80% of the seats on the management councils of the cooperatives should be reserved for peasants owning less than 5 feddans, was modified in 1969 to raise the property ceiling to 15 feddans. Moreover, illiterate peasants were deprived, according to the modified law, of the right to be elected to these councils, despite the fact that they constitute about 95% of the rural masses.

11 Dharm Narain, *op. cit.,* p.50

12 Quantities of cotton marketed through agrarian reform or cooperative channels were as follows (in kantars):

1952/3	27,000	1955/6	237,000	1958/9	403,541
1953/4	84,800	1956/7	311,137	1959/60	454,849
1954/5	162,700	1957/8	369,008		

Source: Agrarian Reform in Nine Years, as quoted in Saab,
   The Egyptian Agrarian Reform, p.117.

introduced in four governorates, but in 1965 the system became compulsory and was extended to cover all governorates producing cotton.

Table 5.2. *Quantities of cotton marketed cooperatively* (000 metric kantars)

Season	Total quantities marketed cooperatively*	As a percentage of the total cotton production
		%
1962/3	1,428	17
1963/4	3,684	42
1964/5	5,561	60
1965/6	9,573	100
1966/7	8,223	100
1967/8	7,696	100
1968/9	7,683	100
1969/70	9,387	100

*including land reform cooperatives.
Source: NBE, *Economic Bulletin,* XXVI-No. 2 (1973), p.138.

Table 5.2 shows the quantities of cotton marketed cooperatively since the system was first introduced outside the land reform areas in the 1962/3 season. These figures indicate that cooperative marketing in the first three seasons was limited to only a sizeable proportion of the total cotton crop, but this proportion increased very rapidly over the years until the entire crop was marketed cooperatively as from the 1965/6 season.

In this system, farmers deliver their cotton to *collecting centres,* where they are registered, weighed and their grades determined. The cotton is then transported to the *ginning mills,* where, after processing, it is pressed into bales. Insurance coverage is provided against all natural disasters and other risks from the moment the cotton is delivered to the collection centres until it is passed on to the local spinners or is exported.[13]

The cotton crop is generally regarded as the main guarantee for loans made by the cooperatives and as the only tangible collateral for money due to them by their members. In consequence, picking of the cotton crop was subject to the prior consent of the *mustrif ta'awni,*[14] who never allowed the peasants to enter the cotton fields until a complete block of 30—50 feddans was fully ripe.[15]

13 See M. Riad El Ghonemy, 'Economic and Institutional Organisation of Egyptian Agriculture since 1952', in P.J. Vatikiotis (ed.), *Egypt since the Revolution* (London: George Allen and Unwin, 1968), p.79; and S.Z. Nassar, 'Socialist Transformation in UAR Agriculture', *L'Egypte Contemporaine,* Vol. LX, No. 337 (July 1969), pp.120—1.

14 The *mushrif ta'awni* (i.e. cooperative supervisor) is usually nominated by the cooperative administration in Cairo; and the elected board of directors of the village cannot reject such a nominee. The *mushrif* exercises effective management in close liaison with the monitoring representative of the Public Organisation for Agricultural and Cooperative Credit.

15 According to the officials, a considerable amount of leakage in the delivery of the crop to the cooperatives would have occurred if the peasants had been allowed to harvest their cotton in the customary manner; this would have given them the opportunity to take away part of their crops through surreptitious picking. See Saab, *The Egyptian Agrarian Reform 1952-1962,* p.96

Table 5.3. *Cooperative marketing of some selected export crops, 1964–70*

Agricultural years	Rice		Onions		Groundnuts		Potatoes		Sesame		Flax straw	
	Quantities marketed (000 dariba)	% of total output	Quantities marketed (000 tons)	% of total output	Quantities marketed (000 tons)	% of total output	Quantities marketed (000 tons)	% of total output	Quantities marketed (000 tons)	% of total output	Quantities marketed (000 tons)	% of total output
1964/5	–	–	241	36	13	26	39	9	5	23	5.5	10
1965/6	901	50	213	31	11	25	70	18	5	31	34.0	63
1966/7	1,090	52	188	29	20	55	54	18	8	80	45.0	86
1967/8	1,226	48	170	33	20	59	n.a.	n.a.	6	70	41.0	60
1968/9	1,277	47	231	46	n.a.	n.a.	n.a.	n.a.	n.a.	n.a.	n.a.	n.a.
1969/70	1,343	49	141	28	24	60	n.a.	n.a.	15	80	n.a.	n.a.

Sources and Notes: CAPMS, *The Annual Bulletin of the Cooperative Activities in the Agriculture Sector*, various issues; percentages computed by the author from CAPMS, *Statistical Handbook* (June 1971), pp.34–5 (on a two-year moving-average basis).

Cooperative marketing of other export crops

Until 1960, other export crops such as rice or onions, were rarely marketed through cooperative channels. Yet by the mid-sixties the agriculture cooperatives have come to play an active part in marketing the other main export crops: rice, onions groundnuts, potatoes, green beans, sesame and other crops. Table 5.3 shows the quantities of the different agricultural export crops marketed cooperatively during the seasons 1964/5 – 1969/70.

In the light of the data presented in Table 5.3, it is important to stress the fact that the system of cooperative marketing was expanding in the 1960s mainly to cover the major *export crops* – apart from cotton – such as rice, onions, ground-nuts, potatoes and flax. In fact, rice comes immediately after cotton as a major foreign exchange earner, and represented about 12 per cent of total export earnings in 1970. On the other hand, onions and potatoes constitute the two major vegetable crops grown for export.

The system of compulsory deliveries

A system of *compulsory deliveries* for wheat was introduced in Egypt in the early 1950s whereby the farmers had to deliver to the state procurement agencies part of their production of the wheat crop at 'adminstered prices' through the medium of 'allocated quotas'. The system was extended in the mid-sixties to cover part of the output of rice and onions.

The system of compulsory deliveries was adopted to mainly in order achieve two important goals:[16]

First,   to ensure a continuous flow of grains, particularly wheat, to feed an ever-
           growing urban population;
Second, to expand exports of rice and onions, which are the main agricultural
           export crops apart from cotton.

The 'allocated'quotas' of different crops to be delivered and their prices are fixed every year by the state. In general, the proportions of the different crops, particularly of rice and onions to be compulsorily delivered to the state agencies are quite high (see Table 5.4).

The prices for compulsory deliveries are usually fixed at a level much lower than those that can be obtained on the free market. Such a difference in prices may well be regarded as the implicit margin of 'indirect taxation' imposed on the required deliveries of these crops. The prices associated with the quotas are shown in Table 5.5 and compared with prices on the free market.

When farmers fail to deliver the 'compulsory quotas' to the state procurement agencies in time they become liable to fines of £E51 for each non-delivered ton of rice and £E12 for each non-delivered ton of onions.[17] The *mushrifs* have the right to open judicial proceedings to establish the responsibilities in such cases. The imposition of such severe fines is clearly intended to curb any attempts by the farmers to dispose freely of the whole of their produce.

16 Nassar, *op. cit.*, p.285
17 Cf. Salem, *op. cit.*, pp.96–7 and 113.

Table 5.4. *Minimum quotas of compulsory deliveries for the "requisition" crops, 1965–70*

Crop	Minimum compulsory deliveries per feddan (in absolute numbers)[1]	Average yields per feddan (for the period 1965–70)	Compulsory deliveries as a percentage of average yields per feddan %	Free retention ratio[2] %
Wheat (ardab)	2	7.25	27.6	72.4
Rice (daribas)	1.5	2.25	66	33.0
Onions (tons)	4	7	57	43.0

Notes:
(1) The figures here represent only 'average quotas'. In practice, these 'quotas' differ widely from one district to another according to the quality and fertility of the soil: (a) in the case of *wheat* they vary between 1 and 3 ardabs per feddan; (b) for *rice*, there exists progressive scale for compulsory deliveries of 1.5 daribas for each of the first five feddans and 1¾ daribas for each feddan over and above the first five; (c) the minimum compulsory deliveries of *onions* are set at 4 tons per feddan in the three governorates of Middle Egypt (i.e. Beni-Sueif, Menia, and Fayoum) and at 6 tons per feddan in the three governorates of Upper Egypt (i.e. Assiut, Souhag, and Quena).
(2) The "free retention ratio" may be defined in the case of rice and onions as the ratio of free marketable surplus. For wheat it means the retention ratio for domestic purposes (i.e. consumption needs of the family, livestock and seed requirements etc.)

Sources:
Nassar, *op. cit.,* Table (7), p.286; A.M. Salem, *The Agricultural Cooperative Marketing* (in the light of local practices) – in Arabic – (Cairo: Dar-el-Maaref, 1968), pp.96–7 and 105; R. Abdel-Rassoul, *Prices and Income Policies in Egyptian Agriculture* (in Arabic), Memo 168 (Internal Series), (Cairo: INP, 1971).

Table 5.5. *Government-procurement prices as compared with free market prices (prices effective during the period 1967–8)*

Crop	Average prices for compulsory purchases (£E)* (1)	Average prices for free retentions (£E) (2)	Price differential (2)/(1) % (3)
Wheat (per ardab)	4†	5.1	127
Rice (per dariba)	20‡	40	200
Onions (per ton)	11	16.5	150

Notes: * Purchase prices listed in col. (1) are only average prices. In practice, purchase prices for the same crop vary according to the quality of produce and the date of delivery.
† The average purchase price for the Hindi wheat was raised to £E5 in the season 1969/70.
‡ Purchase prices for rice differ widely according to the quality: effective purchase prices fixed by state ranged from £E20 up to £E28.5 per dariba.
Source: as in Table 5.4..

5.3 The policy of cotton prices and the regulation of agricultural terms of trade

The agricultural terms of trade are regulated in Egypt by a wide variety of methods both at the *production* level and through various stages of *distribution:* by purchase of all of the cotton crop and the disposal of sizeable portions of other major crops ("requisition crops") through the cooperatives; by state monopoly over the import and distribution of fertilisers and pesticides; and through the provision of supervised agricultural credit.

At the same time, a fairly wide range of agricultural produce and livestock products, as well as the *non-requisitioned* portions of major crops, are marketed mainly through private channels, under government supervision but with little direct intervention in price setting. Hence, the existence of two separate marketing channels for some major crops has led to a *dual price structure* for most of. agricultural products.

In general, it is the prices of cotton and other major cash crops rather than of food prices that most affect agricultural incomes in rural Egypt. As we mentioned earlier most important cash crops (i.e. cotton, rice and onions) are sold to state agencies at 'administered prices' for resale to consumers in urban areas or for export. The government can thus easily regulate the domestic terms of trade by purchasing produce from the farmers at one set of prices (buying prices), and selling it at higher prices (export or consumers' retail prices).

5.3.1 The policy of cotton prices

There exist *three* prices for cotton depending on the various marketing stages: (i) the price paid to cotton growers (producers' prices); (ii) the sale price to local spinners; and (iii) the export price.

Over the period 1950–70, cotton prices passed through four distinct phases. Up to 1952, cotton prices were determined on the *cotton exchange* and therefore fluctuated widely from one year to another.[18] During the second phase (1953–61) control over prices and trade in cotton was exercised at the national level by the Egyptian Cotton Commission (ECC).[19] This period witnessed smaller fluctuations in cotton prices; the spot price per kantar varied between £E12.07 in 1952 and £E15.04 in 1960,[20] with the notable exception of the year 1956 (see Fig. 5.1).

The third phase started with the nationalisation of the cotton trade in 1961 and the closure of the cotton exchange,[21] and since 1962 all sales of raw cotton for export or local consumption have been effected through the ECC, which buys cotton at fixed prices, and fixes selling prices both for export and for local consumption. Thus at the beginning of each crop season the government announce fixed buying, export and domestic selling prices for the whole season.

In view of the existence of numerous varieties and grades, the Government's buying price paid to cotton growers consists of two parts: the base grade price *(rutbat asas)* and the quality difference factor *(farq rutba)* which consists of premiums or discounts of the basic price according to the particular grade of each

---

18 The international trade in cotton has been conducted over the years through a set of highly developed cotton bourses with *future* markets in addition to the *spot* market, and with a well organised system of forward dealing. Future markets, however, have always been suspect as the playground of speculative forces. The Alexandria future market in particular was in the hands of a limited number of powerful dealers. Cf. Hansen & Marzouk, *op. cit.,* p.97.

19 Under legislation approved by the Egyptian Cabinet on 10 June, 1953, no new cotton crop may be exported or delivered to textile mills for local consumption without first obtaining a certificate testifying that such cotton has been bought from the ECC. See *Financial Times:* 12 June, 1953.

20 NBE, *Eco. Bull.,* XXVI–No. 2 (1973), p.131.

21 The Alexandria *futures bourse* was closed in 1961 and the *open spot market* (Minet El-Bassal) in 1962.

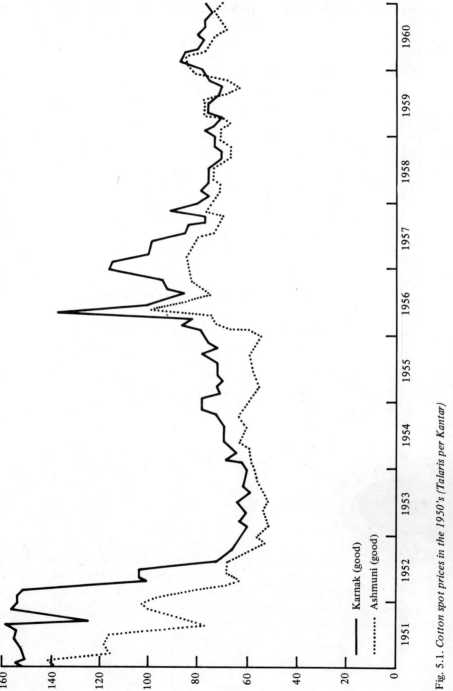

Fig. 5.1. *Cotton spot prices in the 1950's (Talaris per Kantar)*

Source: *The Egyptian Agrarian Reform, 1952–1962* by G.S. Saab, published by Oxford University Press under the auspicies of the Royal Institute of International Affairs.

cotton variety.[22] Moreover, a sum of £E0.718, representing the value of seeds and scarto (cotton scrap), is added to the price of each kantar of ginned cotton.

Fig. 5.2. *Cotton ECC buying prices, domestic selling prices and export prices*

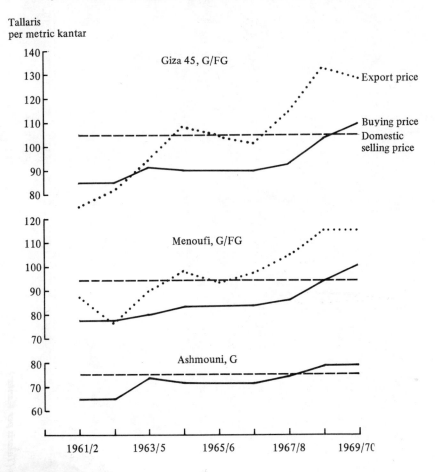

To give an idea of the price relationships fixed by the ECC, we show in Table 5.6 price quotations for the quality 'good/fully good' of some important varieties during the seasons 1960/1 – 1969/70. The buying prices are the prices paid for deliveries from ginning mills. The selling prices for local consumption are are the prices paid by domestic spinners no matter whether they are producing for

22 Cf. El-Ghonemy, 'Economic and Institutional Organisation . . . ', p. 79.

the domestic market or for export.[23]

A glance at Fig. 5.2 immediately reveals that the producers' price received by cotton growers is much lower, in most instances, than the fixed selling price for export or local consumption, thus implying considerable profit margins for the state.[24]

In fact, the selling prices for local spinners remained fairly constant throughout the 1960s while the ECC export quotations changed from year to year according to the state of foreign demand. On the other hand, between 1961/2 and 1966/7, increases in producers' prices paid to cotton growers were in the modest range of 6–11 per cent, i.e. much less than the general rise in the cost of cotton cultivation over the same period. This led to a situation where many farmers found cotton cultivation much less profitable than before, which was a major factor underlying their failure to take up their full area allotments of cotton.

To remedy this situation, the government raised prices paid to cotton growers by three tallaris for all varieties and grades in the 1967/8 season. The buying prices were further increased by 10 tallaris for Giza 45, 8 tallaris for Menoufi and 4 tallaris for Ashmouni in the 1968/69 season. All in all, between 1964/5 and 1969/70, increases in prices paid to farmers for the principal varieties of cotton were in the range of 10–22 per cent.

However, the rise in cotton prices differed from one variety to another. For instance, the prices of extra-long staples tended to increase at a much higher rate than in the case of long and medium varieties. For whereas the price of Menoufi in 1970 was about 21% higher than in 1965, reaching £E19.7 per kantar, the rise in the price of the Ashmouni variety during the same period was only 10%.

Although the government continued to raise the producers' price paid to cotton growers, cotton acreage nevertheless declined steadily, from a peak of 1.99 million feddans in 1961 to 1.5 million feddans in 1971. This persistant contraction in cotton acreage may be attributed to the rise in costs of production after the mid-sixties at rates which outstripped the increase in cotton prices, thus leading to diminished profitability per feddan (see Table 5.7). Consequently farmers tended to allocate their land to subsistence crops or to other more lucrative cash crops (i.e. vegetables) that did not entail the degree of government control and cooperative supervision associated with cotton growing.[25]

23 It is important, however, to note that when the textile industry exports yarn or cloth a *subsidy* is paid by the government corresponding to the difference between the ECC selling price of raw cotton for export and that for local consumption. Domestic consumption is usually concentrated on the cheapest and largely non-exportable qualities (i.e. Ashmouni of quality 'Good'). Cf. Hansen & Marzouk, *op. cit.*, p.105

24 It should be remembered, however, that before World War II and throughout the fifties the producers' prices received by the farmers were much lower than the Alexandria quotations as a result of the margins of the mills and the intermediaries handling the cotton trade. Dr. A. El-Gritly mentions that before World War II the margin between the Alexandria quotations and the producers' prices may have amounted to almost fifty per cent (quoted in Hansen & Marzouk, p.105)

25 Cf. NBE, 'The Role and Prospects of Cotton in the Egyptian Economy', *Eco. Bull.*, Vol. XXVI– No. 2 (1973), pp.122–3.

Table 5.6. Cotton prices, 1961–70 (tallaris per metric kantar)[1]

Marketing season (September – August)

Variety	1961/2			1962/3			1963/4		
	Buying prices	Selling prices to domestic mills	Export prices	Buying prices	Selling prices to domestic mills	Export prices	Buying prices	Selling prices to domestic mills	Export prices
I Extra-long staple[2]									
Giza 45, G/FG	85.0	105.0	75.0	85.0	105.0	82.25	92.5	105.0	96.0
Menoufi, G/FG	77.0	93.5	86.5	77.0	93.5	76.0	79.5	93.5	88.25
II Long staple[3]									
Dandara, G	65.0	79.25	57.5	65.0	75.5	64.25	75.5	75.5	72.75
Giza 47, G/FG	71.0	87.25	64.5	71.0	87.25	68.5	78.5	87.25	78.0
III Medium staple[4]									
Ashmouni, G	65.0	75.25	56.0	65.0	75.5	63.5	73.5	75.5	69.25

Marketing season (September – August)

Variety	1964/5			1965/6			1966/7		
	Buying prices	Selling prices to domestic mills	Export prices	Buying prices	Selling prices to domestic mills	Export prices	Buying prices	Selling prices to domestic mills	Export prices
I Extra-long staple[2]									
Giza 45, G/FG	90.0	105.0	108.5	90.0	105.0	104.0	90.0	105.0	101.0
Menoufi, G/FG	82.5	93.5	98.0	82.5	93.5	92.7	82.5	93.5	95.5
II Long staple[3]									
Dandara, G	72.5	72.5	81.5	72.5	75.5	74.2	72.5	75.5	70.0
Giza 47, G/FG	76.0	87.25	75.5	76.0	87.25	n.a.	76.0	87.25	76.0
III Medium staple[4]									
Asnmouni, G	71.75	75.5	76.5	71.75	75.5	101.0	71.75	75.5	94.0

Variety	Marketing season (September – August)								
	1967/8			1968/9			1969/70		
	Buying prices	Selling prices to domestic mills	Export prices	Buying prices	Selling prices to domestic mills	Export prices	Buying prices	Selling prices to domestic mills	Export prices
I *Extra-long staple*[2]									
Giza 45, G/FG	93.0	105.0	114.5	103.0	105.0	133.0	110.0	105.0	128.0
Menoufi, G/FG	85.5	93.5	104.0	93.5	93.5	115.0	99.5	93.5	115.0
II *Long staple*[3]									
Dandara, G	75.5	73.5	77.5	75.5	73.5	82.0	75.5	73.5	79.0
Giza 47, G/FG	–	–	–	–	–	–	–	–	–
III *Medium staple*[4]									
Asnmouni, G	74.75	75.5	96.0	78.75	75.5	n.a.	78.75	75.5	n.a.

Notes: (1) One *tallari* is equal to £E0.20; one *kantar* is equal to 50 kilograms (110 pounds)

(2) The group of extra long staple varieties accounted for 49% of total cotton acreage in 1961 (some 978,000 feddans). However the area allocated to these varieties declined in later years falling to a figure of 712,000 feddans in 1970 (44%).

(3) The area allocated to this group is third in size after extra-long and medium staples.

(4) The area allocated to this group accounts for about one-third of the total for cotton.

Sources: The Egyptian Public Organisation for Cotton; *Cotton Bulletin*, various issues; Nawal Omar: *Etude de surplus agricole en Egypte de 1952 a 1967*, unpublished Ph.D. thesis submitted to the University of Paris (1970), Table (26), p.250; Abdel-Rassoul, *op. cit.*, pp.42–3.

Table 5.7 *Profitibility per feddan of sown cotton, 1960–70*

Year	Average price per kantar £E	Yield per feddan (kantars)	Value of production per feddan			Production costs per feddan* £E	Net Yield per feddan £E	Net profit per kantar £E
			Value of cotton £E	Value of firewood £E	Total £E			
1960	15.040	5.20	78.210	1.400	79.610	45.245	34.365	6.60
1961	14.580	3.21	45.800	1.500	48.300	49.700	(−) 1.400‡	–
1962	14.840	5.12	75.980	1.500	77.480	51.840	26.640	5.00
1963	15.240	5.12	78.030	2.280	80.310	54.590	25.720	5.02
1964	16.840	5.66	95.310	2.200	97.510	57.681	39.829	7.04
1965	16.120	5.02	80.922	3.370	83.959	64.375	19.584	3.90
1966	16.052	4.40	70.629	3.087	73.716	71.259	2.457	0.558
1967	17.042	4.72	80.438	3.897	83.335	69.920	13.415	2.84
1968	17.463	5.25	91.681	3.623	95.304	70.590	24.714	4.71
1969	18.040	4.85	87.494	3.563	91.057	73.590	17.467	3.60
1970	18.190	5.48	99.681	3.214	102.895	75.660	27.235	4.97

* Inclusive of rent per feddan
‡ Due to heavy damage to the cotton crop inflicted by pests in 1961/2.
Source: Price Planning Agency, *Memo No. 11: Report on cotton* (Cairo: May 1972), Table 17.

5.3.2 Estimation of cotton acreage responses to price change

Here we use simple, lagged regressions of cotton acreage upon price in order to examine acreage responses to price change. We have tried three possible formulations to study the shift in acreage under cotton in response to changes in producers' prices during the period 1960–73.

In choosing the most appropriate *relative* price deflator, the usual practice is to take prices of relavant "substitute" or "rival" crops as possible explanatory variables. Hence, we have estimated three *acreage response functions* for cotton with respect to: (i) changes in the absolute price of cotton; (ii) the relative prices of cotton and rice; and (iii) the relative prices of cotton and wheat.

The three estimated regressions are as follows:

(a) $\quad A_t = 39.136 + 0.690 \, (P_c)_{t-1} - 2.544t \qquad R = 0.74$
$$(0.396) \phantom{(P_c)_{t-1} -} (0.820)$$

(b) $\quad A_t = 115.0 - 0.158 \left(\dfrac{P_r}{P_c}\right)_{t-1} - 0.606t \qquad R = 0.71$
$$(0.119) \phantom{\left(\dfrac{P_r}{P_c}\right)_{t-1}} (0.674)$$

(c) $\quad A_t = 158.88 - 0.559 \left(\dfrac{P_w}{P_c}\right)_{t-1} - 0.987t \qquad R = 0.81$
$$(0.206) \phantom{\left(\dfrac{P_w}{P_c}\right)_{t-1}} (0.373)$$

where

A = index of cotton acreage on 1960 base;

P_c = index of cotton price on 1960 base;

$\dfrac{P_r}{P_c}$ = index of ratio of rice to cotton price on 1960 base;

$\dfrac{P_w}{P_c}$ = index of ratio of wheat to cotton price on 1960 base.

The numbers in parentheses under the estimated coefficients are the computed standard errors. The multiple correlation coefficients are listed after each equation.

Our findings are that there is a significant relationship between the acreage under cotton and its lagged absolute price. In the second equation, we find no significant relationship between the shifts in acreage under cotton and changes in the relative prices of cotton and rice. This is most surprising since cotton and rice are on average the two most profitable field crops for the majority of farmers. It may be due to the existence of technological constraints on shiftability of land within a certain pattern of crop rotations. This factor could affect the magnitude of the acreage response to the relative price change.[26] On the other hand *relative yields* (defined in terms of income per acre) of cotton and rice may be introduced as an explanatory variable instead of *relative prices* in formulating an appropriate acreage response function.

---

26 Cf. J. Bhagwati and S. Chakravarty, 'Contributions to Indian Economic Analysis', *American Economic Review*, Vol. LIX–No. 4 (Supplement), September 1969, p.40.

In the third equation, we find a significant price-induced shift in cotton acreage in response to relative price changes of cotton and wheat. This is also accompanied by an improvement in the ratio of the regression coefficient to its standard error and an increase in the overall degree of determination as a result of replacing $(P_c)_{t-1}$ by $\left(\dfrac{P_w}{P_c}\right)_{t-1}$. This brings us closer to a satisfactory formulation of the cotton acreage response function in the Egyptian context.

Finally, let us note that a more realistic approach to the problem would be to distinguish in the analysis of acreage responses to price change between various groups of landholders by size-class of holdings.

5.4   Behaviour of agricultural terms of trade

The critical question of the *relative* terms of trade between agriculture and other sectors (including its own-inputs) has occasionally been raised in the Egyptian literature. Yet no serious empirical study has been attempted to explore this important question in the light of the facts of the Egyptian experience.

Our analysis in this section will focus on the following two issues:

(1)   What have been the directions and size of the movements in the terms of trade between agriculture and the manufacturing sector and vis-à-vis its own-inputs?

(2)   How far could knowledge of such movements contribute to a better understanding of the types of agrarian policies carried out in 1960s?

Conventionally the index of the agricultural terms of trade is computed as the ratio of a price index of goods sold by farmers (the numerator) and a price index of goods bought by them both for consumption and production purposes (the denominator). We propose here to decompose such a global index of terms of trade into two distinct sets of agricultural/non-agricultural terms of trade, namely:

(1)   The index of the terms of trade between agricultural outputs and agricultural inputs

$$I_m \;=\; \frac{\text{Price index of agricultural goods sold by farmers}}{\text{Price index of manufactured inputs used in farming operations}}$$

(2)   The index of the terms of trade between agricultural outputs and consumer goods and services bought by farmers

$$I_c \;=\; \frac{\text{Price index of agricultural goods sold by farmers}}{\text{Price index of manufactured consumer goods bought by farmers}}$$

Each of these ratios has a different weighting system and different components of *non-agricultural goods*. The importance of the second ratio I_c will depend largely on the proportion of the peasants' income spent on manufactured consumer goods. The kind of data needed to compute the denominator I_c would be a *representative bundle* of manufactured consumers' goods bought by the Egyptian farm population.

5.4.1.   *The direction and size of the movements in the terms of trade for the agricultural sector*

The first question to be raised in this connection is that of types of agricultural products which should be included in our index. In general one can distinguish between three main types of farm produce: (1) field products, (2) fruit and vegetables and (3) animal products.

We propose to concentrate here on the first of these groups, since *field crops* (mainly cotton and cereals) rank first among the components of both plant and total agricultural production.[27] Another point in favour of this choice is that the changes in prices of fruit, livestock and dairy products in the main affect the farm income of the big, rich and well-to-do middle farmers, rather than the great majority of the land-holders in Egyptian agriculture.

The crops included in our index are: cotton, rice, wheat, maize, onions and sugarcane. These are fairly representative of the major agricultural commodities sold by farmers. This index however leaves out some minor crops which can be safely neglected,[28] since their data are not available for the whole period under review and their impact on the farm income is not all that great.

Our analysis of the movement in the terms of trade for the agricultural sector is centred on the relationships between agricultural and non-agricultural commodities (i.e. agricultural inputs and consumers' goods obtained from the manufacturing sector). The question of the *relative* terms of trade within the agricultural sector itself (i.e. between agricultural output and its own-inputs) will be examined separately (see sub-section 5.4.2).

For all indices of terms of trade the year 1960 has been chosen as the base-year, because it represented a turning point in a number of governmental policies concerning agricultural prices as well as the marketing of the major cash crops. The price indices of the bundles of goods produced, bought and sold by the agricultural sector, as well as the weights used to construct the indices of terms of trade are reported in detail in Appendix E.

The principal results of our investigations are given in Table 5.8, and are also shown in Fig. 5.3, where all indices are three-year moving averages, which smooth out some of the year-to-year fluctuations in the movement of terms of trade.

The base-weighted and the 1970-weighted index-numbers are shown separately.[29]

The fact which emerges is that the use of different weights (or rather different base-years) affects only the magnitudes of the aggregative index-numbers; the *pattern* and the *direction* of the movement of the terms of trade for the agricultural sector remain the same.

The notable discrepancy between the two sets of aggregative indices since the mid-1960s is due primarily to the changing weight of rice as the second leading

27 See: CBE, *Economic Review*, XIII–No. 2 (1973), p.138
28 The only important exclusion is that of green fodder (berseem) which cannot be considered as a cash crop for the bulk of farmers.
29 Professor Richard Stone argues against using any particular form of averaging such as the "ideal" formula proposed by Irving Fisher because: "where both the base – and current – weighted index-numbers can be calculated it is desirable that they should be given separately. For the evaluations appropriate to each situation may be so different that the comparison is dominated by the set of valuations which is adopted as the basis of comparison. This fact will emerge if the two index-numbers are given separately but it will be hidden if they are averaged". See: *Quantity and Price Indexes in National Accounts* (Paris: OEEC, 1956), p.39.

Table 5.8 *Indices of terms of trade for the agricultural sector* (on a three-year moving average basis)

Period	(a) Terms of trade between agricultural output and manufactured inputs		(b) Terms of trade between agricultural output and manufactured consumer goods		(c) Overall index of terms of trade between agricultural output and manufactured commodities	
	Base-weighted	1970 weighted	Base-weighted	1970 weighted	Base-weighted	1970 weighted
1960–2	99.6	101.0	98.6	98.4	94.6	94.4
1961–3	98.0	100.0	96.3	96.1	89.1	88.9
1962–4	99.3	101.2	96.9	96.4	86.4	86.0
1963–5	100.1	102.5	93.5	93.3	86.4	88.1
1964–6	103.8	106.7	92.6	93.5	88.3	91.0
1965–7	111.3	118.2	90.4	92.5	90.5	94.6
1966–8	120.9	133.1	91.0	94.1	94.7	98.1
1967–9	131.4	149.5	91.5	94.6	97.9	101.6
1968–70	131.3	149.5	92.5	95.1	97.5	100.7

Source: Appendix E Tables

Fig. 5.3 *Movement in terms of trade for the agricultural sector (three-year moving averages: 1960/62–1968/70)*
    (a) Terms of trade between agricultural output and manufactured agricultural inputs
    (b) Terms of trade between agricultural output and manufactured consumers' goods
    (c) Overall index of terms of trade between agricultural output and manufactured goods

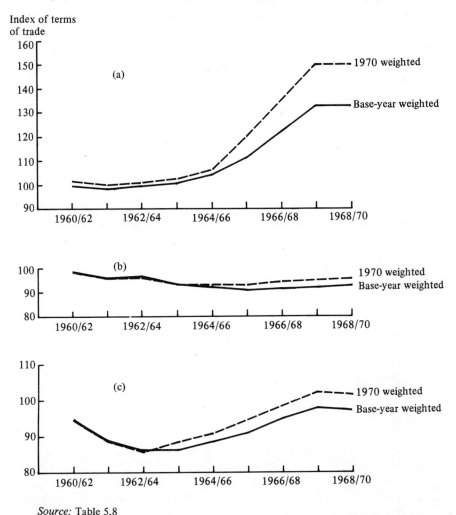

Source: Table 5.8

cash crop in Egyptian agriculture *vis-à-vis* cotton. Thus the use of the 1970–weights tends to exaggerate the terms of trade movements, and conversely the use of the base-period weight somewhat dampens the movements in the terms of trade for the agricultural sector.

On the whole, the recorded time series of the agricultural terms of trade over the period 1960–70 indicate an improvement in the relative prices of agricultural output *vis-à-vis* agricultural inputs obtained from the manufacturing sector. This improvement may be attributed to the effectiveness of the system of distribution of chemical fertilisers at controlled (and sometimes subsidised) prices through the cooperatives under the supervision of the Organisation of Agricultural Credit (O.A.C.)[30] In fact, *the implicit price deflator* for chemical fertilisers indicates a fall of 30% in prices during the ten years under consideration.

As for the movement in the terms of trade between agricultural output and manufactured consumers' goods, there is certainly evidence of a slight deterioration in the mid-1960s, since then they have remained fairly stable. The movement in this index and in that of the official cost-of-living fit fairly well together, taking into account the great weight given to cotton and woollen textiles in the construction of our index of the prices of manufactured consumers' goods (see Appendix E).

Whatever the qualifications in interpreting the data, the general pattern that emerges from our study suggests that domestic terms of trade have not turned greatly against agriculture during the period under consideration. The crucial policy variable in this respect has been the favourable terms of trade between agricultural outputs and manufactured inputs (mainly fertilisers).

5.4.2 The directions of the movements in the terms of trade within the agricultural sector

The recorded series of the terms of trade between agricultural output and inputs originating within the agricultural sector itself (i.e. fodder, seeds, manure) recorded a clear deterioration over the period under consideration (see Fig. 5.4). This is

Fig. 5.4. *Movement in terms of trade between outputs and inputs from the agricultural sector*

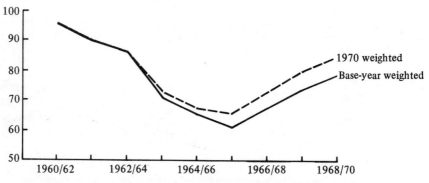

Source: Appendix E, Table E-7 (three-year moving averages)

basically a reflection of the sharp increase in prices of berseem (Egyptian clover), which represent the main component of fodder.[31] This in turn is partly due to the fact that increased demand for berseem, resulting from the attention paid to cattle breeding both for the purpose of land servicing and for meat and dairy products exceeded the scope for expanding its area (and in turn output), owing to the need to utilise the limited available land for the production of food and export crops.[32]

---

30 See: Appendix F on 'The Policy of Fertiliser Prices'.
31 The large increase in berseem prices in the years 1966 and 1967 is mainly attributable to the bad weather of the early winter of the 1966/7 season, which damaged a large part of its cultivated area.
32 See: CBE, "Agricultural Income, 1959/1960 – 1968/69", *Eco. Rev.*, XIII–No. 2 (1973), p.145

Such a movement in relative terms of trade within the agricultural sector is liable to produce a shift in the *internal* distribution of income within the farm sector between different groups of the peasantry, as marketed surplus of berseem seems — according to the 1961 agricultural census data — to be a larger proportion of output for rich and big farmers than for small ones.

According to the 1961 agricultural census data the allocation of the cropped area of berseem between landholdings by size is as follows:

Size-class (feddans)	< 5	5–20	20–50	> 50	Total
	%	%	%	%	%
(a) Permanent berseem	46.5	29.5	8.9	15.1	100.0
(b) Short-term berseem					
(before cotton cultivation	41.2	31.8	10.3	16.7	100.0

We calculated the following *normalised* ratio:

$$\frac{\text{Percentage share in cropped area of clover (berseem)}}{\text{Percentage share in the stock of cattle}}$$

as a rough indicator to identify the 'deficit' and 'surplus' farmers in terms of green fodder, and obtained the following results:

Size-class (feddans)	< 5	5–20	20–50	> 50
Normalised ratio for permanent berseem	0.7	1.2	1.8	3.0
Normalised ratio for short-term berseem	0.6	1.3	2.0	3.3
Identification	net deficit farmers	Self-sufficient or marginally surplus farmers	Net surplus farmers	

Source: Computed from 1961 *Agricultural Census,* Part I — Section 2, Table (27), p.275.

Therefore one would expect that part of the rich and big farmers' green fodder surplus to have been sold to the small 'deficit' farmers who needed more fodder to feed their cattle. In this situation small farmers had to pay more for their purchases of green fodder during the 1960s and this in turn resulted in a further redistribution of agricultural income in favour of the rich and big farmers.

5.5   Summary and conclusions

As we stated earlier, the general pattern that emerges from our study suggests that the domestic terms of trade have not turned greatly against agriculture during the period under consideration. The crucial policy variable in this respect has been the favourable terms of trade between agricultural outputs and manufactured inputs (mainly fertilisers).

While these facts are interesting in themselves, they beg the most relevant question as to what the level of farm incomes might have been if world-market prices for the leading export crops had been allowed to obtain. According to our calculations, the Egyptian farmer in the 1960s received something between 70 and

Table 5.9. *Development of producer and export prices and government profit margins for the cotton crop, 1960–70*

Years	Producers' price (£E per metric kantar) (1)	Average export price (£E per metric kantar) (2)	(1)/(2) (3)	Government's profit margin per kantar (£E) (4)	Quantities exported (000 metric kantars) (5)	Total government revenue (£E million) (6)
			%			
1960	15.0	18.0	83	3.0	8,497	25.5
1961	14.6	18.1	81	3.5	6,740	23.6
1962	14.8	16.7	89	1.9	5,010	9.5
1963	15.2	18.8	81	3.6	6,447	23.2
1964	16.8	19.2	87	2.4	5,835	14.0
1965	16.1	22.3	72	6.2	6,843	42.4
1966	16.0	20.8	77	4.8	6,848	32.9
1967	17.0	20.2	84	3.2	6,043	19.3
1968	17.5	21.8	80	4.3	5,194	22.3
1969	18.0	25.3	71	7.3	4,760	34.7
1970	18.2	26.0	70	7.8	6,438	50.2

Average annual government revenue   27.0

Sources: Col. (2): Central Price Agency, *Cotton Report, op. cit.*, Table 28, p.105
Col. (5): Central Price Agency, *Cotton Report, op. cit.*, Table 24, p.98

Table 5.10. *Price relationships and government profit margins for bleach rice, 1965–70*

Season	Government buying price per ton of rice in husk (£E) (1)	Total cost per ton of bleached rice* (£E) (2)	Average export price (£E) (3)	Government profit margin per ton (£E) (4)	(4)/(3) (5)	Total quantities exported (000 tons) (6)	Total government revenue (£E million) (7)
					%		
1965/6	22.0	35.2	62.1	26.9	43	287	7.7
1966/7	25.4	36.4	65.1	28.7	44	275	7.9
1967/8	25.4	38.8	69.5	30.7	44	395	12.1
1968/9	30.0	43.8	81.4	37.6	46	498	18.7
1969/70	30.0	45.4	73.1	27.7	38	707	19.6

Average annual government revenue   13.2

*inclusive of costs of rice milling and export preparation costs per ton of exported rice.
Source: Price Planning Agency, *Report on Rice*, Tables 43 and 81.

80 per cent of the world market price for his cotton crop (see Table 5.9). As for therice crop, one can contend that an effective export duty amounting to about 44 per cent *ad valorem* was levied on exported rice from the mid-sixties onwards (see Table 5.10).

In this respect, cooperatives have effectively become a means of taxing agriculture indirectly, by permitting the procurement of the main cash crops at tax-element-inclusive prices. The transfers of income from agriculture to the state treasury due to the manipulation of agricultural prices and export duties on farm produce has been estimated at about £E330 million during the period 1965–70, which is equivalent to a 10–11 percent tax on farmers' income.[33]

It may be argued, however, that such a policy package has not resulted in a drastic diversion of income from farmers, since the producers' prices received by cotton growers before World War II and throughout the fifties were much lower than the Alexandria export quotations, because of the margins of the ginning mills and the intermediaries handling the cotton trade (before World War II the margin between Alexandria quotations and the producers' prices may have amounted to 50 per cent). In other words, the new policy package in the 1960s led, in the main, to a drastic squeeze on the profit margins of the intermediaries handling the cotton trade rather than the cotton growers.

Nonetheless, it has been argued, with some force, that the policy of procurement of the major agricultural crops (cotton in particular) at tax-element-inclusive prices had a strong *disincentive* effect which became apparent after the mid-1960s. In fact, the producers' prices of the major agricultural crops (with the exception of onions) remained relatively stagnant throughout the first half of the 1960s and it was only from the mid-sixties onwards that the prices of rice and cereals showed a substantial increase.

Table 5.11 shows the rises in prices of the major agricultural crops marketed cooperatively since the mid-sixties.

These price increases were introduced chiefly in order to stimulate the production of these products. Yet the increase in the price of cotton was still considered too low to induce the farmers to voluntarily increase the area allotted to cotton cultivation.[34]

This reveals a general dilemma facing the planners in most developing countries as they attempt to set the producers' prices of the agricultural crops high enough to provide production incentives, yet low enough to provide for a substantial transfer of the agricultural surplus to government coffers. Somehow a balance has to be

---

33 It has been estimated that the total financial contribution of agriculture to the State treasury amounted to about 16.4 per cent of the total agricultural income during the period 1965–1970. See: A.Z. Sheira, 'Financial Contribution of Agriculture in the UAR', *paper presented at the seminar on prospective regional planning,* held in Warsaw, June 1970, and M. Abdel-Raouf, 'Vertical Expansion in Egyptian Agriculture', *L'Egypte Contemporaine,* Vol. LXIII–No. 350 (Oct. 1972), p.635. We have obtained our estimate by netting out the yields of taxes on land, which represent only about 6.4 per cent of total agricultural incomes. See: J. Lotz, 'Taxation in the U.A.R.', *IMF Staff Papers,* Vol. XII–No. 1 (March 1966), p.145.
34 See: NBE, *Eco. Bull.,* XXV–No. 4 (1972), p.265

Table 5.11. *Changes in prices of major agricultural crops, 1964/5–1969/70*

Crop	Unit	Price in 1964/5 (£E)	Price in 1969/70 (£E)	% Change
Cotton	Kantar	16.9	18.0	6.5
Rice	Dariba	18.0	29.2	62.2
Wheat	Ardeb	4.6	5.8	26.1
Sugarcane	Kantar	0.105	0.131	24.8
Groundnuts	Ardeb	5.0	6.6	32.0
Sesame	Ardeb	10.4	13.9	33.7
Lentils	Ardeb	11.2	16.8	50.0

Source: Ministry of Planning, *Plan Follow-up Report 1969/70*, pp.22–5

struck between drawing resources from agriculture and not discouraging output too much.[35]

It should be remembered in this context that the income effect of favourable terms of trade for food crops is usually small in the case of a country like Egypt, for it is cotton rather than food prices that affect most agricultural incomes.[36] We may further note that one relevant factor in determining the extent of an improvement (or deterioration) in the terms of trade for different groups of the peasantry would be differences in *crop-mixes*. In this respect, it is important to note that the prices of some agricultural products — usually those produced by the rich farmers and handled by private trade, such as livestock, dairy products, fruit and vegetables — have generally tended to rise much faster than the prices of other cash and food crops.

In general, one could argue that the policy package involving cooperative marketing and compulsory deliveries represented, in the main, a method of levying taxation on the incomes of the bulk of small and medium peasants. This is true insofar as the system of *tax-inclusive-procurement* prices of the major cash crops and food-grains discriminatorily taxes farmers who happen to be producers of these specific commodities and thereby pulls financial resources away from their production.

Nonetheless, it must be remembered that an important offsetting factor of the shift in the terms of trade against the small and medium farmer may have been the instituted policies aiming at encouraging agricultural production by public investment in irrigation, drainage, and flood control, and making available fertiliser, pesticides and tractor rentals at low prices and on favourable credit terms. In fact, farmers short of working capital, storage facilities and market information are easily exploited by the merchants who buy their produce; and the prevention of this can be an important offsetting factor.[37]

35 Cf. Little, Scitivsky and Scott, *Industry and Trade in Some Developing Countries*, p.349
36 Cf. R. Mabro, 'Industrial Growth and the Lewis Model . . . ', p.350 (note 38).
37 Little, Scitovsky and Scott, *Industry and Trade in Some Developing Countries*, p.44 note 3.

Finally, it is important to emphasise that agriculture must provide more resources for industrialisation than it would do under *laissez-faire* policies. In fact, land taxation in Egypt has been allowed in the past to wither almost to the point of insignificance.[38] On the other hand, direct taxation of farm incomes proved difficult because of both evasion and political or administrative difficulties. Against this background, regulation of the relative terms of trade between the agricultural and other sectors (i.e. export and manufacturing sectors) has become the most effective instrument of taxing farmers' incomes. Cooperativisation and manipulation of agricultural terms of trade may also be seen as effective devices by which the State was able to increase its inflow of *grain* and the *leading export crops* in order to expand urban employment and maximise the country's foreign exchange earnings.

38 Up to 1959/60 the yield of taxes on land did not exceed 2 per cent of the total agricultural income in Egypt. Cf. comment by A. Mohie-el-dine in *L'Egypte Contemporaine*, LIX–No. 332 (April 1968), p.303.

6

Rural Out-Migration

6.1   Basic rural-urban trends

After the First World War there was a continuous stream of migration from rural
areas to urban centres, especially to big metropolitan centres like Cairo, Alexandria
and the three major cities of the Suez Canal Zone. The proportion of the rural
component in the total population declined continuously from over 80 per cent at
the turn of the century to 60 per cent in 1966, and more recently to 58 per cent
(see Table 6.1).

The decade including World War II, 1937—1947, witnessed an accelerated process
of urbanisation. The war activities undoubtedly stimulated urbanisation by creating
new job opportunities in the large governorates (i.e. the cities of the Suez Canal
Zone), where most of the allied troops were based.[1] In the post-war period, population in both rural and urban areas grew rapidly, but urban areas still showed a
higher rate of acceleration. The basic rural-urban population trends are summarised
in Table 6.1

Table 6.1 *Rural-urban composition of the Egyptian population, 1907—70*

Year	Population Total (000's)	Rural (000's)	%	Urban (000's)	%	Annual compound growth rate (%)* Rural	Urban	Total
1907	11,183	9,058	81	2,125	19	-	-	-
1917	12,670	10,030	79	2,640	21	1.03	2.19	1.26
1927	14,083	10,367	74	3,716	26	0.33	3.48	1.05
1937	15,811	11,429	72	4,382	28	0.98	1.67	1.16
1947	18,806	12,604	67	6,202	33	0.99	3.54	1.75
1960	25,771	16,120	63	9,651	37	1.91	3.46	2.45
1966	29,732	17,690	60	12,042	40	1.56	3.76	2.41
1970**	33,329	19,331	58	13,998	42	2.24	3.83	2.87

Source: CAPMS, *The Increase of Population in the U.A.R. and its Impact on Development,*
     (Cairo: 1969), Table 2.5.1, p. 167.

Notes
*   Computed by the author
**   Estimated figures: see CAPMS, *Internal Migration in Egypt* (in Arabic), Cairo: 1971, p. 9.

Perhaps the most striking feature of these statistics is the fact that while the
absolute size of the Egyptian population has almost tripled since 1907, the size of
the urban population has increased more than sixfold during the same period.

---

1   Cf. R. Mabro, "Industrial Growth, Agricultural Under-Employment and the Lewis
     Model: The Egyptian Case, 1937—1965", *J. Dev. Stud.*, (1967), p. 328.

Estimates of the internal migration flow from rural to urban areas varied from three-quarters to a million people between 1947–1960. Table 6.2 shows the pattern of population shifts, according to the estimates of Donald Mead, between 1947 and 1960. Governorates here are assumed to represent roughly the urban and provinces the rural population. It can be also gleaned from Table 6.3 that net migration flow between the last two censuses (1960 and 1966) amounted to 455,000 people over six years, with the annual flow of migration running at the rate of 75,833 people.

Table 6.2 *Population shifts, 1947–60 (000s)*

Category	Urban-rural changes between 1947 and 1960				
	Population in 1947	Natural increase	Actual increase	Calculated migration	Population in 1960
1. *Governorates*					
Population	3,544	1,316	2,151	+ 835	5,695
Adult males:					
Total	1,113	304	540	+ 236	1,653
Employed	943		469		1,412
In agriculture	27		38		65
Not employed	171		71		242
In services	694		307		1,001
2. *Provinces*					
Population	15,478	5,747	4,912	− 835	20,391
Adult males:					
Total	4,648	1,268	1,032	− 236	5,680
Employed	4,303		879		5,182
In agriculture	3,112		383		3,495
Not employed	345		153		498
In services	899		418		1,317

Source: Donald Mead, *Growth and Structural Change in the Egyptian Economy, op. cit.*

These statistics reveal that much of the rural migration seems to have been pouring into the five big metropolitan governorates (i.e. Cairo, Alexandria and the Canal Zone governorates). However, some provinces which had abundant work opportunities during the period 1960–6, e.g., the mining districts of the Red Sea and the gigantic building sites at Aswan, seem to have attracted a sizeable proportion of the new migrants. The *governorates of repulsion* belong to two categories: (1) the over-populated regions neighbouring the metropolitan areas, e.g. Minufiya and Kalyubia; (2) the overcrowded poor provinces of Upper Egypt, e.g. Menia, Quena, Beni-Sueif.

Moreover the data on the growth of towns between 1960 and 1966 indicate a considerable expansion of the city of Giza and the semi-urban centre of Choubra-el-Kheima in the greater Cairo conurbation. Other provincial towns, apart from Aswan, seem to have attracted migrants during this period: the semi-urban centre of Mehalla-al-Kobra, Assiut which benefited from its status of regional capital in Upper Egypt, and also Zagazig and Suez.[2]

Although the metropolitan areas do not offer abundant work opportunities in the 'formal sector', the attraction of the larger cities lies in their capacity to provide

2 CAPMS: *Statistical Handbook* (Cairo, June 1970), p. 13. See also Mabro, *The Egyptian Economy*, pp. 199–200.

110

Table 6.3 *Net internal migration of the population between governorates, 1960–65 (000s)*

Governorates	Males	Females	Total
Cairo	+ 140	+ 134	+ 274
Alexandria	+ 37	+ 35	+ 72
Port-Said	+ 4	+ 4	+ 8
Ismailia	+ 6	+ 6	+ 12
Suez	+ 10	+ 10	+ 20
Daietta	− 6	− 5	− 11
Dakahlia	-	− 2	− 2
Sharkia	− 9	− 11	− 20
Kalyubia	− 2	− 4	− 6
Kafr-El-Sheikh	− 16	− 11	− 27
Gharbia	− 22	− 23	− 45
Munufia	− 36	− 38	− 74
Behera	− 8	− 5	− 13
Giza	+ 23	+ 23	+ 46
Beni-Suef	− 29	− 25	− 54
Fayum	− 19	− 13	− 32
Menia	− 40	− 32	− 72
Asyut	− 4	− 7	− 11
Suhag	− 15	− 13	− 28
Qena	− 31	− 29	− 60
Aswan	+ 14	+ 5	+ 19
Frontier governorates	+ 3	+ 1	+ 4

+ refers to immigration to the governorate.
− refers to emigration to other governorates

Source: CAPMS, *Increase of Population in the U.A.R. and its Impact on Development*, p. 176

Table 6.4 *Population and growth of towns, 1960–6*

Towns	Population in 1960 (000s)	Population in 1966 (000s)	Percentage increase	Presumed direction of net migration[*]
Cairo	3,353	4,220	25.85	+
Giza	419	571	36.28	+
Choubra-el-Kheima	101	173	71.29	+
Greater Cairo	3,873	4,964	28.12	+
Alexandria	1,516	1,801	18.80	+
Port Said	245	283	15.51	−
Suez	206	264	28.15	+
Ismailia (city)	116	144	24.13	+
Tanta	200	230	15.00	−
Mehalla-al-Kobra	188	225	19.70	+
Mansourah	167	191	14.37	−
Assiut	127	154	21.25	+
Zagazig	125	151	20.80	+
Damanhour	127	146	14.96	−
Fayum	112	134	19.64	+
Aswan	63	128	103.17	+
Minia	100	113	13.00	−

Note: [*] On the assumption of a uniform natural increase (15.74 per cent during 6 years).
Source: Mabro, *The Egyptian Economy 1952–1972*, Table 9.2, p. 200.

better income prospects and more flexible employment opportunities in the 'informal sector'.

In this respect it has been observed that the bigger the city the faster its population growth, in spite of the fact that natural increase is quite similar throughout the whole country. This has led to a pronounced *over-urbanisation* of the big cities (i.e. of 100,000 and over). Cairo and Alexandria alone account for about 20% of the total population and are, together with the canal zone cities (Suez, Port Said and Ismailia), growing at a much faster rate than other cities.

According to the census of 1960 the two big metropolitan cities, Cairo and Alexandria, accounted for more than 52 per cent of the urban population. In 1966 these two cities accounted for 55 per cent of the urban population.[3] Hence it seems appropriate, in the case of Egypt, to think in terms of the growth of *metropolitanism* rather than in terms of a generalized process of urbanisation.

6.2   The determinants of rural out-migration

Rural-urban migration is usually explained in terms of a contrast between the "pull" and "push" factors. There is now a wide consensus of opinion among economists working in this field that while the earlier urbanisation of the advanced industrialised countries was mainly motivated by "pull" factors, rural migrants being attracted by the increasing employment opportunities in the towns, urbanisation in most underdeveloped countries is achieved mainly by "push" factors, that is, by the deteriorating conditions in rural areas forcing migrants to seek a livelihood in the city.[4]

In the Egyptian case, it is possible to identify *two types of rural migrants*:[5] the 'bright youths who migrate in search of education or wider opportunities' and the 'have-nots of the village'. The latter are numerically dominant and constitute the basic migration stream.

In the first case, the *selective migrants* enter the urban life by way of two main paths. One is through *the education system*, the other through *military service*. Education influences 'the desire to migrate' of educated youth with rural background, for higher education turns a rural-born youth into an urban dweller from the moment he joins the university or other institution of higher education. The second impetus to selective migration has been military service, as more and more villagers appear to be relocating permanently in the city after their term of duty. In fact, skills learned by conscripts in the service give them a valuable competitive edge in urban employment.[6]

3   Cf. Mostafa H. Nagi, "Internal Migration and Structural Changes in Egypt", *The Middle East Journal* vol. 28 No. 3, summer 1974, p. 273.
4   See on this point Galal Amin, *Urbanisation and Economic Development in the Arab World*, American University of Beirut, 1972, p. 15, K. Davis and H. Golden, "Urbanization and the Development of Pre-Industrial Areas", in *Economic Development and Cultural Change* (Oct. 1954); B. Hoselitz, *Sociological Aspects of Economic Growth*, (The Free Press of Glencoe, N.Y. 1960); and D. Kamerschen, "Further Analysis of Over-Urbanization", *Economic Development and Cultural Change*, (Jan. 1969). For more details see also ILO, *Why Labour Leaves the Land*, (Geneva, 1960).
5   Cf. Janet Abu-Lughod, 'Migrant Adjustment to City Life: The Egyptian Case', *American Journal of Sociology*, Vol. 67 (1), 1961, p. 23.
6   Cf. Janet Abu-Lughod, 'Rural Migration and Politics in Egypt' in *Rural Politics and Social Change in the Middle East*, edited by R. Antoun and I. Harik (Bloomington: Indiana University Press, 1972), p. 317.

Although while education and military service seem to be the major determinants of the stream of selective migration, 'push factors' may be dominant for landless labourers and members of the poorer landed families. In other words, the basic stream of rural migration in Egypt seems to be mainly motivated by "push factors", forcing an increasing number of the 'have-nots' to seek refuge in the cities in order to escape the hard economic conditions prevailing in the countryside. The fact that the larger proportion of rural migrants comes from the poorer strata is borne out by an ILO-INP sample survey in rural areas. It appeared from an interview of 422 migrants that 26 per cent came from families earning less than £E50 a year before migration; 40 per cent from the £E51-75 bracket; 22 per cent from families with an income of £E76-100 and 6 per cent only from those with an income higher than £E100.[7]

On the other hand, INP-ILO rural employment survey provided further information on the nature of "push factors" driving rural inhabitants to migrate to urban areas.[8] The village of Omar Shahin was selected as a 'sample village', since it is the oldest in the Tahrir Province as far as collective rural migration is concerned. The total number of household heads in this village was 156 and the total population 960. A questionnaire was designed to investigate conditions before and after migration and to determine the relative weights of the 'push' and 'pull' factors involved in the migratory process. The findings of this experimental study with respect to the relative importance of different 'push factors' are summarised in Table 6.5.

Table 6.5 *Distribution of household heads according to push factors of migration − based on an experimental study conducted in the village of Omar Shahin − Tahrir province*

Push factors	% of Household heads (out of 156)
Landlessness	86
Lack of rented land	53
Lack of agricultural operations	37
Lack of other occupations	32
Independent income	65
Absence of specialisation	3
Absence of markets	-
Family feuds	1
Revenge	-
Liberation from traditions	-
Broken family ties	2
External marriage	-
Work personal relations	-
Housing conditions	26
Health problems	12
Lack of social services	11
Lack of educational services	7
Lack of recreational services	3
Transportation problems	1
Ambition	15
Other reasons	3

Source: Final Report on Employment Problems in
Rural Areas in U.A.R., p. 29.

7 INP/ILO, *Research Report on Employment Problems in Rural Areas*, (Cairo: 1965−68), Report B, as quoted in Mabro, *The Egyptian Economy 1952−1972*, p.202.
8 INP/ILO, *Final Report on Employment Problems in Rural Areas*, (Cairo: 1968).

It is clear from this table that while most respondents have complex reasons for migrating, the strongest push factor driving them to migrate is their *state of land-lessness*. This factor ranks first and influences 86% of the household heads. The second factor in relative ranking is the desire to have an independent life and income away from the extended family, mentioned by 65% of the respondents. The third push factor is the lack of rented land in the region of origin, 53% of the emigrants were unable to rent land in their original villages and were, therefore, driven to migrate in search of opportunities better than that of being a seasonal agricultural labourer.[9]

Having suggested that 'push factors' are responsible for the bulk of internal migration in Egypt, we now turn to discuss very briefly the importance of 'pull factors' in the Egyptian case. It must be emphasised at the outset that the urban centers act as magnets attracting the rural migrants not so much for purely economic reasons[10] but, more importantly, because of 'psychic' motivations deeply rooted in the desire of the younger members of the rural community to break away from the rigid socio-cultural traditions prevailing in the village.[11] These latter 'psychic' factors, as opposed to pure economic motives, should be regarded as the major 'pull factor' affecting the process of rural out-migration in Egypt.

Most of the attraction of city life lies in the fact that extensive medical, educational and other services are concentrated in big cities. Moreover, the fruits of technical progress as well as modernisation are to be found and enjoyed only in the metropolis. This latter aspect was accentuated by the increasing role of government in economic and public life in recent years, for big metropolises like Cairo, Alexandria, Giza and the Canal Zone towns, are cities characterised mainly by being the political and cultural centres and seats of administration.[12]

6.3   Summary and conclusions

In the light of the foregoing analysis, it seems reasonable to argue that the deter-minants of rural migration in the case of Egypt are not particularly related to the

---

9 *Ibid.*, p. 30.
10 Economists writing in the neo-classical tradition present the prospective urban migrants as maximisers of expected utility. They postulate that rural-urban migration will continue so long as the expected urban real income, at the margin, exceeds real agricultural product; and that migration will cease only when the expected income differential is zero. Such an approach considers the rural-urban real wage differential to be the main inducement mechanism pulling the population to the cities. See in particular J.R. Harris and M.P. Todaro, "Migration, Unemployment and Development: A Two-Sector Analysis", *American Economic Review*, (March 1970), pp. 126–42.
11 *Age selectivity* of young adults, males and females, among rural migrants has been found to be statistically significant in the Egyptian case. See K.C. Zachariah, 'Sex-Age Pattern of Population Mobility in the U.A.R.: With Some International Comparison', *Paper presented to the I.U.S.S.P. Conference* (London: 1969).
12 Cf. Amin, *Urbanisation and Economic Development*, 17.

urban/rural wage differential and the probability of finding a job in a Todaro-type model.[13] In most instances, 'push factors' in rural areas and the flexibility of the 'informal sector' in towns combine to enable migration to occur.[14]

As a matter of fact, rural-urban migration in Egypt has proceeded at a rate far beyond the absorptive capacity of industry and particularly of the manufacturing sector. Over a period of 11 years (1952–63), the growth of Egyptian industry created new employment opportunities for only 350,000 persons, meanwhile the population of Cairo alone was increasing by more than this every three years.[15]

Presumably most rural migrants to towns try to create jobs for themselves in the 'informal sector', using this sector as *a transit route* to the modern sector. Hence, the gravitational pull of the big metropolises like Cairo, Alexandria, Giza and the Canal Zone towns lies in their capacity to offer much greater and more flexible opportunities in the 'informal sector' than any provincial town.[16]

Finally, let us note, that the process of *selective migration* (i.e. education-linked and military service-linked migration) adds greatly to rural-urban imbalances by leaving behind the uneducated, the least skilled, and very young and the very old.

13 There is now a wide consensus of opinion among economists familiar with the Egyptian situation that economic pressures in rural areas force people to move to the cities in search of employment and livelihood. To put it differently, rural-urban migration is mainly a consequence of the 'push' from the countryside, rather than the demand for labour by developing industrial activities in the cities, or 'pull' factors. See Davis and Golden, "Urbanization and the Development of Pre-industrial Areas", in D. Heer (ed.), *Readings on Population*, (New Jersey: Prentice-Hall, 1968), p. 50; Mabro, *The Egyptian Economy 1952–1972*, p. 202; Nagi, 'Internal Migration and Structural Changes in Egypt', 268.
14 Mabro, *The Egyptian Economy, 1952–1972*, p. 202.
15 Cf. Amin, *Urbanisation and Economic Development in the Arab World*, p. 12.
16 The role of the 'informal sector' in metropolitan areas in absorbing rural migrants has not as yet received the attention it deserves in the case of Egypt.

7

Conclusion

The agrarian problem in Egypt before 1952 was essentially one of extreme inequality in the distribution of landownership and of growing rural poverty. The production relations prevailing in Egyptian agriculture were *transitional* between feudalism and capitalism. For while, in most of the Egyptian countryside, the characteristically feudal bonds of servitude had been eliminated and the closed system of natural production had been replaced by production for the market, the dominant relations of production were not strictly capitalist in character.[1]

The 1952 land reform was a potent force in bringing about the disintegration of the old agrarian structure. It led to the demise of the old class of big landowners and provided one of the major impulses for change in the agrarian structure. Indeed agrarian-change did not stop with land distribution and legal measures to free the peasantry from servility to their landlords, as in the case of the Mexican revolution after 1910. Rather, the Egyptian policy-makers went all the way to create new conditions under which small cultivators would be freed from economic and political dependence on landlords, moneylenders and village merchants.[2] This led to the emergence of a new set of agrarian relations more conducive to growth and development.

We propose here to offer an overall assessment of the socio-economic dynamics of the process of agrarian transition in Egypt in the post-reform era, seen from various angles. The conclusions which follow from our analysis in the preceding chapters may be arranged in the following taxonomic way.

7.1   The impact of the land redistribution programme

The series of 'agrarian reforms', which were prompted by the unequal ownership distribution, disparity of incomes and unsatisfactory tenancy arrangements before 1952, released almost a million feddans for redistribution and improved the social and economic conditions of 342,000 families. Priority in the distribution of land was given to tenants and permanent wage labourers from the expropriated estates, then to farmers with large families, and finally to the poorest members of the village.

These land reforms did not aim to satisfy the land hunger of all tenants and land-less labourers. Given the area of land for redistribution, the policy choice was between

1 Hussein, *Class Conflict in Egypt: 1945–1971*, p. 19.
2 Iliya F. Harik, "Mobilization Policy and Political Change in Rural Egypt", in R. Antoun and I. Harik (eds.), *Rural Politics and Social Change in the Middle East* (Indiana Univ. Press, 1972), p. 287.

arbitrary selecting a limited number of peasants to become small farmers with viable holdings or giving sub-viable plots to the entire landless peasantry. It is arguable, from a purely economic point of view, that distribution of land to the landless in small sub-viable holdings would have increased the buying back of food, and would also have worsened output response, due to lack of farming experience.[3]

Nonetheless, while distribution of land to former tenants and permanent labourers is justified on efficiency grounds, benefits could have been extended to larger numbers of landless families if the ceiling on ownership had been lowered to 25 feddans in the second stage of the reform in 1961.[4] This solution was ruled out for ideological and political reasons which mainly derived from the socio-economic nature of the new regime itself. In reality, decisive action against the thin top layer of absentee big landowners is politically much easier than against the top 10 per cent of landowners (including the rich peasantry) who usually oppose fiercely any further downward adjustment of the land ceiling.

Therefore the most serious limitations of the land redistribution programme arise from the position of the landless labourers. Complementary measures, in the form of regulation of work conditions and minimum wages for the *tarahil* (casual migrant rural labourers), could have improved the living standards of the landless and further corrected the distributional bias of the reform. But such measures were never enforced. Public schemes of rural works in the 1960s helped to expand employment opportunities for casual labour and hence did much to relieve the plight of the landless. Nonetheless, the magnitude of the problem is such that only a sustained programme of industrial expansion could entirely relieve the landless labourers.

The rising number of landless households since the mid-1960s suggests the spectre of a new agrarian crisis, which is caused by the exhaustion of the equalising effects of the land redistribution programme as well as the failure of the supply of new cultivable land to keep pace with rapid population growth.

7.2   Agrarian transition and the differentiation of the peasantry

The operation of historical socio-economic forces differentiates, within the varied mass of the peasantry, the *rich*, the *middle* and the *poor* peasants. Under the post-reform system of agrarian relations, the rich peasants (and some of the middle peasants) were transformed into capitalist farmers, relying largely on hired labour, producing essentially for the market, and using modern cultivation methods and machinery for large-scale farming. At the other end of the scale, the majority of the peasants who were either landless or poor peasants operating small plots of land (less than two feddans) depend largely on agricultural labour for their livelihood. An important socio-economic feature of this latter group of peasantry is that they combine a multiplicity of casual occupations in the process of earning their livelihood.

On all counts, the group of rich peasants displays certain strikingly similar socio-economic features, which facilitate the study of their transformation into a class of

---

3   This view was put forward by Michael Lipton in "Towards a Theory of Land Reform", in D. Lehmann (ed.) *Agrarian Reform and Agrarian Reformism* (London: Faber and Faber, 1974), p. 284.
4   See Mabro, *The Egyptian Economy 1952–1972*, p. 73

capitalist farmers. In fact, the rich peasants occupy a dominant position in the new agrarian system on account of the advantages of large-scale farming (viz, a higher rate of marketable surplus); their superior resource endowment position; their easy access to agricultural credit at favourable terms; and the use of their political power and good relations with local officials to consolidate their position *vis-à-vis* the small and poor peasants and landless labourers. A glance at the statistics of the changes in landownership (see Ch. 1, Table 1.15) reveals the interesting fact that the class of rich peasants has, since 1952, increased its area of owned land by a net purchase of 161,000 feddans, which forms 19.8 per cent of their current owned farm area.

At the other end of the spectrum, the stock of capital owned by the small and poor sections of the peasantry (according to our classification) is very low, and invariably embodies an old technology tied to traditional methods of farming. The poor peasants' households typically own a small plot of land which cannot come anywhere near providing them with the means of the subsistence for the year. The general tendency has been for this group of poor peasants to combine the cultivation of their small plots of land with several other casual occupations, in order to escape complete ruination.

In sum, the historical essence of the process of differentiation of the Egyptian peasantry lies in the greater polarisation of the differentiated peasantry, thus transforming the rich surplus — making peasants into a dynamic class of capitalist farmers at one end of the scale, while squeezing, and eventually proletarianising, the poor and landless peasants. In this process, the rich and middle peasants have become the innovators and the chief carriers of the new technology in Egyptian agriculture. The changes in the agrarian structure in the post-land-reform era have thus helped to enhance 'capitalistic' developments in Egyptian agriculture and to rationalise both the land and labour markets in rural areas.[5] These movements away from the old semi-feudal agrarian structure have been of great importance to the integration and expansion of the home market for industrial goods and services.

7.3   The impact of intra-rural redistribution of income on the integration and expansion of the home market

The changes in the distribution of agricultural income among a broad section of the rural population (as a result of the redistribution of land from big to small farmers and the regulation of tenancy contracts so as to raise the tenant's share in net output) constituted a necessary condition for an enlarged home marked for manufactures in the vast rural areas, thus giving a new impetus to the industrialisation process in Egypt. In fact the reduction in income disparities resulted in a significant rise in the purchasing power of the new owners, tenants and other small farmers, hence leading to an enlargement of the home market for consumer goods and services.

Similarly, the transformation of the 'rich' and 'middle' peasantry into a class of

---

5   In the post-reform era, leasing-out to tenants, particularly by absentee landlords was severely penalised, which led to an increase in wage-labour-based cultivation.

capitalist farmers helped to enlarge the market for means of production (i.e. farm machinery, chemical fertilisers etc.), thus giving an important impetus for the expansion of import-substituting industries at home. The high annual rate of growth in the consumption of chemical fertilisers in Egyptian agriculture led to a great expansion in the total production capacity for manufacturing chemical fertilisers.[6] Tractors factories were also established, but these are mainly *assembly operations*,[7] about which there is no clear information as to the share of imported components.

All in all, it seems fair to say that the growth of intersectoral transactions for the purposes of agricultural production, as well as rural households' consumption, will promote industrial development further and hence will lead to a rapid expansion in the forces of production in society as a whole.

7.4   Cooperativisation and the disposal of farm produce

The massive cooperativisation campaign launched in Egyptian agriculture in the late 1950s was conceived as an essential component of an overall development strategy aiming at achieving rapid industrialisation and high rates of growth for the national economy. In this connection, Egyptian policy-makers placed great emphasis on the restructuring of landholdings into efficient-sized units backed by cooperative organisation where scale effects made it desirable. While farmers continued to retain both ownership and the responsibility for cultivating their own plots, they were required to follow a number of practices: crop consolidation, triennial rotation, and cooperation in certain activities, such as fumigation of crops and pest control.[8]

This set of policies was particularly successful in improving the yields of *cotton* and the basic *food crops*, as can be easily gleaned from Table 7.1.

In reality, these changes in the management of production through the cooperative system have affected the individual cultivator far more than land redistribution *per se*. For whether the cultivator is an owner of land or leases it from the owners, he has no choice but to deal with the village cooperative, the only source available for credit, seeds, fertilisers and pesticides. After the 1961 cotton disaster, responsibility

6   Egypt currently has six fertiliser factories with a total production capacity of over 1,800,000 tons. The domestic production facilities are concentrated in *nitrogenous* fertilisers, although the country has started the manufacture of *phosphatic* fertilisers. Taking four-year moving averages, it is remarkable to observe how the relative shares of domestic production and imports of nitrogenous fertilisers moved over the decade 1957–68.

	1957–60		1964–8	
	000 tons of N	%	000 tons of N	%
Domestic production	38	20	151	63
Imports	110	80	102	37
Total	148	100	253	100

Source: O.E.C.D. Development Centre, *Fertilizer Distribution in the Arab Republic of Egypt*, (Paris, 1972), p. 93.

7   We estimate that since 1965 home production of tractors has amounted to about 50 per cent of the country's total annual availability of tractors.

8   See Mabro, *The Egyptian Economy 1952–1972*, pp. 74–5.

Table 7.1 *Indices of yields for some selected crops, 1952–70* (base: average 1948–51 = 100)

Agricultural Years	Cotton	Wheat	Maize	Millet	Barley	Rice
1952	102	101	101	107	107	88
1960	116	133	106	118	132	131
1965	124	143	167	142	137	132
1970	141	150	180	156	124	143

Source: Mabro, *The Egyptian Economy 1952–1972*, Table (4.7), p. 81.

for combatting pests in the cotton crop was taken away from cultivators and placed in the hands of the cooperatives. However, it would be wrong to regard the cooperative system in Egyptian agriculture as a partial move towards *collectivisation* of production, for actual cultivation is still in the hands of the individual farmer and income from land is not communally shared.

Finally, it should be noted that the main drawback of the system of 'supervised cooperatives' is that it leads to serious bureaucratic distortions and inefficiencies,[9] and that it leaves little or no room for independent initiatives by the peasants themselves in formulating the major policies affecting their daily life and future, as the elected board members of the co-operative societies are ranked below the agronomists (*mushrifs*) and their staff.

On the other hand, the cooperativisation package has effectively become a means of taxing agriculture indirectly, by permitting the procurement and marketing of the main cash crops at *tax-element-inclusive prices.* If one adopts Sanghivi's distinction between the *optional* and *obligatory* surplus, it may be argued that the cooperativisation policy has succeeded in increasing the size of the 'obligatory surplus' necessary to pay back the peasants' input loans in kind and to meet other financial obligations due to the state (i.e. land tax). Thus cooperativisation can be seen as a clever institutional arrangement by which the State was able to increase its inflow of *grain* and the major *export crops* in order to expand urban employment and maximise the country's foreign exchange earnings.

As has become evident from our analysis, *agricultural prices* were used more deliberately from the early 1960s as an effective instrument of taxing farmers' incomes indirectly and thus extracting a financial surplus from agriculture. While this is broadly true, it should be remembered that the "squeeze on Egyptian agriculture" in the 1960s was accompanied by the allocation of important public funds to the agricultural sector in the form of public investment in big developmental projects, such as flood control, irrigation and drainage.

The relevant measure of the magnitude of surplus transfers from agriculture would be the *net* investible surplus squeezed out of the agricultrual sector to finance capital formation and public expenditures in other sectors of the economy. If due allowance is made for public funds rechannelled into the agricultural sector in the form of basic public investment, the net transfers of financial surplus out of agriculture would have amounted only to about 5–7 per cent of the total agricultural income during the period 1965–70.[10]

9 Micro-surveys indicate that in many instances bureaucratic inefficiencies result in inadequate supplies of pesticides at crucial times and that some corrupt officials create artificial shortages in order to benefit from black-market operations.

10 See Abel-Raouf, "Vertical Expansion of Agriculture in the UAR", pp. 635–6.

In practice, there are tangible limits to the efficacy of the intersectoral terms of trade as an instrument for increasing state revenues, because of the possible *disincentive effects* which become operative after a certain critical level of unfavourable terms of trade to agriculture.

7.5   The political dynamics of agrarian transition

Following the implementation of land reforms and the consequent erosion in the power of the *landed aristocracy*, and the *mercantile rural élite* (cotton merchants and village brokers), the group of rich and middle peasants emerged as a new rural élite with dominant political and economic power in the new agrarian system.

Opposed to this fairly large group of rich and middle peasantry are the much larger (though not well-organised) masses of poor peasantry and landless labourers who rely mainly on selling their labour power to earn their livelihood.

The position of small peasants (with holdings of 3–5 feddans) is more complicated, as it is just possible that they might eventually support the poor peasantry in order to break the hold of rich and middle peasants over the local power structure in the village. However, there would almost certainly be widespread opposition among small peasants to the various forms of collectivisation which would be necessary to ameliorate the conditions of the landless in a substantial and irreversible way.

Thus, given the existing configuration of social forces in rural Egypt, an alliance of interests between the rich and middle peasantry seems 'natural' or at least highly congenial. Together they control most of the productive assets in Egyptian agriculture (62% of the farm area and about 80–90 per cent of the stock of farm machinery), and they tend to submerge their objective differences and make common cause against the interests of the rural poor.

All in all, since the 1952 revolution the major change in the village-level power structure has been the replacement of one class of notables by another, while small and poor peasants made very limited progress in assuming political leadership roles. Land reform struck at the power basis of the royal family, the landed aristocracy and very large landlords, but not that of the rich peasants and village notables.[11]

It has been argued, with some force, that the Nasser regime's success in controlling the countryside despite the hostility of the big landlords and the old mercantile rural élite, was attributable to the presence of a class of rich farmers as a competing élite in the countryside.[12] However, the profound structural changes in the economic and political system during 1961–2 unleashed important conflicts of interest between the regime and the new rural élite, which became much more clearly exposed during the second half of the sixties.

Moreover, by the mid-1960s it had become clear to the authorities in Cairo that the new rural élite obstructed the effective implementation of the regime's agrarian policies in the countryside. It has also become clear that, even though it was

11   Harik, *op. cit.*, p. 304.
12   *Ibid*, p. 307

fourteen years since the 1952 revolution, instances of oppression in villages were still to be found, with hardly any available local recourse to justice.[13]

The regime's assessment of the situation during 1965–6 resulted in a change in policy designed to encourage the small peasantry (holders of less than 5 feddans) to assume a new political role in the countryside and to be trained to become a new competing élite. This became the guiding principle behind the reforms in the provincial structure of the Arab Socialist Union (the single political party) during 1965–6.[14] Under the new reforms, the Arab Socialist Union village branch, known as the Committee of Twenty (because it consisted of twenty elected officers) was by-passed, and a new body called the Leadership Group was created to function as the main organ responsible for party activities, with its members selected by the district party secretary in consultation with trusted local party militants.

The main purpose of these changes at the village level was to take political initiative away from the Committee of Twenty, thus neutralising the rich peasantry, which dominated these committees by placing their peasant clients in office. The chairman of the leadership Group and its secretary were, as a rule, selected from amongst the small peasantry in the village.[15] The new party reforms have created well-informed local cadres, who are able to explain the regime's reforms and policies to the rural masses.

In effect, the reforms in the structure of the Arab Socialist Union made in 1965 were limited to the changes required for the party to assume a new political role in implementing the official policy line in the countryside and in checking the influence of the old and new rural élites. Ideological indoctrination and political participation were therefore encouraged as catalysts to speed up the implementation of national policy and to enable the rural masses to protect themselves and national goals from the obstructive tactics of the rural élite.

However, the new political structures did not eliminate class conflicts in rural Egypt, but simply subsumed and organised them under a set of patronising constraints. Political competiton, rivalry and class conflict continued to exist openly among various groups of the peasantry.

The outcome of this class conflict is by no means clear. By the end of the 1960s, however, there were clear indications, that because of the new compromise between the urban and rural élites with the regime the balance of power in rural Egypt had shifted once again in favour of the rich and middle peasants.[16]

This shift has become even more apparent in the early 1970s, with the dogged

---

13 In May 1966 a left-wing militant in the Delta village of *Kamshish*, who had spent years supporting the rights of small and poor peasants against the local big landlords and rich peasants, was assassinated. The incident was serious enough for the authorities to set up a special committee to investigate the remnants of feudalism throughout the countryside. The hearings of the committee revealed serious and flagrant irregularities. See for illustrative cases the minutes of the "Committee for Liquidation of Feudalism", published in the Egyptian press starting 8 July 1966.

14 Harik, *op. cit.*, p. 306.

15 *Ibid.*, p. 307.

16 Small farmers (holders of less than 5 feddasn) have been granted by law the majority of seats on boards of agricultural cooperative societies. This situation has given rise to continuous intrigue by rich farmers to discredit the cooperative system. Under pressure from the rich farmers the law was modified in 1969 to allow the middle peasants to sit on the boards of agricultural cooperative societies instead of the small peasants.

and highly successful defence of the interests of the new rural bourgeoisie by the kulak lobby in the People's Assembly. This new situation is likely to result in sharpening class contradictions between the poor peasantry and landless peasants on the one hand, and the rich peasantry on the other. The social struggles in the 1970s will undoubtedly mark a new chapter in the history of agrarian transition in Egypt.

APPENDICES

Appendix A

The Agrarian Reform Law No. 50 of 1969

Law No. 50 of 1969 was promulgated on 16 August stipulating that no person shall possess more than 50 feddans of agricultural as well as fallow and desert land, and that no one family shall possess more than 100 feddans of such lands (Art. I.). By the family is meant the husband, wife and minor children, even though they be married. Included in the husband's family are his minor children through previous marriage. If the husband is already dead, then the family comprises his wife and their minor children, unless the wife has remarried since the husband's death; in this case the minor children are to be considered as forming an independent family (Art. II). Members of the family whose property exceeds the limit prescribed by the law are entitled to dispose of the excess area within 100 feddans for the whole family, provided that no one member shall own more than 50 feddans (Art. IV para. 1). As an exception to the provisions of Articles I and II, a grandfather can transfer to his grandchildren born to a deceased son the ownership of some of the area in excess of the limit set for his individual holding, on condition that holding of any one of them shall not exceed 50 feddans and the property of the family to which they belong shall not exceed 100 feddans (Art IV, para 2).

With regard to the indemnity due to expropriate owners, Articles IX and X introduce new principles: (a) the indemnity is to be paid *in cash* in ten annual instalments, (b) no interest is to be paid to the owners. This is different from the procedure provided by the previous land reform laws, which made the indemnity payable in interest-bearing state bonds redeemable within a much longer period.

Appendix B

The impact of public development schemes on employment opportunities for casual agricultural labourers

It is widely agreed that those who benefited least from the agrarian reforms were the casual agricultural labourers. In distributing the land, preference was given to those actually cultivating the land as tenants or permanent labourers. *Permanent* labourers were eligible to receive land, but not all casual labourers could receive a holding.

At first casual labourers, passed over by the land redistribution measures, may have become temporarily worse off, since the break-up of large estates caused a reduction in demand for their labour affecting approximately 5–10 per cent of farm labourers. This reduction in employment opportunities for casual labourers has been reported by several writers studying the Egyptian agrarian reforms.[1] Various factors may account for the failure of the land reforms to expand the employment opportunities for hired casual labourers.[2]

First, the new beneficiaries of the land reforms tended to employ *self-employed* farm labourers than the expropriated landowners. For most employment on the newly distributed plots of land consists mainly of family labour. In other words, new beneficiaries tended to *maximise family self-employed labour*;
Second, there was a general slackening in agricultural investment by big landowners not directly affected by the land reform. Many of these owners, unsure about the future of their holdings, slowed down their investment in drainage and irrigation works and subsequently reduced the demand for hired casual labourers.
Third, many of the large-scale farmers perferred to break-up their holdings *voluntarily* and sell it out — in small plots — to small farmers, who usually operate an intensive system of farming, relying mainly on family labour.

In short, because of these redistributive effects, the Egyptian agrarian reforms, while succeeding in maximising the utilisation of self-employed family labour on small farms, aggravated the problems of open employment of landless labourers.

Nonetheless, the consequent initial reduction in employment opportunities was offset later in the early sixties by the new demand for casual labour generated by the construction of the High Dam and the new land reclamation schemes.

Work on the High Dam started in 1960 and it is estimated that the constuction phase and other related projects have provided a total of 155.2 million man-days of employment.[3] It is also estimated that an additional 215.2 million man-days were provided through irrigation and drainage projects and for construction of new barrages on the Nile. After the completion of the High Dam, it is estimated that the irrigation sector, the river fleet, and the new factories could provide permanent employment for more than 400,000 labourers (see Table B-1).

1   See among others: Warriner, *Land Reform and Economic Development, op.cit.;* P. Pissot, 'La reforme agraire en Egypte', *Bull. Soc. Francaise d'Economie Rurale,* (Oct. 1959): Saab, *The Egyptian Agrarian Reform, op.cit.,* Ch. VIII.
2   Cf. Saab, *op.cit.,* p.123; and M.H. Nagi, *Labour Force and Employment in Egypt: A Demographic and Socio-economic Analysis,* (New York; Praeger, 1971), p.105
3   ILO, *Rural Employment Problems in the U.A.R.,* (Geneva, 1969), p.79.

According to these figures, about 45.6 million man-days of casual employment were offered each year, on average, during the construction stage of the High Dam. However, it is exceedingly difficult to obtain any reliable estimate as to the likely number of labourers actually employed. The principal difficulty encountered arises from the lack of any data on the time-phasing of the 455.9 million man-days of employment offered over a period of ten years.

To give only a rough estimate, let us assume that employment opportunities were provided on various types of construction activities in half-monthly units of 12-day work periods for different periods averaging 3 years per labourer. The total number of man-days worked by each labourer would thus be 864 (i.e. 12 days multiplied by 24 half-monthly units for three years). By dividing the total of 455.9 million man-days

Table B-1 *Labour and wages for the High Dam and dependent projects*

Project	Construction stage		Working stage	
	Wages (million £E)	Labour (million man-days)	Annual Wages (million £E)	Labourers (0005)
High Dam and related projects	80.8	155.2	0.04[1]	0.2[1]
Barrages on the Nile	20.0	40.0	0.06	0.3
Irrigation of newly reclaimed land	80.7	220.2	4.3	21.0
Agriculture on newly reclaimed land	...	...	100.0	400.0
Navigation section	4.3	5.5	0.8	2.0
Factories running full capacity	25.0	35.0[2]	5.3	16.0
Total	210.8	455.9	110.5	439.5

[1] Only High Dam workers.
[2] 130,000 workers
Source: *ILO Report, op.cit.*, p.80

by the presumed average number of man-days worked by each labourer, we obtain the figure of 527,663 as the number of casual labourers likely to have benefited from the new employment opportunities opened up by the construction stage of the High Dam and other dependent projects.

These rough estimates indicate that about half a million casual labourers could have benefited from the new employment opportunities — for periods of varying lengths. However, the real employment benefits may have been spread more *widely* or more *thinly* than our arbitrary figures suggest.[4]

Land reclamation has been another source of major temporary employment benefits. During the operation of the National Production Council (1953—9), 79,000 feddans were reclaimed at an annual rate of 13,000 feddans of new land. Under the first five-year plan (1960/1—1964/5), 536,000 feddans were reclaimed at an accelerated pace of 107, 000 feddans per annum.[5]

4 Some estimates put the number of casual rural labourers employed during the High Dam construction period at 300,000 Cf. *ILO Report*, p.108
5 Cf. *ILO Report*, p.80.

An integrated programme of horizontal agricultural expansion was proposed under the second five-year plan (1965/6–1969/70), proceeding at an annual rate of about 140,000 feddans of reclaimed land. Projected employment figures during the reclamation stage as well as the estimated labour requirements in the cropping stage are given in Table B-2.

It should be emphasised that these are no more than 'target figures', and in no way reflect the real employment benefits accruing as a result of the actual progress in the implementation of the reclamation projects. Official statistics claim however that the total area actually reclaimed during the period 1960/1 up to 1969/70

Table B-2 *Target employment figures in reclamation projects during second five-year plan, 1965/6–1969/70*

Year	Reclamation		Cropping		Total	
	Workers (000)	Wage Bill (million £E)	Workers (000)	Wage Bill (million £E)	Workers (000)	Wage Bill (million £E)
1965/66	51.8	5.036	101.3	8.324	153.1	13.360
1966/67	63.3	6.986	138.5	10.914	201.8	17.900
1967/68	54.3	5.843	162.5	13.150	216.8	13.993
1968/69	72.4	7.750	161.1	14.130	233.5	21.880
1969/70	79.8	8.442	158.0	14.912	237.8	23.354
Annual Average	64.3	6.8	144.0	12.3	208.3	19.1

Source: INP/ILO, *Research Report on Employment Problems in Rural Areas UAR,* (Report E on Impact of National Development Projects) (Cairo, 1965), p. 89.

amounted to 884,300 feddans.[6] In other words, the actual progress in land reclamation proceeded at a moderate pace of 88 thousand feddans per annum, only about half the target figure for the period.

It is therefore safe to conclude that only half of the 'projected' employment figures for both the reclamation and cropping stages actually materialised.

On the whole, and in the absence of further evidence, it is extremely difficult to assess whether the new employment opportunities, created as a result of the implementation of the construction and reclamation schemes actually made up for the reduction in employment opportunities for casual agricultural labourers formerly employed on the expropriated estates and not benefiting from the redistribution of land.

6 CAPMS, *U.A.R. Statistical Handbook,* (Cairo, June 1971) p. 58.

Appendix C

On Wage Determination in Rural Egypt

The question of the way in which agricultural wages are determined in 'labour surplus economies' remains highly controversial in modern literature on development. On the one hand one meets the familiar marginal productivity argument, according to which the money-wage rate is governed by the value of the marginal product of labour in agriculture. On the other, there are those who argue that such wages are determined *institutionally,* usually with reference to some notion of *subsistence wages.*[7]

Professor Bent Hansen has been the mose persistent writer, in his attempts to show that rural wages in Egypt behave in accordance with the marginal productivity theory of distribution.[8] Hansen's interpretations of the Egyptian empirical evidence have been challenged by Donald Mead[9] and more recently by James Hanson.[10]

In his most recent study Hansen uses the wage data and the recent evidence provided by the *Rural Employment Survey* – conducted jointly by the I.L.O. and I.N.P. of Cairo in 1964/5 – to give an empirical basis to his 'marginal productivity' thesis of wage determination in Egyptian agriculture.

This survey was based on a sample of 48 villages. Labour records and information on wages and working-time were collected every week from the beginning of June 1964 to the end of June 1965. The information collected mainly reflected the personal views of the village heads (*oumdas*) about the daily wages and working-time of rural labourers, typical in the village for the week in question.[11]

In many instances the wage records were not complete. For some villages, information was completely lacking. For others information was missing for the slack season where, during certain weeks, there had been no wages to record. None-theless, despite these shortcomings, there can be little doubt that the collected wage statistics throw an interesting light on wage behaviour in rural Egypt.

7 Cf. W.A. Lewis, 'Economic development with unlimited supplies of labour' *Manchester School* (May 1954); J.C.H. Rei and G. Ranis, *Development of the Labour Surplus Economy: Theory and Practice* (Homewood, Illinois 1964).

8 See in particular B. Hansen, "Marginal Productivity Wage Theory and Subsistence Wage Theory in Egyptian Agriculture", *Journal of Development Studies,* vol. 2 (July 1966); B. Hansen, "Employment and Wages in Rural Egypt" *Amer. Econ. Rev.,* (June 1969), pp. 298–313.

9 Cf. D. Mead, *Growth and Structural Change in the Egyptian Economy,* (Homewood. Illinois: 1967), pp.80–98.

10 J. Hanson, "Employment and Rural Wages in Egypt: A reinterpretation", *Amer. Econ Rev.* (1971), pp. 492–99

11 Cf. INP/ILO, Employment Problems in Rural Areas, U.A.R.: *Report D on Wages Income and Consumption in Rural Areas,* prepared by B. Hansen, A. Sedki, and Y. Moustafa, (Cairo, Dec. 1965), p.1.

Table C-1 shows the frequency distribution of villages in the sample by size of average daily wages. In addition, the table gives the breakdown of these average daily wages by different sex and age groups.

The fact that the distribution of wage data in this sample is not truncated, or squeezed up against a traditional subsistence minimum, but fairly normal, provides — according to Hansen — sufficient empirical evidence to disprove the subsistence wage hypothesis in wage determination.[12] Nonetheless — as Hanson has pointed out — if we decide to use the wage data, but omit the six villages in *Fayoum* — which are the only observations from Upper Egypt[13] — the distribution becomes a *truncated-half of the normal distribution* [see Figs. (C-I) and (C-II)]

The inescapable conclusion which follows is that neither the hypothesis that the wage data are normally distributed, nor the hypothesis that they are distributed as a truncated half of the normal distribution, can be rejected on the basis of the

Table C-1 *Distribution of villages in the sample by sex-age groups and size of daily wages (annual averages)*

| Piastres per day | Number of villages with annual average of daily wages | | | | | |
| | All villages with records | | | Villages with records for 50 weeks and over | | |
	Men	Women	Children	Men	Women	Children
4–5.9	–	3	8	–	–	4
6–7.9	–	4	4	–	–	2
8–9.9	–	4	16	–	4	6
10–11.9	6	8	13	6	6	7
12–13.9	1	6	5	1	3	–
14–15.9	4	10	–	2	2	–
16–17.9	12	3	–	7	1	–
18–19.9	11	–	–	7	–	–
20–21.9	8	–	–	5	–	–
22–23.9	3	–	–	2	–	–
24–25.9	2	–	–	1	–	–
26–27.9	1	–	–	–	–	–
Total number of villages	48	38	46	31	16	19

Source: Report D, op.cit., p.7

12 Cf. "Employment and Wages in Rural Egypt", pp.306–7.
13 This procedure is fully justifiable since the six observations from the *Fayoum* villages may be regarded as odd observations, and cannot be regarded as representative of the whole of *Upper Egypt*. For Fayoum, an oasis separated from the main Nile Valley by some ten km. of desert, exhibits rather peculiar features, and the low level of wages (as well as rents) is mainly attributable to the poor quality of soil in this area.

empirical evidence provided by the rural employment sample survey for the Delta region.[14]

A more careful analysis, however, should allow for variations in the money cost of the subsistence bundle of goods between different regions. In other words, it would be more appropriate to deflate the data on money wages by some index of regional prices in order to reach a more meaningful conclusion about the process of wage determination in rural Egypt, as wage differentials between regions may simply reflect regional differences in cost of living. Unfortunately we know of no systematic study of regional differences of costs-of-living for Egypt, but one can only suspect that there exists significant differences between the areas covered by the rural employment survey.

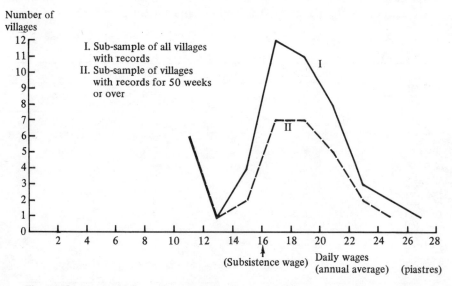

Fig. C-I *Non-truncated form of a sample distribution of villages by size of daily wages*

14 Hanson (pp.496–97) performed a Kolmogorov-Smirnov test of the goodness of fit to a hypothesised distribution on the observations from the remaining 25 Delta villages with records for 50 weeks and over. "Under the null hypothesis that *the sample was drawn from a normal distribution* with mean and standard deviation of 18.79 and 2.71 piastres per day, respectively, the largest difference between the cumulative frequency of the sample and the hypothesized normal distribution was 0.20. This is a smaller difference than one would get under the null hypothesis 95 per cent of the time and so we cannot reject the null hypothesis.

"For the *truncated distribution* the observed frequency table of daily wages was inverted between the second and third classes, and the resulting set of new sample observations was summed by classes. This procedure resulted in a normal distribution which is symmetric about a mean of 15.95 piastres per day, with a standard deviation 3.92. Under the null hypothesis that *the sample was drawn from the right tail of this distribution*, we find that the largest difference between the cumulative frequency of the sample and that expected under the null hypothesis is also 0.20. Again we cannot reject the null hypothesis at the 5 per cent level of significance."

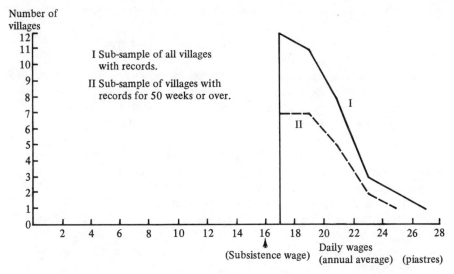

Fig. C-II *Truncated form of the sample distribution of villages by size of daily wages*

In conclusion, the wage statistics collected in the rural employment survey[15] while throwing an interesting light on wage behaviour in rural Egypt, by no means provide decisive evidence against an 'institutional' theory of wage determination. We further note that neither the wage statistics collected in the survey nor Professor Hansen's analysis justify an acceptance of a marginal productivity theory of distribution. As Hanson correctly remarked, in his comment on Hansen, "disproving the traditional subsistence wage theory is not the same as proving that distribution is regulated by marginal products".[16]

However, Professor Hansen's analysis remains a valuable contribution to our knowledge in this area in so far as he establishes rather conclusively that *seasonal* fluctuations of labour demand (during the peak seasons) are the major determinant of the fluctuations in money wage rates in rural Egypt.[17]

Lastly, one should stress the need for further empirical work in this area, as more systematic evidence needs to be collected over longer periods and covering much of the country.

15 The reader should bear in mind the limitations of the source-data on which the survey was based. The fact that the labourers and the employers were not *directly* asked about wages received or paid makes the collected wage statistics open to serious errors due to respondents' biases.
16 Hanson, *op. cit.*, p. 496.
17 The employment pattern in Egyptian agriculture — as revealed by the survey's labour records — shows the occurrence of *two* distinguishable seasonal peaks; one in May-June and one in September. The first peak is related to the *wheat and maize harvest,* the second to the *cotton harvest.* The highest daily wage rate during the peak seasons (i.e. the *harvest wage-rate*) may well be twice or three times the lowest daily wage during the slack season. Cf. *Report D, op.cit.,* p.5

Appendix D

Wage differentials by sex, age and regions in rural Egypt

Perhaps the most illuminating set of statistics on the rural labour force is that based on the sample survey which was conducted jointly by the Institute of National Planning of Cairo and the International Labour Office in 1964–5. Table D-1 presents an overall summary of these data, compared with the findings of the 1960 population census.

Apart from differences due to timing, etc., it seems obvious that the census data classified many more people as not in the labour force. The differences between census and sample survey findings are mainly attributable to differences in definition, e.g. as to the extent to which a farm woman who does household chores for part of the year and farm work when necessary is or is not counted in the labour force. Similarly, the important role played at certain times of the agricultural year by children – especially in cotton picking – raises a general problem of both statistics and basic measurement of labour force and unemployment.

We prefer the sample survey findings to those of the census, because the former are based on actual interviews with working people regarding the hours spent in

Table D-1 *Manpower in rural Egypt (%)*

	According to 1960 population census		According to 1964–5 the INP-ILO sample survey	
Total rural population	100		100	
In labour force	31		46	
Employed		31		42
Unemployed		0		4
Not in labour force	44		24	
Housewives		25		13
In school		19		11
Unable to work	25		30	
Children under 6		19		19
Disabled, elderly, etc.		6		11

Source: The Agricultural Potential of the Middle-East (New York, 1971) p.49.

productive employment. Thus it is reasonable to maintain that a large proportion of housewives omitted, as well as children undercounted, by the census were included in the sample survey.

The ILO/INP wage survey revealed (see Table D-2) that the average daily wage for women tends to be about two-thirds, and for children half, of that paid to men, despite the fact that the average working hours are much the same for men, women and children, namely around 8 hours per day.[18]

Similar wage differentials were observed as early as the thirties and seem to have been fairly constant over a longer period.[19] These basic trends have sometimes

18   *Report D, op. cit.*, p.5
19   cf. Hansen, *AER* (1969), p.308.

Table D-2 *Annual averages of wages and working hours for men, women and children (13 villages in the Delta, 1964/6)*

	Men	Women	Children
Wages per day (piastres)	18.9	12.1	9.6
Percent of men's wages	100	64	51
Wages per hour, (millièmes)	23.3	15.5	11.9
Percent of men's wages	100	67	51
Working hours per day	8.1	7.9	8.1
Index (men = 100)	100	97	100
Percentage shares in the permanent wage-labour force	67	8	25
Percentage shares in the 'casual' wage-labour force	49	17	34

Source: Report D, op.cit., p.4.

been interpreted as being mainly determined by rigid 'institutional factors' related to conventional rules and values governing the process of social division of labour between men, women and children in rural Egypt.

The rural employment survey also pointed to the existence of substantial wage differences between various regions, as there is a systematic tendency for wages to be relatively lower in Upper Egypt than in the Delta Governates (see Table D-3).

Table D-3 *Wage differentials by regions 1964/65* (annual averages)

	Men piastres/day	Women piastres/day	Children piastres/day
I. *Delta*			
Menoufia	21.4	13.0	10.0
Beheira	18.5	12.5	9.8
Gharbia	18.7	11.6	9.6
Average for Delta villages	19.5	12.4	9.8
II. *Upper Egypt*			
Assiout	17.6	11.7	9.8
Kenna	20.4	11.9	9.0
Fayoum	11.7	6.1	5.1
Average for Upper Egypt villages	16.6	9.9	8.0

Source: Report D, op.cit., p.7.

This table shows that the Menoufia region (near Cairo) comes top, and Fayoum at the bottom. Nonetheless, by far the most important fact is the existence of such large wage differentials for men and women between the *Delta* and *Upper Egypt* Governates.

On the whole it may be a fair generalisation to contend that the structure of *sex, age* and *regional* wage differentials has remained much the same as before the revolution. In 1950, children's daily wages were about 55 per cent of men's wages, a differential which remained much the same up to 1964/5. Wages in the Delta Governates were in 1950 about 25 per cent higher than in Upper Egypt; a cruder average based on the rural employment survey in 1964/5 points to a slightly smaller difference. *This may perhaps be taken as an indication that no significant changes took place in the structure of wage differentials in rural Egypt in the post-1952 period.*

133

Appendix E

The choice of prices and weights used for computing the indices of agricultural terms or trade

One of the principal difficulties in any empirical study of the behaviour of domestic terms of trade is the choice of appropriate *prices* and *weights* for the sales and purchases of the different sectors in the national economy.[20]

In general the relevant price series for a study of movement in the terms of trade would be:

(i)   Actual 'ex-farm prices' paid to the growers of the major crops, to be used as a good approximation to 'harvest prices' or 'producers' prices';

(ii) the farm level prices (the ex-factory plus trade and transport margins) to be used for purchases by the agricultural sector of manufactured inputs (i.e. fertilisers, insecticides, diesel oil etc.). In the case of *Imported* fertilisers and insecticides, the appropriate prices to be used are c.i.f. prices plus duties plus appropriate trade and transport margins;

(iii) *retail* prices of the manufactured consumers' goods sold in rural areas seem to be appropriate. However, *wholesale* prices for these goods are, in general, more accurately reported in the official statisics.

When one turns to the weighting system to be used, one runs into the familiar difficulties of the index number problem. For various alternative weighting schemes may well yield different results. Nonetheless, in general, the appropriate weights to be used should reflect the production (or sale) of output by the agricultural sector and its purchases of the other sectors' goods. At any rate the weights can be varied by adopting different *weighting schemes* for the sale and purchase of each good in the base-year, or simply by changing the base-year.

We now turn to a discussion of the main price series and weights used in the calculation of our three ratios of the agricultural terms of trade reported in chapter 5.

Prices

(a) *prices of agricultural products.*

In estimating the price series for the six selected field crops we converted them into index-numbers with reference to the base-year 1960. The prices used are *ex-farm* prices which reflect average producers' prices for all grades whether delivered through government procurement system or sold to the co-operatives or on the free market.

In fact, the data included in *the commodity reports* prepared by the *Central Agency for Price Planning* provide enough background material to enable us to check the consistency and reliability of the price data reported in other series and publications.

---

20   See: S.R. Lewis, Jr. and S.M. Hussain, *Relative Price Changes and Industrialization in Pakistan,* 1951–64 (Karachi: Pakistan Institute of Development Economics, Monograph No. 16, June 1967), Appendix on Method, pp. 26–32.

(b) prices of manufactured agricultural inputs

There are two types of price series that can be used for this purpose. The set of price deflators *implicit* in the GNP statistics for the agricultural sector and the wholesale price indices.

We prefer to use the *implicit* price deflator series in our calculations rather than the wholesale price indices, as they are roughly more representative of the prices paid by the farmers to obtain these inputs.

The Egyptian GNP statistics are published by sectors of origin, both in *current* and in *constant* prices. The difference in the derivation of the two estimates is that, in the one case, current input quantities are multiplied by *current* prices, while in the other, the same quantities are multiplied by *constant* prices. The set of implicit price-deflators is therefore obtained by calculating the ratio of the two series.

(c) prices of manufactured consumers' goods

The main source of data on types of goods and services purchased by farmers and their relative importance is the results of the 1964/5 family budget survey. Retail price series in rural areas should be fairly representative of the prices paid by the farmers. Nonetheless, in the absence of reliable retail price series, wholesale price data are used, not without some distortion of the behaviour of terms of trade.

Weights

One of the principal difficulties of this study was the determination of appropriate weights for the sales and purchases of the various commodity groups.

1. Agricultural commodities

The weights for the agricultural sector's output were calculated on the basis of gross value of output at current prices and then adjusted in such a way as to reflect *marketings* for different crops.

The reason for calculating a set of weights based on *marketings* instead of gross *production* is that one would expect a systematic bias due to the fact that certain crops, particularly cash crops, have greater proportions of production marketed than staple food crops.[21]

Making some crude assumptions as to the marketing ratios of different crops included in our index for agricultural output, we decided to use the following average marketings ratios for all years under consideration:

Crop	Marketing ratio (%)	Remarks
Cotton	100	
Rice	66	covers the parts of the crop
Onions	60	marketed both through the
Wheat	40	cooperative channels and under
Sugarcane	90	the system of compulsory
Maize	30*	deliveries.

*Ratio based on the 1958/9 family budget survey data for the auto-consumption of maize after making an allowance of 10% over the above 'auto-consumption' requirements.

21   Lewis and Hussain, Appendix B, p.50.

2. Agricultural inputs

To derive appropriate weights for the purchases of manufactured agricultural inputs by the agricultural sector, it was first necessary to obtain estimates of the cost structure of the input requirements in Egyptian agriculture *at constant prices*. We then calculated the percentage weights to be assigned to various inputs (manufactured or non-manufactured) as presented in Tables E-1 and E-2.

3. Manufactured consumers' goods

From the family budget survey of 1964–5 we were able to obtain a percentage distribution of total expenditure on consumption for all rural households in the sample. We were then able to compute the ratio to total expenditure of the sum spent on each commodity group included in our index. The percentage expenditures on such manufactured commodity groups add up to 21.9%. Weights were then calculated as percentages from this fraction of total expenditure. The commodity groups, their percentage of expenditure and the weights assigned are shown in Table E-5.

Weighted price indices

If the weights and prices are defined as described above, we propose to use the following system of notation for the weighted aggregative price indices for each year:

(a) *Index of prices of goods sold by the agricultural sector:*

$$= \sum_{r}^{n} P_{rj}^{a} \cdot W_{ro}^{a} \qquad \text{(for each year } j)$$

where

P_{rj}^{a} is the producers' price of the rth crop sold by the agricultural sector (a) in the year j.

W_{ro}^{a} is *the percentage weight* of the rth crop in the base-year (and W_{rt}^{a} in the year 1970).

(b) *Index of prices of 'manufactured inputs' bought by the agricultural sector:*

$$= \sum_{s} P_{sj}^{m} \cdot W_{so}^{m} \qquad \text{(for each year } j)$$

where

P_{sj}^{m} is the implicit price deflator of manufactured inputs (m) of item s in the year j.

W_{so}^{m} is the *percentage weight* of input s bought by the agricultural sector in the base-year (and W_{st}^{m} in the year 1970).

136

(c) *Index of prices of 'agricultural inputs' produced and used within the agricultural sector:*

$$= \sum_{k} P_{kj}^{a} \cdot W_{ko}^{a} \qquad \text{(for each year } j)$$

where

P_{kj}^{a} is the implicit price deflator of inputs originating in the agricultural sector (a) of the type (k) in the year j.

W_{ko}^{a} is the *percentage weight* of input k used by the agricultural sector in the base-year (and W_{kt}^{a} in the year 1970).

(d) *Index of prices of manufactured consumer goods bought by the farm population:*

$$= \sum_{c} p_{cj}^{m} \cdot W_{co}^{m} \qquad \text{(for each year } j)$$

where

p_{cj}^{m} is the index number of the wholesale price of the consumer good (c) bought from the manufacturing sector (m) in the year j.

W_{co}^{m} is the ratio of the expenditure on the commodity (c) to total expenditure in the base-year (1964/5).

(e) *Overall index of prices of manufactured goods purchased by the farm population:*

$$= \sum_{l} P_{lj}^{m} \cdot W_{lo}^{m} \qquad \text{(for each year } j)$$

where

P_{lj}^{m} is the index number of the price of the good l bought from the manufacturing sector (m) in the year j.

W_{lo}^{m} is the ratio of the expenditure on the commodity l to total expenditure on manufactured goods in the base-year (1964/5).

The four synthetic ratios of terms of trade for the agricultural sector for any year j, with the base year (1960) equal to 100, are written as

(I) $\displaystyle I_{(m)}^{j} = \frac{\sum\limits_{r} P_{rj}^{a} \cdot W_{ro}^{a}}{\sum\limits_{s} P_{sj}^{m} \cdot W_{so}^{m}}$ (for all $j = 1961, \text{--------}, 1970$)

(II) $\displaystyle I_{(a)}^{j} = \frac{\sum\limits_{r} P_{rj}^{a} \cdot W_{ro}^{a}}{\sum\limits_{k} P_{kj}^{a} \cdot W_{ko}^{a}}$ (for all $j = 1961, \text{--------}, 1970$)

(III) $\displaystyle I_{(c)}^{j} = \frac{\sum\limits_{r} P_{rj}^{a} \cdot W_{ro}^{a}}{\sum\limits_{c} P_{cj}^{m} \cdot W_{co}^{m}}$ (for all $j = 1961, \text{--------}, 1970$)

(IV) $\displaystyle I_{(l)}^{j} = \frac{\sum\limits_{r} p_{rj}^{a} \cdot W_{ro}^{a}}{\sum\limits_{l} p_{lj}^{m} \cdot W_{lo}^{m}}$ (for all $j = 1961, \text{--------}, 1970$)

Table E-1 *Price indices for agricultural commodities and non-agricultural inputs (1960 = 100)*

Classification of goods	1960	1961	1962	1963	1964	1965	1966	1967	1968	1969	1970
I. Agricultural commodities(1)											
Cotton	100	97	99	101	112	107	107	113	116	120	121
Rice	100	100	100	100	106	118	149	167	175	172	158
Wheat	100	99	100	101	103	105	114	130	113	114	135
Maize	100	97	87	102	106	102	121	140	110	124	127
Onions	100	140	165	115	117	130	130	142	142	127	157
Sugar-cane	100	100	100	100	100	100	125	125	125	125	125
Aggregative index numbers											
1960 weights	100.0	98.4	99.6	101.2	109.8	107.7	114.1	123.0	122.1	125.4	127.2
1970 weights	100.0	98.4	99.1	101.0	109.0	108.2	117.6	127.4	126.4	129.4	129.9
II. Non-agricultural production inputs(2)											
Chemical fertilisers	100	91	88	93	91	96	101	73	71	71	70
Insecticides	100	118	400	368	361	316	268	235	207	208	327
Fuel and lubricants	100	107	109	111	107	113	111	133	142	141	143
Aggregative index numbers											
1960 weights	100.0	96.1	103.0	106.1	103.4	107.2	108.7	94.1	94.3	94.0	97.4
1970 weights	100.0	94.0	100.3	103.8	101.3	105.0	107.4	86.4	85.0	84.9	87.9

Notes: (1) The Price indices for agricultural commodities reflect average producers' prices for all grades sold to cooperatives or on free market.

(2) *Implicite* price deflators derived from the estimates of National Income originating in agriculture.

Sources: For Prices of Agricultural Commodities, CAMPS, *Price Planning Agency*, Memo No. 31 (April 1974).
For Non-Agricultural production inputs, CAMPS, *Estimates of National Income for the Agricultural Sector 1965* (Cairo, 1967), pp. 6–8; *Estimates of National Income for the Agricultural Sector 1970* (Cairo, 1972), pp. 12–14.

Table E-2 *Implicit price deflators for inputs from the Agricultural sector* (1960 = 100)

Years	Natural fertilisers	Fodder	Seeds	Aggregative index numbers	
				1960 weights	1970 weights
1960	100	100	100	100.0	100.0
1961	92	115	106	105.2	104.1
1962	105	111	104	107.4	107.2
1963	123	130	101	121.2	121.2
1964	122	157	100	132.6	131.4
1965	122	269	126	187.6	181.6
1966	92	299	142	194.1	185.3
1967	91	283	141	186.5	178.3
1968	99	209	129	154.0	149.3
1969	99	222	134	160.8	155.6
1970	98	225	131	161.1	155.7

Source: CAMPS, *Estimates of National Income for The Agricultural Sector*, various issues.

Table E-3 *Wholesale price indices[1] for principal manufactured commodities consumed by the farm population in Egypt*

Commodity groups	1960	1961	1962	1963	1964	1965	1966	1967	1968	1969	1970
Sugar, tea and coffee	100	100	105	111	111	132	132	146	146	146	138
Edible oils and fats	100	97	99	102	97	101	122	137	140	139	134
Soap and other chemicals[2]	100	102	102	106	108	109	110	113	113	113	114
Cotton and woollen textiles	100	98	103	108	110	124	124	124	132	132	132
Aggregative index numbers	100.0	98.9	103.3	108.3	108.9	123.5	125.6	132.5	136.4	136.3	133.0

(1) With the original base-year (1939 = 100)
(2) Includes soap, matches, jute, sulphuric acid, caustic soda and alcohol.
Source: Year Book of the Federation of Egyptian Industries (1972 issue), p. 12.

Table E-4 *Weights for output and inputs of the agricultural sector*

Classification of goods	Weights	
	base-period weights %	1970-weights %
I. *Agricultural commodities*		
Cotton	68	58.0
Rice	10	17.5
Wheat	8	8.0
Maize	8	9.0
Onions	2	1.3
Sugarcane	4	6.2
II. *Non-agricultural inputs*		
Chemical fertilisers	70	83
Insecticides	3	3
Fuel and lubricants	27	14
III. *Inputs from the agricultural sector*		
Natural fertilisers	34	39
Fodder	44	40
Seeds	22	21

Table E-5 *Weights for manufactured goods consumed by the farm population*

Commodity group	Expenditure percentages*	Weights
	%	%
Sugar, tea and coffee	8.0	36.5
Edible oils and fats	2.2	10.0
Soap and other chemicals	1.7	7.8
Cotton and woollen textiles	10.0	45.7

* Computed from the 1964/5 family budget survey (average of the four rounds).

Table E-6 *Weights for total purchase of manufactured goods by the agricultural sector*

Commodity groups	Total value of purchases at current prices (£E million)	Weights %
I. *Inputs*		
Chemical fertilisers	38.1	22.4
Chemical insecticides	10.4	6.1
Fuel and lubricants	12.4	7.3
II. *Consumer goods*		
Sugar, tea and coffee	39.2[1]	23.1
Edible oils and fats	11.2[1]	6.6
Soap and other chemicals	8.4[1]	4.9
Cotton and woollen textiles	50.4[1]	29.6
Total	170.1	100.0

[1] Figures obtained by multiplying average *per capita* consumer expenditure on each commodity group by an approximate figure representing the farm population in 1964/65 (i.e. 14 million).

Table E-7 *Indices of terms of trade for the agricultural sector, 1960–70*

Years	(a) Terms of trade between agricultural output and manufactured agricultural inputs		(b) Terms of trade between agricultural output and inputs from the agricultural sector		(c) Terms of trade between agricultural output and manufactured consumers' goods		(d) Overall index of terms of trade between agricultural output and all manufactured goods	
	Base-weighted	1970 weighted	Base-weighted	1970 weighted	Base-weighted	1970 weighted	Base-weighted	1970 weighted
1960	100	100	100	100	100	100	100	100
1961	102	105	94	95	99	99	99.5	99.5
1962	97	99	93	92	96	96	84.2	83.8
1963	95	97	83	83	93	93	83.7	83.5
1964	106	108	83	83	101	100	91.4	90.7
1965	100	103	57	60	87	88	84.0	90.1
1966	105	109	59	63	91	94	89.4	92.1
1967	131	148	66	71	93	96	98.1	101.6
1968	129	149	79	85	90	93	96.5	100.7
1969	133	152	78	83	92	95	99.2	102.4
1970	131	148	79	83	96	98	96.8	98.9

Source: Tables E-1, E-2 and E-3.

141

Appendix F

The policy for fertiliser prices[22]

F.1   The fertiliser distribution system

Before 1960 the importation and distribution of fertilisers in Egypt was carried out by various private agencies, as well as some public-sector fertiliser firms, such as the Egyptian Agricultural Society and the Agricultural Credit and Cooperative Bank (A.C.C.B.). In 1960 the government prohibited importation of fertilisers by the private sector, although the Egyptian Agricultural Society continued to appoint some individual distributors to act as fertiliser agents.

In 1964, as a result of the farmers' complaints that they could not get the fertilisers they needed, the Agricultural Development Committee issued a decree forbidding the private sector to deal in fertilisers. In 1965, the Agricultural and Cooperative Credit Organisation (A.C.O.) was given the exclusive franchise for procuring and wholesaling fertilisers in Egypt. The supply of fertilisers (whether locally produced or imported) has thus become highly *centralised* at the national level. A.C.O., together with the Ministry of Agriculture, determine every agricultural year the quotas to be shipped to each governorate on the basis of the land areas to be cultivated and the types of crop rotations practised.

According to these rotations, the acreage for each group of crops in each season is fixed and hence the 'fertilisers quotas' for each particular crop are also fixed. Thus the quotas to be sold – at low fixed prices – to each farmer are decided on the basis of the data shown in his *farm holding card*, which is issued by the Ministry of Agriculture.[23]

The working of such a centralised distribution system was made feasible by the existence of a supervised credit system, in which a loan-cum-fertiliser package[24] ensures that the fertiliser component in the 'production loan' is actually put to the use for which it was intended (ignoring black-market resale operations) when issued in kind.

F.2   Fertiliser prices

Fertiliser prices are controlled at each stage of the distribution chain. Implementation of a uniform price policy throughout the country is facilitated by the centralisation of fertiliser distribution in one national organisation since 1965 A.C.O.

At the producer level, prices are determined on a cost-plus basis. The cost figures are first worked out by the producer, to cover production costs and transport to the A.C.O. designated depots. These figures are then checked by a cost accountant

---

22   This account is based on the important and comprehensive study of Ezz-el-dine Hammam and M.G. Abu-el-Dahab, *Fertilizer Distribution in The Arab Republic of Egypt,* edited by Eric O. Deguia (Paris: OECD Development Centre, 1972).

23   It should be noted, however, that if a farmer decides to buy an extra amount over and above his quota, he is allowed to buy the extra quantities at higher prices within the following limit: 100 kg of nitrogenous fertiliser (15.5 per cent nitrogen) per acre for all field crops and orchards; a farmer can obtain any amount of phosphatic fertilisers with no limitations.. Cf. Hammam and Abu-el-Dahab, p. 34–5

24   See Appendix G on "The Rural Credit System since 1952'.

Table F-1 *Structure of controlled prices at each stage of distribution 1969/70*

(£E)

Fertiliser	Local			Imported		
	Producer's price delivered to major railhead station[1]	A.C.O.'s wholesale price to cooperatives[2]	Cooperatives' retail price to farmers	Accumulated price delivered to major railhead station[3]	A.C.O.'s wholesale price to cooperatives[4]	Cooperatives' retail price to farmers
Superphosphate (15% P_2O_5)	11.500	12.875	13.500	17.120	12.875	13.500
Calcium Nitrate (15.5% N)	22.600	24.750	26.000	-	-	-
Ammonium Sulphate (20.6% N)	27.500	27.600	29.000	23.700	27.600	29.000
Calcium Ammonium Nitrate (26% N)	31.300	34.635	36.135	26.150	34.635	36.135
Urea (46% N)	-	-	-	41.050	-	-

Notes:

(1) It appears that the negotiated producer's price delivered to major railheads includes basic fertiliser cost plus allowed margin to producer, transport and handling to delivery points near A.C.O. depots. It would seem highly probable that this price also includes the F.P.S.O. stabilising margin

(2) Includes tax of one Egyptian pound paid by the A.C.O. and A.C.O.'s operating overheads.

(3) It appears that this includes cif prices, packing, and transport up to major points near A.C.O.

(4) This item includes the tax of £E1 paid by the A.C.O. and A.C.O.'s operating overheads, and appears include the F.P.S.O. stabilising margin to bring import prices to the level of the fixed locally-produced fertiliser prices.

Source: Hammam and Abu-el-Dahab, p. 64.

and a technician from the Ministry of Industry. The margin added to these costs is determined by the Ministry. Once the price is accepted by the factory it is obliged to deliver stocks at the agreed prices.

At the wholesale level, prices (i.e. the price charged by the A.C.O. to cooperative societies) are determined on a cost-plus basis. Cost here includes the producer's delivered price, transport and storage costs (before reaching cooperatives) and the costs of financing credit sales. The margin added to these costs is determined by the Ministry of Agriculture.

At the retailer level, prices are also determined on a cost-plus basis, and a reasonable mark-up which covers cooperatives' expenses for storing and marketing is fixed by the Ministry of Agriculture. Thus, prices are uniformly fixed throughout the country. Table F-1 shows the price structure of the different kinds of fertilisers at the three levels, for both those produced locally and those imported.

F.3   Subsidies

No direct subsidies exist, although in essence an *indirect subsidy scheme* operates through the Fertiliser Price Stabilisation Fund.[25] The specialised agency established for this purpose is the Fertiliser Prices Stabilisation Office (F.P.S.O.).

The main function of the F.P.S.O. is to stabilise fertiliser prices, whether stocks are locally produced or imported. Retail prices are fixed by the government which negotiates with the local producing companies. Any differences between procurement prices and stiuplated retail prices (which may exist as a result of the stabilisation process) are compensated for by the office. If selling prices are fixed below the purchase price, the F.O.S.O. pays the difference to the supplier. On the other hand, if the selling prices are set at a higher level than the purchase price the office collects the difference.

Similarly, in connection with imported fertilisers, the office assumes responsibility for the differences which may exist between import prices plus internal distribution expenses and the fixed selling prices. If these prices and expenses are higher than the selling price, the office pays the difference to the importing organisations. On the other hand, if the selling prices are set higher than the import prices the office collects these differences. The F.P.S.O. pools these funds to "subsidise" fertiliser where procurement prices are above specified selling prices.

The sources of the F.P.S.O.'s revenue are:
(1)   *The customs duty* paid on imported fertilisers.
(2)   *Differences in price* which accrue through the stabilisation process (i.e. collected surplus between selling prices and purchase price).
(3)   The government budget.

F.4   Fertiliser levies

High distribution margins were observed, up to 40 per cent over *ex-factory prices* (see Table F-2). This is due to the system of double levies: a tax of £E1 per metric ton which is paid to the Ministry of Finance, and an "equalising" margin collected (or sometimes paid out) by the F.P.S.O.

25   *A price stabilisation fund for fertilisers* was established in May 1960, to stabilise prices locally. The aim of the fund is to ensure that farmers do not abstain from using fertilisers because of rises in import prices or production costs.

Table F-2 *Prices and distribution margins of locally produced fertilisers*

(£E per metric ton)

Producer's negotiated ex-factory price	Average transport cost	Producer's negotiated delivered price	Tax	Net margin	Wholesale price to cooperative	Retail margin	Cooperative's price to farmers	Total margin between ex-factory price and retail price	Margin as % of ex-factory price
9,700	1,800	11,500	1,000	0,375	12,875	0,625	13,500	3,800	40
20,800	1,800	22,600	1,000	1,150	24,750	1,250	26,000	5,200	25
25,700	1,800	27,500	1,000[1]	0,100	27,600	1,400	29,000	3,300	12–17
29,500	1,800	31,300	1,000	2,335	34,635	1,500	36,135	6,575	22

Note:

Information available from the text tells us that ammonium sulphate is delivered in bulk form and that the ACO must then pack the materials into 100 kg containers; it is also known that bagging costs £E3,000 per m.t. of fertiliser and that the ACO pays a tax of £E1 per m.t. handled. Hence if £E27,000 is the negotiated price for the producer – i.e. for ammonium sulphate delivered in bulk to major ACO depots, and if ACO sells to coops at £E27,000 then it is implicit that ACO receives FPSO equalising funds as follows:

Delivered price	27,500	
Packing	3,000	
Tax	1,000	
Accumulated cost to ACO	31,500	
FPSO "subsidy"	4,000	less
Real cost paid by ACO	27,500	
Margin	0,100	
ACO wholesale price to cooperatives	27,600	

If however the bagging and tax items are included in the delivered price, then the cost of structure for ammonium sulphate might be as follows:

Ex-factory	21,700
PMSM	1,800
Bagging	3,000
Tax	1,000
	27,500
Margin	100
Price to cooperatives	27,600

Source: Hammam and Abu-el-Dahab, p. 113.

145

Appendix G

A Note on the Rural Credit System Since the Agrarian Reform in 1952

G.1   The allocation of rural credit through supervised cooperatives

The attempts made at reforming the rural credit system in Egypt before the revolution of 1952 produced only meagre results. The basic reason for this was the prevailing semi-feudal interests, which acted as major constraints on the effectiveness of policies intended to reform the rural credit system.

Rural credit organisations with very limited funds continued to advance credit on the conventional banking principle of 'credit-worthiness'. This in effect meant that only a small fraction of the limited rural credit funds could go to smallholders; the chief beneficiaries were the bigger landlords.[26] It is, therefore, not surprising that private money-lenders, who relied primarily on the custom of poorer peasants, continued to flourish side by side with the formal rural credit organisations before 1952.

The reform of the rural credit system, which brought about a significant reduction in the power of private money-lenders in the countryside, was made possible only tbe the social and political changes which followed the revolution of 1952.

Under the new supervised agricultural credit system, first introduced in 1957, loans are advanced against the security of crops, instead of land, as was the case before.[27]

On the other hand, the new 'supervised cooperatives', which initially operated only in land reform areas, became the model for cooperative farming and crop consolidation, and the marketing of the principal cash crop. In 1957 the government initiated a five-year programme to extend the cooperative system throughout the country; by the end of it, in 1962, its success was such that the cooperatives had become the sole suppliers of agricultural credit, and cooperative membership was compulsory for all farmers.[28] In other words, the agricultural cooperative societies became the only channel through which rural credit facilities could be extended to the farmers.

26 Following the Great Depression of the early thirties Government intervention became a necessity in order to relieve small peasants of part of the burden involved. Efforts were therefore made to regulate short-term agricultural credit, leading to the establishment of the Agricultural Credit Bank under the auspices of the Government in 1931 to meet the credit requirements of small peasants. The so-called 'small owners', who could benefit from cash loans, were initially defined as owners of 30 feddans or less. But pressure from the richer landlords resulted in successive redefinition of the term 'small owners' to include bigger landlords. Thus in 1933 'small owners' were redefined as holders of 90 feddans or less and in 1937 as holders of 200 feddans or less. See Eprime Eshag and M.A. Kamal, 'A Note on the System of the Rural Credit in U.A.R. (Egypt), *Bulletin of the Oxford University Institute of Economics and Statistics,* Vol. 20., No.2 (May 1967), pp.99–100.

27 Cf. El-Ghonemy, 'Economic and Institutional Organisation....., *op.cit.,* p.79; CBE *Economic Review,* XII-No.1 (1973), p.13.

28 Eshag and Kamal, *op.cit.,* p.101.

As from 1961 all loans from the Agricultural and Cooperative Bank became free of interest.[29] But the major step in the evolution of the rural credit system was taken in 1964 by the conversion of the Agricultural and Cooperative Credit Bank into an Organisation for Agricultural and Cooperative Credit. Its function is primarily to achieve central planning of agricultural and cooperative credit within the framework of general state policy, to supply the funds necessary for the extension of such credit and to provide the necessary prerequisites for agricultural production.[30]

The offices and branches of the Agricultural and Cooperative Credit Bank in the various governorates were consequently transformed into provincial banks for agricultural and cooperative credit under the supervision of the new organisation. Moreover, closer links were established between cooperative societies and these banks, leading to an integration of the system of rural credit and the system of cooperative marketing of agricultural produce.

The most notable feature of the new rural credit scheme lies in its great emphasis on short-run loans in *kind*. Such loans in kind — seeds, fertilisers, insecticides etc. — are made to each farmer according to the area of the farm and the type of crop planted. The amount of cash loans allocated to each farmer is determined by reference to his cash outlays in production. In fact the volume and value of short-run loans in kind and in cash has increased more than twenty times during the period 1952–66 (see Table G-1). On the other hand, the link between short-term agricultural credit and fertiliser distribution is close and obvious. In fact fertiliser loans are the most important component of short-term lending by the Organisation for Agricultural and Cooperative Credit (see Table G-2).

G.2   Credit and differentiation

It has unfortunately not been possible to obtain adequate information on the distribution of credit between the smallholders and the bigger landlords in recent years. The only data available relate to distribution of agricultural loans by purpose and type. These disaggregated figures available for certain years in the 1960s reveal a typical pattern. Short-term cash loans, which represent 30 to 40 per cent of total loans, are particularly biased in favour of the larger landowners and capitalist farmers who operate with wage-labour.[31]

In addition to short-term loans, medium-term loans, repayable in 5 to 10 years, are also advanced to farmers for the purchase of agricultural machinery and cattle, and for land improvement operations, such as the construction of irrigation and drainage canals, as well as orchard planting. The medium-term loans, which represent about 2 per cent of the total agricultural credit, go in the main to bigger landholders and capitalist farmers who are likely to undertake the type of investment projects mentioned above.[32]

29 Interest on loans was re-established in 1967 and fixed at 4.5 per cent. At present a commission of 3% is charged on all loans granted by the bank, and a penalty amounting to 5% is charged in case of overdue debts. See CBE, *Economic Review*, XIII – No. 1 (1973), p.15.

30 *Ibid.,* p.12.

31 Mabro, *The Egyptian Economy 1952–1972*, pp. 77–8.

32 Eshag and Kamal, *op.cit.,* p.103

Table G-1 *Loans granted by the E.O.A.C.C.*[1] *to cooperatives classified by loan duration, 1952–1966*

Year	Type of loan						Total
	Short-term	% of total	Medium-term	% of total	Long-term	% of total	
1952	3,276,461	96.4	123,233	3.6	-	-	3,399,694
1961–1962	41,443,588	97.9	374,208	2.1	13,422	-	42,331,218
1962–1963	51,810,857	96.1	2,058,477	3.8	33,500	.1	53,902,834
1963–1964	56,347,789	94.8	3,089,944	5.2	-	-	59,437,733
1964–1965	62,811,907	96.2	2,514,818	3.8	-	-	63,326,725
1965–1966	78,222,369	98.4	1,288,281	1.6	-	-	79,510,650

(1) Egyptian Public Organisation for Agricultural and Cooperative Credit.
Source: Hammam and Abu-el-Dahab, p. 32.

Table G-2 *Quantities and value of fertilisers advanced to farmers on a short-term loan basis and their ratio to total value of short-term loans, 1956–67*

Year	Quantity (in thousand metric tons)			Value	
	Nitrogenous fertilisers	Phosphatic fertilisers	Total	Value (million £E)	Ratio to total value of short-term loans
1956	347	62	409	5.682	35%
1957	467	82	549	6.963	38%
1958	557	96	653	8.283	42%
1959	584	105	689	10.608	44.5%
1960	681	178	859	12.608	46.5%
1961/2	820	194	996	14.750	45.3%
1962/3	1,091	220	1,311	22.397	44%
1963/4	1,278	252	1,053	20.447	40.4%
1964/5	1,682	290	1,971	25.328	43.2%
1965/6	-		1,761	34.728	48.5%
1966/7	-		1,386	38.032	46%

Source: Ibid., p. 72.

Cooperative finance has thus made it both economic and possible for the rich peasants to invest in fixed agricultural investment to a greater extent than it would have been possible if they had had to rely entirely on their own investible surpluses. The low rates of interest charged by the cooperative in relation to the borrowing rate of interest in the village market are crucial in this respect.

At the other end of the spectrum, poor peasants — usually short of cash — tend to divert the short-run loans made to them to other purposes, to such an extent that they are often compelled to use bad seeds, little fertilisers, etc. This in turn leads to low crop yields and to an inevitable accumulation of big unsettled debts owed to their cooperatives. Anxious to reduce these debts, the *mushrifs* usually cut down the loans, so that poor peasants fall back on the private money-lenders in the village and sink further into debt and misery.[33]

This aspect of differentiation can be indirectly inferred from the fact that the loan arrears which the rich farmers (i.e. owning more than 25 feddans) owed to *the Public Organisation of Agricultural Credit* in 1966 amounted to £E60 million, i.e. 75% of the total arrears, which totalled £E80 million.[34]

A far more serious aspect of the process of credit differentiation lies in the fact that many privileges are enjoyed exclusively by the rich farmers, by virtue of certain laws and regulations. For instance, in the system for insurance of livestock only the owner of at least 3 head of cattle is formally eligible to insure his livestock, and subsequently to obtain a ration of 150 kg fodder at the low (subsidised) price fixed by the state. The poor peasant who cannot insure his livestock is deprived of such privileges. Not only does he have no right to any compensation if his cattle perish, but he is also forced, in most cases, to buy his fodder on the black market. On the other hand, only owners of more than 15 feddans are eligible to buy selected seeds (hybrid maize, mexican wheat varieties etc.) at subsidised prices.[35]

33 See Saab, *op. cit.*, p.83.

34 See Adel Ghoneim, 'Notes on the Evolution of Economic and Class Relations in the Egyptian Countryside', *Al-Tali'ah* (September 1966), p.68. See also *Al-Ahram*, 28 Nov. 1967.

35 See the survey conducted by the leftist monthly magazine, *al-Tahli'ah*, and published in the September issue, 1966.

G.3   Cooperative accounting[36]

Each smallholder is given an account book (*bataqa*) in which are entered his name, the exact area of his holding, and all his financial transactions with his cooperative. On the credit side are entered all payment in kind (i.e. the crops delivered for bulk disposal) and in cash which an operator makes to the authorities or to his 'local' cooperative. On the debit side were entered all the loans, in cash and in kind, and services with which he is provided, as well as the money due for the holding.

As from 1957, accounts have been balanced at the end of each financial year in June. This annual accounting is purely formal, and as far as a peasant is concerned, the real accounting takes place only in October, once his cotton crop has been picked, weighed and stored in the cooperative warehouses. His account will be then credited with a loan equal to 90 per cent of the value of cotton as determined by the prevailing prices, or with its full value if its price has already been fixed by a sale contract with his cooperative. It is then and only then that the peasant is allowed to cash any surplus (commonly referred to as cotton surplus).[37]

When the definitive prices of the cotton crop are fixed at a later date, the difference between the loan made on the basis of current market prices and the value of the cotton as fixed by subsequent sale is to be credited to the landholder's account and a cash payment usually follows early in January.

Nonetheless, with the exception of a few well-managed cooperatives, delay in accounting and in the payment of cash surpluses from cotton is the rule, and peasants frequently complain that they can not follow up on their accounts and that surpluses are paid to them only after several months delay.

In short outstanding debts, the illiteracy of the vast majority of the smallholders, who find it difficult to grasp the accounting system, and delay in drawing up accounts, form the main obstacles to a smooth and rapid settlement of outstanding liabilities.

In spite of all the shortcomings of the new 'supervised rural credit scheme', there is little doubt that it has succeeded in weakening the hold of usurers (village money-lenders, and the village cotton brokers who used to buy crops in advance from small landholders against cash with a big discount) which was so strong in rural Egypt before 1952. Increases in the volume and changes in the terms of rural credit, are among the most important achievements of the new scheme.

36 This section draws heavily on Saab's analysis, contained in *The Egyptian Agrarian Reform*, Ch. V1.

37 The 'cotton cash surplus' is to be settled after deducting from the value of the crop disposed of the sums due for: (1) the annual land tax; (2) repayment of the loans in kind and in cash granted by the cooperative; (3) any other services provided by the cooperative; (4) the iradat al-gam'iya (commissions and contributions to the income of the cooperative).

Appendix H

Housing Conditions in Rural Areas

There is little doubt that housing conditions in rural areas represent an important and significant aspect of the problem of rural-urban disparities. We shall confine our analysis here to the conditions prevailing in the dwellings of the *fellahin*, without concerning ourselves with the houses of the notables and rich peasants.

Rural families in Egypt usually build their dwellings themselves as part of their off-seasonal activities. The staple building material of the typical fellah house is a mixture of the Nile valley soil, chopped straw from the fellah's standard crops, and Nile water. This may be smeared on both sides of a framework of maize stalks, palm leaves or reeds, to make the mud walls of the poorest type of house. But more often it is poured into wooden moulds to make raw bricks (*tub akhdar*) which are dried in the sun and then used for building.[38]

The space provided by a typical fellah house, representing 74.3 per cent of the total stock of rural dwellings, does not usually exceed on average one hundred square metres. This dwelling — floors, walls, roof — by its very squatness is part of the earth. The trunks of palm trees are used for roof beams and in most instances the doorways of the fellah house contains no door; the loophole windows may have neither glass nor woodwork.

In order to be able to assess the quality of 'rural housing', we should *first* include data on the construction material of the houses, and *second* we should indicate whether or not certain amenities are available within or outside the house.

Table H-1 *Proportion of houses according to material predominant in the floor, walls and roof in rural areas*

	% of houses
1. *Floor material*	
Earth	95
Other	5
2. *Walls' material*	
Red brick and other	12.1
Mud brick	87.9
3. *Roof material*	
Concrete or timber	11.7
Palm leaves or reeds	88.3

Source: Mahmoud Abdel-Raouf, 'On The Reconstruction of the Egyptian Village', (in Arabic), *Socialist Studies*, Vol. 3, No. 7 (July 1974), p. 23.

On the question of construction material, we propose to analyse the material used for the floor, walls and roof of houses in rural areas (see Table H-1).

Looking at this table we observe that 95 per cent of the total rural population lives in houses with an earth floor. It is also clear that kiln-baked bricks (red brick) or lime-stone rubble is a far superior building material for walls compared with the

38   Cf. Ayrout, *The Egyptian Peasant*, pp.115–6.

mud bricks used in the construction of 88 per cent of rural dwellings, since it keeps out dampness from the soil which undermines the walls.

On the availability of basic amenities within the dwelling units in rural areas we have the following information:

	%
(a) Proportion of dwelling units lacking internal fixed bath	96.6
(b) Proportion of dwelling units lacking internal WC	62.5
(c) Proportion of dwelling units lacking proper kitchen	95.6

Source: As in Table (H-1).

152

References

I Books and Articles

Abdallah, Hassan *U.A.R. Agriculture* (Cairo 1965); Arabic.

Abdel-Fadil, M. "Les coopératives agricoles en R.A.U.", *Options Méditerraniennes* (Paris: April 1971).

Abdel-Malek, Anouar *Egypt, Military Society,* translated by Ch. Lam Markmann (New York, Random House, 1968).

Abdel-Meguid, A.R. "The Agrarian Structure in Egypt", *L'Egypte Contemporaine,* Vol. LI, No. 300 (April 1960).

Abdel-Raouf, Mahmoud "Vertical Expansion in Egyptian Agriculture", *L'Egypte Contemporaine* Vo. LXIII No. 350 (Oct. 1972).

Abdel-Raouf, Mahmoud "On the reconstruction of the Egyptian Village" (in Arabic), *Socialist Studies,* Vol. 3 No.7 (July 1974).

Abu-Lughod, Janet "Migrant Adjustment to City Life: The Egyptian Case", *American Journal of Sociology,* Vol. 67 (1) (1961).

Abu-Lughod, Janet "Rural Migration and Politics in Egypt", in *Rural Politics and Social Change in the Middle East,* ed. by R. Antoun and I. Harik (Bloomington: Indiana University Press, 1972).

Amer, Ibrahim *The Land the peasant: The Agrarian Question in Egypt,* in Arabic (Cairo, 1958).

Amin, Galal *Food Supply and Economic Development with special reference to Egypt.* (London: Frank Cass & Co., 1964).

Amin, Galal *Urbanization and Economic Development in the Arab World,* (American University of Beirut, 1972).

Anis, M.A. *National Income of Egypt,* (special number of *L'Egypte Contemporaine,* Nos. 261–262, Nov.–Dec. 1950.

Artin, Yacub *La propriété foncière en Egypte,* (Cairo, 1883).

Atkinson, A.B. "On measures of Inequality", *Journal of Economic Theory,* Vol. 2 (1970).

Ayrout, H.H. *The Egyptian Peasant* (Boston: Beacon Press, 1963).

Baer, Gabriel *A History of Landownership in Modern Egypt, 1800–1950* (London: Oxford University Press, 1962).

Bardhan, P.K. "On the Minimum Level of Living and the Rural Poor", *Indian Economic Review,* (April 1970).

Bhaduri, A. "Agricultural Backwardness under Semi-Feudalism", *Economic Journal,* (March 1973).

Bhagwati J and Chakravarty, S. "Contributions to Indian Economic Analysis", *American Economic Review,* Vol. LIX, No. 4, (Supplement), Sept. 1969.

Bhardawaj, Krishna *Production Conditions in Indian Agriculture,* Univ. of Cambridge, Dept. of Applied Economics: Occasional Paper, No. 33, (Cambridge Univ. Press, 1974).

Bose, Swadesh R. "Trend of Real Income of the Rural Poor in East Pakistan", in K. Griffen & Azizur R. Khan (eds.), *Growth and Inequality in Pakistan* (London: Macmillan, 1972).

Clark, C. and Haswell, M. The Economics of Subsistence Agriculture, 4th ed., (London: Macmillan 1970).

Clawson, M.; Landsberg, H.; Alexander, L.T. (eds) *The Agricultural Potential of the Middle East,* (New York: American Elsevier Publishing Company, Inc., 1971).

Davis, K. and Golden, R. "Urbanization and the Development of pre-industrial areas", *Economic Development and Cultural Change,* (Oct. 1954).

Eckstein, A. "Land Reform and Economic Development", *World Politics,* Vol. 3 (1955).

El-Ghonemy, M.R. *Resource Use and Income in Egyptian Agriculture Before and After the Land Reform with particular Reference to Economic Development,* Unpublished Ph.D. thesis, (North Carolina State Univ., USA: 1954).

El-Ghonemy, M.R. "Economic and Institutional Organisation of Egyptian Agriculture since 1952", in *Egypt since the Revolution,* P.J. Vatikiotis (ed), (New York': Praeger, 1968).

El-Kholie, Osman A. "Disparities of Egyptian Personal Income Distribution as reflected by Family Budget Data", *L'Egypte Contemporaine,* Vol. LXIV No. 354 (Oct. 1973).

Elliott, Charles "Income Distribution and Social Stratification: Some Notes on Theory and Practice", *Journal of Development Studies,* Vol. 8 No.3 (April 1972).

Elliot, Charles *Patterns of Poverty in the Third World* (New York: Praeger Publishers, 1975)

El-Shafei, A.N. "The Current Labour Force Sample Survey in Egypt (U.A.R.)", *The International Labour Review,* Vol. 82, (1960).

Engleman, Konrad *Building Co-operative Movement in Developing Countries,* (New York: Praeger, 1968).

Eshag, Eprime and Kamal, M.A. "A note on the system of the Rural Credit System in UAR (Egypt)", *Bulletin of the Oxford University Institute of Economics and Statistics,* Vol. 20 No. 2, (May 1967).

Eshag, Eprime and Kamal, M.A. "Agrarian Reform in the United Arab Republic (Egypt)", *Bulletin of the Oxford University Institute of Economics and Statistics,* Vol. 30 No. 2 (May 1968).

Falcon, W.P. "Farmer response to price in a subsistence economy: The case of West Pakistan", *American Economic Review,* Vol. LV No.3, (May 1964).

Gadallah, Saad *Land Reform in Relation to Social Development in Egypt,* (Univ. of Missouri, USA: 1962).

Ghoneim, Adel "Notes on the Evolution of Economic and Class Relations in the Egyptian Countryside", *Al-Tali'ah,* (Sept. 1966).

Hansen, B. "Marginal Productivity Wage Theory and Subsistence Wage Theory in Egyptian Agriculture", *Journal of Development Studies,* Vol. II (July 1966).

Hansen, B. "Distributive Shares in Egyptian Agriculture, 1897–1961" *The International Economic Review,* Vol. 9 No.2, (June 1968).

Hansen, B. "Employment and Wages in Rural Egypt", *American Economic Review,* (June 1969).

Hansen, B. "Economic Development in Egypt", in C.A. Cooper and S.S. Alexander (eds), *Economic Development and Population Growth in the Middle East,* (Rand Corporation Study). (New York, 1972).

Hansen, B. and Harzouk, G.A. *Development and Economic Policy in the UAR (Egypt),* (Amsterdam: North-Holland Publishing Company; 1965)

Hanson, J. "Employment and Rural Wages in Egypt: A reinterpretation", *American Economic Review,* (1971).

Harik, I.F. "Mobilization Policy and Political Change in Rural Egypt", in Antoun, R and Harik, I. (eds) *Rural Politics and Social Change in the Middle East* (Bloomington: Indiana University Press, 1972).

Harris, J.R. and Todaro, M.P. "Migration, Unemployment and Development: A two sector Analysis", *American Economic Review,* Vol. 60, (March 1970).

Hoselitz, B. *Sociological Aspects of Economic Growth,* (New York: The Free Press of Glencoe, 1960).

Hussein, H.M. "Pilot Survey of Family Budgets in Egypt", *The International Labour Review,* Vol. 78 No. 3 (Sept. 1958).

Hussein, H.M. and El-Sayeh, M.A. "The 1958–1959 Family Budget Sample Survey in Egypt (U.A.R.)", *Bulletin de L'Institut de Statistique,* tome XXXVIII, 2ne Livraison. (Tokyo, 1961).

Hussein, Hosni "Tarahil Labourers" (in Arabic), *Al-Tali'ah,* Vol. 7 No. 1 (Jan. 1971).

Hussein, Mahmoud *Class Conflict in Egypt 1945–1970,* (New York: Monthly Review Press, 1973).

Joy, Leonard "Food and Nutrition Planning", *Journal of Agricultural Economics,* Vol. XXIV No. 1 (Jan. 1973).

154

Kamerschen, D. "Further Analysis of Over-Urbanization", *Economic Development and Cultural Change,* (Jan. 1969).

Lehmann, D. (ed) *Agrarian Reform and Agrarian Reformism, (Studies of Peru, Chile, China and India).* (London: Faber & Faber, 1974).

Lenin, V.I. *The Development of Capitalism in Russian,* 2nd ed. (Moscow Progress Publishers, 1964).

Lewis, S.R. Jr. and Hussain, S.M. *Relative Price Changes and Industrialization in Pakistan, 1951–·64,* (Karachi: Pakistan Institute of Development Economics, Monograph No, 16 June 1967).

Lewis, W.A. "Economic Development with Unlimited Supplies of Labour," *The Manchester School,* (May 1954).

Little, Scitovsky & Scott *Industry and Trade in Some Developing Countries,* (London: Oxford Univ. Press, 1970).

Lotz, J. "Taxation in the U.A.R." *IMF Staff Papers,* Vol. XII No. 1 (March 1966).

Mabro, R. "Industrial Growth, Agricultural Under-Employment and the Lewis Model: The Egyptian Case, 1937–65", *Journal of Development Studies,* Vol. 4 (1967).

Mabro, R. "Employment and Wages in Dual Agriculture," *Oxford Economic Papers,* Vol. 23 No. 3 (Nov. 1971).

Mabro, R. *The Egyptian Economy, 1952–1972,* (Oxford: Clarendon Press, 1974).

Mansfield, Peter *Nasser's Egypt,* 2nd ed. (London, 1969).

Marchal, J. and Ducros, B. (eds) *The Distribution of National Income,* (London: 1968).

Marei, Sayed "The Agrarian Reform in Egypt", *The International Labour Review,* Vol. 69 No.2 (Feb. 1954).

Marei, Sayed *Egyptian Agrarian Reform,* (Cairo, 1957).

Marei, Sayed "UAR Overturning the Pyramid", CERES - FAO Review, Vol. 2 No. 6 (Nov–Dec. 1969).

Mead, D. *Growth and Structural Change in the Egyptian Economy,* (Homewood: Illinois, USA, 1967).

Mohieldine, A. *Agricultural Investment and Employment in Egypt since 1935,* Unpublished Ph.D. Thesis, (London: 1966).

Nagi, M.H. *Labour Force and Employment in Egypt: A Demographic and Socio-Economic Analysis,* (New York: Praeger, 1971).

Nagi, M.H. "Internal Migration and Structural Changes in Egypt", *The Middle East Journal,* Vol. 28 No.3 (Summer 1974).

Narain, Dharm "Ratio of interchange between agricultural and manufactured goods in relation to capital formation in under-developed economies", *The Indian Economic Review,* Vol. III No. 4 (August 1957).

Nassar, S.Z. "Socialist Transformation in UAR Agriculture", *L'Egypte Contemporaine,* Vol. LX No. 337, (July 1969).

Nuti, D.M. "Social Choice and the Polish Consumer", *Cambridge Review,* (May 1971).

O'Brien, Patrick *The Revolution in Egypt's Economic System from Private Enterprise to Socialism 1952–65,* London: Oxford Univ. Press, 1966).

Omar, Nawal *Etude du Surplus Agricole en Egypte de 1952 à 1967,* Unpublished Ph.D. Thesis, Paris University, (1970).

Oweis, J.S. "The impact of Land Reform on Egyptian Agriculture, 1952–1965", *Intermountain Economic Review,* Vol. II No. 1 (Spring 1971).

Owen, Wyn "The double developmental squeeze on agriculture", *American Economic Review,* Vol. LVI No. 1 (March 1966).

Pasinetti, L.L. *A new Theoretical Approach to the Problem of Economic Growth,* Pontificiae Acadamiae, Scientirarum Scripta Varia (Rome 1965).

Pissot, P. "La reforme agraire en Egypte", *Bulletin de Societé Francaise d'Economie Ruralé* (October 1959).

Ranis, G. and Fei, J.C.H. *Development of the Labour Surplus Economy: Theory and Practice,* (Homewood, Illinois, U.S.A., 1964).

Raid, Hassan *L.Egypte Nassérienne,* (Paris, 1964).

Robinson, Joan *The Accumulation of Capital,* (London: Macmillan, 1956).

Saab, G.S. *The Egyptian Agrarian Reform, 1952–1962,* (London: Oxford University Press, 1967).

155

Salem, A.M. *The Agricultural Cooperative Marketing (in the light of local practices),* In Arabic, (Cairo: Dar el Maaref, 1968).

Sanghvi, P. *Surplus Manpower in Agriculture and Economic Development,* (London: Asia Publishing House, 1969).

Seers, D. "The Meaning of Development", *International Development Review, Vol. 11* (1969).

Sheira, A.Z. "Financial Contribution of Agriculture in the U.A.R.", *Paper presented at the Seminar on Prospective Regional Planning,* held in Warsaw (June 1970).

Sraffa, P. Introduction to the *Works and Correspondence of David Ricardo,* Vol. I (Cambridge University Press, 1951).

Warriner, Doreen *Land Reform and Development in the Middle East,* (London: Oxford University Press 1957).

Warriner, Doreen *Land Reform in Principle and Practice,* (London: Oxford University Press, 1969).

Zachariah, K.C. "Sex-Age Pattern of Population Mobility in the UAR: With some International Comparison", *Paper presented to the I.U.S.S.P. Conference* (London: 1969).

II Official Publications

A. Egyptian Official Publications

Central Agency for Price Planning
Report on Cotton, Memo No. 11: (Cairo, May 1972)
Nutritional levels in relation to Prices, Memo No. 12: (by F. Shalaby and M.F. Moustafa): (Cairo, June 1972)
Report on Rice, Memo No. 13: (Cairo, August 1972)
Distribution of Personal Incomes, Memo No. 18: (Cairo, January 1973)
Agricultural Pricing Policy in Theory and Practice, Memo No. 31: (Cairo, April 1974)
Central Agency for Public Mobilization and Statistics (CAPMS)
Annual Bulletin of the Cooperative activities in the Agricultural Sector, (various issues)
Bulletin of Public Mobilisation and Statistics, (various issues)
Cultivated Areas in ARE in 1969, Ref. No. 30/413 (November 1972)
1964/1965 Family Budget Survey, Doc. 20/221 (Cairo, 1969)
The Increase of Population in the UAR and its impact on development, (Cairo, 1969)
Internal Migration in Egypt, (Cairo, 1971)
National Income Estimates for the Agricultural Sector 1965 (Cairo, 1967)
National Income Estimates for the Agricultural Sector 1970, (Cairo, 1972)
Statistical Handbook of ARE (1952–70), (Cairo, June 1971)
Statistical Indicators of UAR (1952–64), (Cairo, 1965)
Year Book, various issues
Central Bank of Egypt Economic Review
"Changes in the Pattern of Landownership in UAR (1952–65)", Vol. VIII No.3/4 (1968)
"Animal Production in UAR", Vol. IX nos. 3/4 (1969)
"Agricultural Credit in Egypt", Vol. XIII No. 1 (1973)
"Agricultural Income 1959/60–1968/69", Vol. XIII No. 2 (1973)
Central Committee of Statistics
Sample Survey of Family Budgets in the Egyptian Region 1958–59, (Cairo, April 1961)
Egyptian Public Organization for Cotton
The Cotton Bulletin, (Monthly) various issues
The Federation of Egyptian Industries
Year Book, various issues
Institute of National Planning (INP)
Abdel – Rassoul, Ragaa – *Agricultural Prices and Income Policies,* Memo 168 (Internal series), (June 1971)
Allam, S.T., *Agricultural Prices: Bases of Setting and Control,* Memo 1022 (October 1972)

El-Tomy, M. *Summary of a Preliminary Study of the Economic Effects of the Agrarian Reform Law in UAR* , Memo 356 (1963)

Hamman, Ezz-el Dine *The real impact of the Agrarian Reform on the Distribution of Income between Landowners and Tenants in UAR,* Memo 492 (1964)

Hansen, B. Sedki, A and Moustafa, Y – *Wages, Incomes and Consumption in Rural Areas,* Report D on Employment Problems in Rural Areas (1965)

Zaghloul, Fathia *A cost of living index for rural labourers, 1913– 61,* Memo 557 (1965)

Final Report on Employment Problems in Rural Areas UAR, (Cairo, 1968)

Ministry of Agriculture

Third Agricultural Census, 1950, compiled by Department of Statistics and Census, (Cairo, 1958)

Fourth Agricultural Census, 1961, (Cairo, 1967)

Monthly Bulletin of Economics and Statistics, various issues

Ministry of Planning

Follow-up and Evaluation Report on the First Five-Year Plan, Part I, (Cairo, February 1966)

Plan Follow-up Report 1969/70

National Bank of Egypt Economic Bulletin

"Agrarian Reform in Egypt", Vol. 3 (1952)

"The Egyptian Economy: 1959/60–1969/70" Vol. XXV No. 4, (1972)

"Food Consumption in the UAR", Vol. XXII No.4 (1969)

"The Preliminary Results of the 1965 Family Budget Study in the UAR", Vol. XX No. 3 (1967)

"The Role and prospects of Cotton in the Egyptian Economy", Vol. XXVI No. 2 (1973)

"A Study of Agricultural Costs" Vol. XVI Nos. 1/2 (1963)

B. Other Official Publications

F.A.O.

Report of the Second Committee on "Calorie requirements", *Nutrional Studies,* No. 15 (1957)

F.A.O.'s *Indicative World Plan for the Near East,* (Rome, 1966)

National Grain Policies (Rome, 1963).

National Grain Policies (Rome, 1969)

I.L.O.

Rural Employment Problems in the U.A.R., (Geneva, 1969).

Why Labour Leaves the Land, (Geneva, 1960).

I.M.F.

Arab Republic of Egypt *Recent Economic Development,* Document – SM/72/135 (Washington, June 1972).

Arab Republic of Egypt *Recent Economic Development,* Document – SM/73/101 (Washington, May 1973).

Arab Republic of Egypt *Recent Economic Development,* Document – SM/74/182 (Washington, July 1974)

O.E.C.D.

Abu el Dahab, M.G. and Hamman, Ezz el Dine *Fertilizer Distribution in the Arab Republic of Egypt,* edited by E.O. DeGuia, (Paris: O.E.C.D. Development Centre, 1972).

Stone, Richard *Quantity and Price Indexes in National Accounts,* (Paris: O.E.C.D., 1956)

U.N.

Distribution of Income and Economic Growth (concepts and issues), U.N. Research Institute for social development, Report by N. Baster, (Geneva: 1970).

Economic Development and Income Distribution in Argentina, (New York: 1969).

Economic Survey of Asia and the Far East 1971, (Bangkok: 1972).

Income Distribution in Latin America, (New York: 1971).

Progress in Land Reform, U.N. Department of Economic and Social Affairs, (New York: 1956).

Newspapers and Periodicals

Al-Ahram (Daily)   *Al-Ahram al-Iqtisadi* (Bi-monthly)

Al-Ta'awun (Weekly)   *Al-Tali'ah* (Monthly)

Dirassat Ishtrakia (Monthly)